Modern Critical Views

Chinua Achebe
Henry Adams
Aeschylus
S. Y. Agnon
Edward Albee
Raphael Alberti
Louisa May Alcott
A. R. Ammons
Sherwood Anderson
Aristophanes
Matthew Arnold
Antonin Artaud
John Ashbery
Margaret Atwood
W. H. Auden
Jane Austen
Isaac Babel
Sir Francis Bacon
James Baldwin
Honoré de Balzac
John Barth
Donald Barthelme
Charles Baudelaire
Simone de Beauvoir
Samuel Beckett
Saul Bellow
Thomas Berger
John Berryman
The Bible
Elizabeth Bishop
William Blake
Giovanni Boccaccio
Heinrich Böll
Jorge Luis Borges
Elizabeth Bowen
Bertolt Brecht
The Brontës
Charles Brockden Brown
Sterling Brown
Robert Browning
Martin Buber
John Bunyan
Anthony Burgess
Kenneth Burke
Robert Burns
William Burroughs
George Gordon, Lord
  Byron
Pedro Calderón de la Barca
Italo Calvino
Albert Camus
Canadian Poetry: Modern
  and Contemporary
Canadian Poetry through
  E. J. Pratt
Thomas Carlyle
Alejo Carpentier
Lewis Carroll
Willa Cather
Louis-Ferdinand Céline
Miguel de Cervantes

Geoffrey Chaucer
John Cheever
Anton Chekhov
Kate Chopin
Chrétien de Troyes
Agatha Christie
Samuel Taylor Coleridge
Colette
William Congreve & the
  Restoration Dramatists
Joseph Conrad
Contemporary Poets
James Fenimore Cooper
Pierre Corneille
Julio Cortázar
Hart Crane
Stephen Crane
e. e. cummings
Dante
Robertson Davies
Daniel Defoe
Philip K. Dick
Charles Dickens
James Dickey
Emily Dickinson
Denis Diderot
Isak Dinesen
E. L. Doctorow
John Donne & the
  Seventeenth-Century
  Metaphysical Poets
John Dos Passos
Fyodor Dostoevsky
Frederick Douglass
Theodore Dreiser
John Dryden
W. E. B. Du Bois
Lawrence Durrell
George Eliot
T. S. Eliot
Elizabethan Dramatists
Ralph Ellison
Ralph Waldo Emerson
Euripides
William Faulkner
Henry Fielding
F. Scott Fitzgerald
Gustave Flaubert
E. M. Forster
John Fowles
Sigmund Freud
Robert Frost
Northrop Frye
Carlos Fuentes
William Gaddis
Federico García Lorca
Gabriel García Márquez
André Gide
W. S. Gilbert
Allen Ginsberg
J. W. von Goethe

Nikolai Gogol
William Golding
Oliver Goldsmith
Mary Gordon
Günther Grass
Robert Graves
Graham Greene
Thomas Hardy
Nathaniel Hawthorne
William Hazlitt
H. D.
Seamus Heaney
Lillian Hellman
Ernest Hemingway
Hermann Hesse
Geoffrey Hill
Friedrich Hölderlin
Homer
A. D. Hope
Gerard Manley Hopkins
Horace
A. E. Housman
William Dean Howells
Langston Hughes
Ted Hughes
Victor Hugo
Zora Neale Hurston
Aldous Huxley
Henrik Ibsen
Eugène Ionesco
Washington Irving
Henry James
Dr. Samuel Johnson and
  James Boswell
Ben Jonson
James Joyce
Carl Gustav Jung
Franz Kafka
Yasonari Kawabata
John Keats
Søren Kierkegaard
Rudyard Kipling
Melanie Klein
Heinrich von Kleist
Philip Larkin
D. H. Lawrence
John le Carré
Ursula K. Le Guin
Giacomo Leopardi
Doris Lessing
Sinclair Lewis
Jack London
Robert Lowell
Malcolm Lowry
Carson McCullers
Norman Mailer
Bernard Malamud
Stéphane Mallarmé
Sir Thomas Malory
André Malraux
Thomas Mann

Modern Critical Views

Katherine Mansfield
Christopher Marlowe
Andrew Marvell
Herman Melville
George Meredith
James Merrill
John Stuart Mill
Arthur Miller
Henry Miller
John Milton
Yukio Mishima
Molière
Michel de Montaigne
Eugenio Montale
Marianne Moore
Alberto Moravia
Toni Morrison
Alice Munro
Iris Murdoch
Robert Musil
Vladimir Nabokov
V. S. Naipaul
R. K. Narayan
Pablo Neruda
John Henry Newman
Friedrich Nietzsche
Frank Norris
Joyce Carol Oates
Sean O'Casey
Flannery O'Connor
Christopher Okigbo
Charles Olson
Eugene O'Neill
José Ortega y Gasset
Joe Orton
George Orwell
Ovid
Wilfred Owen
Amos Oz
Cynthia Ozick
Grace Paley
Blaise Pascal
Walter Pater
Octavio Paz
Walker Percy
Petrarch
Pindar
Harold Pinter
Luigi Pirandello
Sylvia Plath
Plato

Plautus
Edgar Allan Poe
Poets of Sensibility & the
 Sublime
Poets of the Nineties
Alexander Pope
Katherine Anne Porter
Ezra Pound
Anthony Powell
Pre-Raphaelite Poets
Marcel Proust
Manuel Puig
Alexander Pushkin
Thomas Pynchon
Francisco de Quevedo
François Rabelais
Jean Racine
Ishmael Reed
Adrienne Rich
Samuel Richardson
Mordecai Richler
Rainer Maria Rilke
Arthur Rimbaud
Edwin Arlington Robinson
Theodore Roethke
Philip Roth
Jean-Jacques Rousseau
John Ruskin
J. D. Salinger
Jean-Paul Sartre
Gershom Scholem
Sir Walter Scott
William Shakespeare
 Histories & Poems
 Comedies & Romances
 Tragedies
George Bernard Shaw
Mary Wollstonecraft
 Shelley
Percy Bysshe Shelley
Sam Shepard
Richard Brinsley Sheridan
Sir Philip Sidney
Isaac Bashevis Singer
Tobias Smollett
Alexander Solzhenitsyn
Sophocles
Wole Soyinka
Edmund Spenser
Gertrude Stein
John Steinbeck

Stendhal
Laurence Sterne
Wallace Stevens
Robert Louis Stevenson
Tom Stoppard
August Strindberg
Jonathan Swift
John Millington Synge
Alfred, Lord Tennyson
William Makepeace Thackeray
Dylan Thomas
Henry David Thoreau
James Thurber and S. J.
 Perelman
J. R. R. Tolkien
Leo Tolstoy
Jean Toomer
Lionel Trilling
Anthony Trollope
Ivan Turgenev
Mark Twain
Miguel de Unamuno
John Updike
Paul Valéry
Cesar Vallejo
Lope de Vega
Gore Vidal
Virgil
Voltaire
Kurt Vonnegut
Derek Walcott
Alice Walker
Robert Penn Warren
Evelyn Waugh
H. G. Wells
Eudora Welty
Nathanael West
Edith Wharton
Patrick White
Walt Whitman
Oscar Wilde
Tennessee Williams
William Carlos Williams
Thomas Wolfe
Virginia Woolf
William Wordsworth
Jay Wright
Richard Wright
William Butler Yeats
A. B. Yehoshua
Emile Zola

Modern Critical Views

GEORGE GORDON,
LORD BYRON

Edited and with an introduction by

Harold Bloom
Sterling Professor of the Humanities
Yale University

CHELSEA HOUSE PUBLISHERS
New York ◊ Philadelphia

Printed and bound in the United States of America

10   9   8   7   6   5   4   3   2

∞ The paper used in this publication
meets the minimum requirements of the
American National Standard for Permanence
of Paper for Printed Library Materials, Z39.48–1984.

Library of Congress Cataloging-in-Publication Data
Main entry under title:

George Gordon, Lord Byron.

(Modern critical views)
Bibliography: p.
Includes index.
1. Byron, George Gordon Byron, Baron, 1778–1824 —
Criticism and interpretation — Addresses, essays,
lectures. I. Bloom, Harold. II. Series.
PR4388.G44   1986   821'.7   85–28079
ISBN 0–87754–683–5

Contents

Editor's Note

This volume gathers together a representative selection of the best criticism available upon the poetry of George Gordon, Lord Byron. The editor is grateful to Kevin Pask for his assistance in research, and for his critical judgment.

The essays comprising this book are reprinted in the chronological order of their original publication, with the exception of the editor's introduction, a version of which appeared as the chapter on Byron in the revised edition of *The Visionary Company* (1971). As an overview of most of Byron's major poems, it serves here to highlight much that is problematic in Byron's achievement.

With G. Wilson Knight's eloquent rumination on Byron's central conflict, "torn between history and tragic insight," the chronological sequence begins in something of Byron's own exuberant mode. Knight is followed here by the equally distinguished critic, Northrop Frye, whose emphasis upon the interweaving of Byron's life and Byron's writings is refreshingly direct and necessary.

Another generation of Byron critics is represented in the essays by George M. Ridenour, Leslie Brisman, and Michael G. Cooke. Ridenour finely describes Byron's poetic stance in 1816, when in the company of Shelley he had to absorb the strong influences of Rousseau and of Wordsworth. Brooding upon Byron's "romantic origins," Leslie Brisman offers a remarkable reading of *Cain* and an equally perceptive account of *Lara*, each as a prelude to a brief but illuminating consideration of *Manfred*. *Don Juan*, Byron's masterpiece, is analyzed by Michael G. Cooke from a perspective that provides a useful contrast to that employed by the editor in his own exegesis of *Don Juan* in this book's introduction.

A still younger generation of Byron critics completes this volume, with the essays by Sheila Emerson, Peter J. Manning, and Jerome Christensen. Sheila Emerson's reading of *Childe Harold* III is a distinguished instance of an eclectic version of our contemporary "language"-oriented criticism of poetry. With Peter J. Manning's "textualist" study of the radical publisher William Hone's pirated adaptation of Byron's *Corsair*, we receive another engaging example of a current mode of cultural criticism, somewhat in the spirit of Walter Benjamin. Finally, Jerome Christensen's masterly juxtaposition of *Don Juan* and Byron's drama,

Marino Faliero, provides a kind of intratextual poetics of satire from within Byron's own work, and shows the High Romantic companion of Shelley as Pope's true heir, who can be seen as "taking on Pope's power without his authority."

Introduction

PROMETHEAN MAN

Childe Harold's Pilgrimage

Byron's pilgrimage as poet will be introduced here by a study of this series of poems, as we might regard them. Cantos I and II (1812) are merely a descriptive medley, mixing travel and history. Canto III (1816) is a poem in the confessional mode of Rousseau and Wordsworth, and marks Byron's first imaginative maturity. Canto IV (1818) attempts a synthesis of the two previous poems. In it, Byron and Italy are alternatively obsessive themes, and fail to balance, so that Canto III remains probably the best poem of the sequence.

The entire series Byron called *A Romaunt*, and both the title and the verse form (the Spenserian stanza) derive from the romance tradition. The quest-theme of romance previously internalized by Blake and Wordsworth appears again in Shelley's *Alastor* and Keats's *Endymion* under Wordsworth's influence. Canto III of *Childe Harold* manifests a more superficial Wordsworthian influence, probably owing both to Byron's relationship with Shelley in 1816 and to his own reading of *The Excursion*. The theme of a quest away from alienation and toward an unknown good is recurrent in the Romantics, and Byron would have

1

come to it without Wordsworth and Shelley, though perhaps then only in the less interesting way of Cantos I and II.

The alienation of Harold in Canto I is hardly profound, though peculiarly relevant both to Byron's time and to ours:

> Worse than adversity the Childe befell;
> He felt the fulness of satiety.

He has run through Sin's long labyrinth, is sick at heart, and more than a little weary. So are we as we read Cantos I and II, though this is more the fault of his imitators than it is of Byron. Too many Byronic heroes have moved across too many screens, and Byron's rhetoric in Cantos I and II is not yet supple enough to keep us from making the association between the master and his disciples:

> Yet oft-times in his maddest mirthful mood
> Strange pangs would flash along Childe Harold's brow,
> As if the memory of some deadly feud
> Or disappointed passion lurk'd below:
> But this none knew, nor haply cared to know;
> For his was not that open, artless soul
> That feels relief by bidding sorrow flow,
> Nor sought he friend to counsel or condole,
> Whate'er this grief mote be, which he could not control.

Most of what follows, in these first two cantos, has been described, quite aptly, as "the rhymed diary of two years' travel." What counts in these cantos is the first emergence of Byron's Romantic hero, Promethean Man, who will reach his culmination as Manfred and Cain, and then be replaced by Don Juan. Manfred and Cain are ravaged humanists, though they acquire some diabolical coloring. Childe Harold is scarcely even a vitalist until Canto III, and ends his quest in Canto IV by implying that the posture of pilgrimage is itself a value worth the affirming. We can agree, provided this pilgrimage has an imaginative element, an energy of vision and creation powerful enough to convert its spiritual emptiness into a deliberate theme. This is in fact Byron's great achievement in the third and fourth cantos; his faltering Prometheanism becomes the vehicle for myth. The myth concerns the condition of European man in the Age of Metternich, and is presented in and by the person of the Pilgrim, a complex wanderer who shares only a name with the Childe Harold of the Romantic guidebook that is Cantos I and II.

Canto III opens with Byron's departure into voluntary exile, as he regrets the loss of his child, left behind with the estranged Lady Byron. The poet gives himself to the ocean's guidance, and is content to go "wher'er the surge may

sweep." As he is borne on by wind and water, he states the nature of his alienation. No wonder awaits him; his deeds have pierced the depth of life. His heart
has grown hard, having endured too much love, sorrow, fame, ambition, strife.
Most important, his thought is now turned away from ordinary reality and
towards the refuge of "lone caves, yet rife with airy images," and the visionary
shapes of "the soul's haunted cell." Fleeing England, he escapes into his poem,
and affirms a therapeutic aesthetic idealism:

> 'Tis to create, and in creating live
> A being more intense, that we endow
> With form our fancy, gaining as we give
> The life we image, even as I do now.
> What am I? Nothing: but not so art thou,
> Soul of my thought! with whom I traverse earth,
> Invisible but gazing, as I glow
> Mix'd with thy spirit, blended with thy birth,
> And feeling still with thee in my crush'd feeling's dearth.

Thought seeks refuge in the creation of poetry, for by it we gain more life,
even as Byron gains in the life he images. His own limitations are transcended
as he blends himself with the birth of what he creates. Rousseau, in Shelley's
Triumph of Life, returns from this transcendental illusion to the reality of natural
limitation. Byron is so wavering in his own aspiration that he turns from it in his
very next stanza:

> Yet must I think less wildly: — I *have* thought
> Too long and darkly, till my brain became,
> In its own eddy boiling and o'erwrought,
> A whirling gulf of phantasy and flame.

Yet to cease in this wild thinking is to submit one's thoughts to others, and
Byron says of his Childe Harold *persona*:

> He would not yield dominion of his mind
> To spirits against whom his own rebell'd.

This might be Manfred speaking. And again like Manfred, Harold turns to
the mountains for companionship, for "they spake a mutual language." But between the Pilgrim and the Alps lies "an Empire's dust," the legacy of the fallen
Titan, Napoleon. The poem pauses to brood on the fate of Prometheanism, and
to read in Napoleon the same spirit, "antithetically mixt," that reigns in the
Pilgrim. Napoleon is either "more or less than man," yet falls through an aspiration beyond man's hope:

But quiet to quick bosoms is a hell,
And *there* hath been thy bane; there is a fire
And motion of the soul which will not dwell
In its own narrow being, but aspire
Beyond the fitting medium of desire;
And, but once kindled, quenchless evermore,
Preys upon high adventure, nor can tire
Of aught but rest; a fever at the core,
Fatal to him who bears, to all who ever bore.

Blake or Shelley would not have acknowledged that desire had a fitting medium, though Shelley frequently emphasizes its fatality to him who bears it. Byron is already caught between admiration and disapproval of those whose "breath is agitation," of "all that expands the spirit, yet appals." Unlike Wordsworth but like Shelley, he seeks the summits of nature not for their own sake but because they show "how Earth may pierce to Heaven, yet leave vain man below." Nor does Byronic solitude much resemble the Wordsworthian kind. Wordsworth goes apart the better to hear humanity's still sad music emanate from nature. Byron desires to be alone that he may "love Earth only for its earthly sake." If he lives not in himself, it is only to become a portion of the nature around him, and so to evade the burden of being a man, "a link reluctant in a fleshly chain."

Rather unfairly, Byron attributes the same desire to Rousseau, a greater Promethean than Napoleon or Byron:

His love was passion's essence: — as a tree
On fire by lightning, with ethereal flame
Kindled he was, and blasted; for to be
Thus, and enamour'd, were in him the same.

The fire stolen from Heaven both kindles and blasts, and in Rousseau, human love is one with the stolen flame and in turn becomes existence itself. Byron praises Rousseau as inspired, but dismisses him as "phrensied by disease or woe," an anticipation of modern Babbitry toward Rousseau's genius. Byron's ambivalence is a necessary consequence of the extraordinary view of the natural world that *Childe Harold's Pilgrimage* develops. Every element given to man is simultaneously a way to moral greatness and divine blessing, and also a quicker way to self-deception and damnation. Every human act that widens consciousness increases both exaltation and despair. No other poet has insisted on maintaining both views with equal vigor, and one can wonder if Byron ever justifies his deliberate moral confusion by fully converting its aesthetic consequences into personal myth.

In Canto IV Byron reaches Rome, the goal of his Pilgrimage, and is moved by its aesthetic greatness to intensify his statement of negations. The mind is diseased by its own beauty, and this auto-intoxication fevers into false creation. So much for the Romantic Imagination. Disease, death, bondage become an obsessive litany:

> Our life is a false nature—'tis not in
> The harmony of things,—this hard decree,
> This uneradicable taint of sin,
> This boundless upas, this all-blasting tree
> Whose root is earth, whose leaves and branches be
> The skies which rain their plagues on men like dew—
> Disease, death, bondage—all the woes we see,
> And worse, the woes we see not—which throb through
> The immedicable soul, with heart-aches ever new.

As Mr. Flosky says in Peacock's *Nightmare Abbey*, after hearing Mr. Cypress (Byron) paraphrase this stanza, we have here "a most delightful speech, Mr. Cypress. A most amiable and instructive philosophy. You have only to impress its truth on the minds of all living men, and life will then, indeed, be the desert and the solitude." But this is to miss, however wittily, the direction of Byron's rhetoric, which does not seek to persuade, but to expose. Mr. Cypress is a marvelous creation, and we are sad to see him depart "to rake seas and rivers, lakes and canals, for the moon of ideal beauty," but he is a better satire upon Childe Harold than he is on Byron the Pilgrim. Mr. Cypress sings a song that ends as Childe Harold might be pleased to end, knowing that "the soul is its own monument." Byron as the Pilgrim of Eternity refuses to yield the human value of his life to his own vision of all-consuming sin:

> But I have lived, and have not lived in vain:
> My mind may lose its force, my blood its fire,
> And my frame perish even in conquering pain;
> But there is that within me which shall tire
> Torture and Time, and breathe when I expire;
> Something unearthly, which they deem not of,
> Like the remember'd tone of a mute lyre,
> Shall on their soften'd spirits sink, and move
> In hearts all rocky now the late remorse of love.

What survives, as in Shelley, is "like the remember'd tone of a mute lyre." In this case, that means the continued reverberation of this stanza, which accurately predicts its own survival. Seeking an image for such aesthetic immortality,

Byron turns to the plastic art around him in Rome. Gazing at the Apollo Belvedere, he sees the statue with the approving eye of neoclassic aesthetics, a doctrine of stoic and firm control, of the selected moment or incident that shall be both representative and exemplary:

> Or view the Lord of the unerring bow,
> The God of life, and poesy, and light—
> The Sun in human limbs array'd, and brow
> All radiant from his triumph in the fight;
> The shaft hath just been shot—the arrow bright
> With an immortal's vengeance; in his eye
> And nostril beautiful disdain, and might
> And majesty, flash their full lightnings by,
> Developing in that one glance the Deity.

In the next stanza this statue's informing conception is called "a ray of immortality." Just as Byron, in this poem, makes no attempt to reconcile his conviction of the value of human aspiration with his conviction of sin, so he does not try to bring into harmony this neoclassic aesthetic and Rousseau's vision of art as expressive therapy or Wordsworth's more active theory of a poet's creation. A subsequent stanza demonstrates Byron's awareness of the conflict within his own views:

> And if it be Prometheus stole from Heaven
> The fire which we endure, it was repaid
> By him to whom the energy was given
> Which this poetic marble hath array'd
> With an eternal glory—which, if made
> By human hands, is not of human thought;
> And Time himself hath hallow'd it, nor laid
> One ringlet in the dust—nor hath it caught
> A tinge of years, but breathes the flame with which 'twas wrought.

The Promethean fire we "endure" rather than enjoy, for its origin is illicit; it was stolen. We repay the Titan for the gift of creative energy by a work like this statue, but though the work is of human hands, it is not of human thought. Byron is enough of a Romantic to credit the artist with Pomethean energy, but is also too uneasy about the autonomy of Imagination to credit timelessness to a merely human conception. The statue breathes the stolen flame that wrought it, but the aid of more than human inspiration vivifies it.

The timelessness of art ends the wanderings of Byron's Pilgrim, for he comes to rest before the beauty of Rome, his search accomplished. Byron concludes the poem by offering his Pilgrim to the reader as a means of aesthetic grace of the kind the statue of Apollo has supplied to the Pilgrim himself:

> Ye! who have traced the Pilgrim to the scene
> Which is his last, if in your memories dwell
> A thought which once was his, if on ye swell
> A single recollection, not in vain
> He wore his sandal-shoon and scallop-shell;
> Farewell! with *him* alone may rest the pain,
> If such there were—with *you*, the moral of his strain.

The Pilgrim has been a catharsis for his creator, who has sought by his creation to transvalue exile and wandering into an essential good appropriate for a generation whose Titanic force is spent. In an age of reaction and repression the heroic spirit must roam, must indulge the residue of a Promethean endowment, but without yielding to it utterly. Somewhere in the endurance of human art an ultimate value must lie, but Byron cannot give a final assent to any view of human nature or art available to him. In this powerful skepticism that refuses to be a skepticism, but throws itself intensely at rival modes of feeling and thought, the peculiar moral and aesthetic value of Byron's poetry comes into initial being. *Childe Harold's Pilgrimage* has passion and conflict without balance. We turn elsewhere in Byron to find both a clearer exaltation of the Promethean and a firmer control of the critical attitude that seeks to chasten and correct this immense energy.

"Prometheus"

In July 1816, in Switzerland, Byron wrote a short ode in three strophes, "Prometheus." Composed at the same time as the third canto of *Childe Harold's Pilgrimage*, this ode gathers together the diffused Titanism of the romance, and emphasizes the heroic rather than the sinful aspect of Prometheus' achievement and fate. Yet even here there is a troubled undersong, and a refusal to neglect the darker implications of the fire stolen from Heaven. The overt celebration of human aspiration is properly dominant, but is all the more impressive for the juxtaposition of Byron's darker intimations. The gift of fire is the basis of Byron's art and theme, but the gift is unsanctioned by the withdrawn but responsible Power that has lawful possession of energy. Byron's entire poetic career at its most serious—here, in *Manfred, Cain, Don Juan, The Vision of Judgment*—can be understood as an attempt to justify the theft of fire by creating with its aid, while never forgetting that precisely such creation intensifies the original Promethean "Godlike crime." Byron, in this, writes in the line of Milton's prophetic fears, as do Blake in *The Marriage of Heaven and Hell* and Shelley in *Prometheus*

Unbound. The fallen Angels in *Paradise Lost* compose poetic laments and cele-
brations for their Fall and of their deeds respectively, while Satan journeys
through Chaos. Milton rises with immense relief from the abyss he so powerfully
creates, and the temptations of Prometheanism constitute the dangers he has
escaped. The invocations in *Paradise Lost* exist to establish Milton's hope that his
inspiration is Divine, and not Promethean and hence Satanic. Byron has no such
hope; his inspiration is both glorious and sinful, and his creation glorifies
human aspiration (and his own) and increases human culpability.

The ode "Prometheus" defies the sufferings consequent upon such guilt,
though it recognizes their reality:

> Titan! to whose immortal eyes
>   The sufferings of mortality,
>   Seen in their sad reality,
> Were not as things that gods despise;
> What was thy pity's recompense?
> A silent suffering, and intense;
> The rock, the vulture, and the chain,
> All that the proud can feel of pain,
> The agony they do not show,
> The suffocating sense of woe,
>   Which speaks but in its loneliness,
> And then is jealous lest the sky
> Should have a listener, nor will sigh
>   Until its voice is echoless.

This begins as the Prometheus of Aeschylus, but the emphasis on the pride
of silent suffering starts to blend the Titan into the figure of Byron the Pilgrim of
Eternity, who does not show his agony, but whose sense of radical sin is suffocat-
ing, and who speaks to the mountains in the glory of mutual solitude. This first
strophe commends Prometheus as an accurate as well as compassionate observer
of human reality, the function Byron tries to fulfill in his poetry. The start of the
second strophe dares to attribute directly to the Titan the Byronic conflict of
negations:

> Titan! to thee the strife was given
>   Between the suffering and the will,
>   Which torture where they cannot kill.

Prometheus suffers most, like Byron, in the conflict between his sympathy
for and participation in human suffering, and the impious drive of his will in
gloriously but sinfully bringing relief to humanity. Byron's will cannot bring fire

to us, but can create an art that returns the Titanic gift with the b
of a poem, itself a mark of creative grace but also an agency of fu
as it increases our guilt. This rather vicious circularity, a distinctive ꜰeatu.
Byron's view of existence, is very evident in *Childe Harold's Pilgrimage* and
enters into the final strophe of "Prometheus." Byron rises to his theme's power
with a firmness of diction and mastery of rhythm that his lyrical verse does not
often manifest:

> Thy Godlike crime was to be kind,
>   To render with thy precepts less
>   The sum of human wretchedness,
> And strengthen Man with his own mind;
> But baffled as thou wert from high,
> Still in thy patient energy,
> In the endurance, and repulse
>   Of thine impenetrable Spirit,
> Which Earth and Heaven could not convulse,
>   A mighty lesson we inherit.

The Titan's kindness was "Godlike," yet remains a crime. The Promethean
gift would have strengthened Man by making the human mind immortal, but
the gift's full efficacy was baffled by God. The stolen fire, thus imperfectly
received, is itself a torture to us. What survives unmixed in our Titanic inheritance is the emblem of "patient energy," the endurance that will make Manfred's
Spirit impenetrable. Prometheus and Man alike fall short of perfection, and so
share one tragic fate, but they share also in a triumphant force:

> Thou art a symbol and a sign
>   To mortals of their fate and force;
> Like thee, Man is in part divine,
>   A troubled stream from a pure source;
> And Man in portions can foresee
> His own funereal destiny;
> His wretchedness, and his resistance,
> And his sad unallied existence:
> To which his Spirit may oppose
> Itself—and equal to all woes,
>   And a firm will, and a deep sense,
> Which even in torture can descry
>   Its own concenter'd recompense,

Triumphant where it dares defy,
And making Death a Victory.

What is confused, here and throughout Byron, is the attitude toward divinity. The "inexorable Heaven" of the second strophe, which creates for its own pleasure "the things it may annihilate," is nevertheless to be identified with the "pure source" from which Prometheus and Man are only troubled streams. Byron insists upon having it both ways, and he cannot overcome the imaginative difficulties created by his spiritual shuffling. Man's destiny is "funereal," for his "sad unallied existence" is detached from God; such are the consequences of Man's Promethean fall. Byron is like Blake's Rintrah, a voice presaging a new revelation but too passionate and confused to speak its own clear truth. The concentrated requital for Man's tortured striving is merely the glory of a defiant defeat. It is only by making Heaven altogether remote that Byron goes further in *Manfred*, where a defiant Titanism at last attains to its imaginative limits.

Manfred

Manfred, Byron thought, was "of a very wild, metaphysical, and inexplicable kind." The kind is that of Goethe's *Faust* and Shelley's *Prometheus*, the Romantic drama of alienation and renewal, of the self purged by the self. *Faust* strives for the universal, and *Prometheus* is apocalyptic; *Manfred* is overtly personal, and is meant as a despairing triumph of self, and a denial of the efficacy of even a Titanic purgation. The crime of Manfred is that of Byron, incest deliberately and knowingly undertaken.Oedipus gropes in the dark, the light bursts upon him, and outwardly he allows the light to pass judgment upon him. Manfred, like Byron, claims the right of judging himself.

The Manfred we first encounter in the drama has elements in him of Faust and of Hamlet. The setting is in the Higher Alps, where he has his castle. The opening scene is as it must be: Manfred alone, in a Gothic gallery, and midnight the time. By his deep art he summons a condemned star, his own, and attendant spirits. He asks forgetfulness of self; they offer him only power, and suggest he seek his oblivion in death, but refuse to vouchsafe he will find it there. They serve him only with scorn for his mortality; he replies with Promethean pride. His star manifests itself as Astarte, his sister and mistress, but she vanishes when he attempts to embrace her, and he falls senseless. A spirit song is sung over him, which marks him of the brotherhood of Cain.

The second scene is the next morning out on the cliffs. Manfred, alone, soliloquizes like Milton's Satan on Mount Niphates. But Byron's reference here is a deliberate and critical parody. Satan on Niphates has his crisis of conscience and realizes the depth of his predicament, but refuses to believe that he can escape the self he has chosen, and so is driven at last to the frightening inversion "Evil, be thou my good." Manfred, like Satan, sees the beauty of the universe, but avers that he cannot feel it and declines therefore to love it. But he then proceeds to declare its felt beauty. Like Hamlet, and curiously like Satan, he proclaims his weariness of the human condition:

> Half dust, half deity, alike unfit
> To sink or soar.

He desires to sink to destruction, or soar to a still greater destruction, but either way to cease being human. His attempted suicide is frustrated by a kindly peasant, but the wine offered to revive him has blood upon the brim, and his incestuous act is made directly equivalent to murder:

> I say 'tis blood — my blood! the pure warm stream
> Which ran in the veins of my fathers, and in ours
> When we were in our youth, and had one heart,
> And loved each other as we should not love,
> And this was shed: but still it rises up,
> Colouring the clouds, that shut me out from heaven.

With his crime established, Manfred descends to a lower valley in the Alps, where he confronts a cataract that he identifies with the steed of Death in the Apocalypse. In a marvelous invention, he calls up the Witch of the Alps, a Shelleyan spirit of amoral natural beauty. To her he speaks an idealized history of the outcast Romantic poet, the figure of the youth as natural quester for what nature has not to give, akin to the idealized portraits of self in Shelley's *Alastor* and Keats's *Endymion*. But the incest motif transforms the quester myth into the main theme of *Manfred*, the denial of immortality if it means yielding up the human glory of our condition, yet accompanied by a longing to transcend that condition. The Witch stands for everything in *Manfred* that is at once magical and preternatural. She scorns the Mage for not accepting immortality, and offers him oblivion if he will serve her. With the fine contempt that he displays throughout for all spirits that are not human, Manfred dismisses her. At no time in the play is Manfred anything but grave and courteous to his servants, the poor hunter, and the meddling Abbot who comes to save his soul. To the machinery of the poem, which he himself continually evokes, he is hostile always. This is most striking when he glides arrogantly into the Hall of Arimanes, the chief of dark spirits, and a veil for the Christian devil.

Arimanes is a Gnostic Satan; like Blake's Satan, he is the god of the natural world, worshiped by the three Fates and by Nemesis, who is a very rough version of the dialectical entity Shelley was to call Demogorgon. Manfred refuses to worship Arimanes, but the dark god nevertheless yields to the poet's request and the Phantom of Astarte appears. Manfred asks her to forgive or condemn him, but she declines, and cannot be compelled by Arimanes, as she belongs "to the other powers," the infinitely remote hidden god of light. But at an appeal from Manfred which is both very human in its pathos and essentially Calvinistic in its temper, she yields just enough to speak her brother's name, to tell him "tomorrow ends thy earthly ills," and to give a last farewell. She leaves a momentarily convulsed Manfred, who is first scorned and then grimly valued in a fine dialogue of demonic spirits:

> *A Spirit*. He is convulsed—This is to be a mortal
> And seek the things beyond mortality.
> *Another Spirit*. Yet, see, he mastereth himself, and makes
> His torture tributary to his will.
> Had he been one of us, he would have made
> An awful spirit.

The final act rejects Christian comfort with an intensity that comes from a ferocious quasi-Calvinism. The Abbot seeks to reconcile Manfred "with the true church, and through the church to Heaven," but Manfred has no use for mediators. The last scene is in the mountains again, within a lonely tower where Manfred awaits his end. The Spirits of Arimanes come to claim him, as the Abbot utters ineffectual exorcisms. In two remarkable speeches, Manfred's Prometheanism manifests its glory. By power of will he thrusts the demons back, in repudiation of the Faust legend, and dies his own human death, yielding only to himself:

> The mind which is immortal makes itself
> Requital for its good or evil thoughts,—
> Is its own origin of ill and end—
> And its own place and time: its innate sense,
> When stripp'd of this mortality, derives
> No colour from the fleeting things without,
> But is absorb'd in sufferance or in joy,
> Born from the knowledge of its own desert.

The ultimate model here is again Milton's Satan, who hails his infernal world and urges it to receive its new possessor:

> One who brings
> A mind not to be chang'd by Place or Time.
> The mind is its own place, and in itself
> Can make a Heav'n of Hell, a Hell of Heav'n.

Marlowe's Mephistopheles tells his Faustus that "where we are is hell." The Devil is an inverted Stoic; we have an idea of ill, and from it we taste an ill savor. Iago with his blend of the Stoic and the Calvinist is closer to Manfred; both beings, like Webster's Lodovico, could say of their work that they had limned their night pieces and took pride in the result. Manfred is a Gothic poet who has written his own tragedy with himself as protagonist. The Machiavellian villain plots the destruction of others, whether he himself be man like Iago or demon like Mephistopheles. But, as Northrop Frye remarks in his theory of myths, "the sense of awfulness belonging to an agent of catastrophe can also make him something more like the high priest of a sacrifice." Frye points to Webster's Bosola in *The Duchess of Malfi* as an example. In the Romantic period this figure becomes a high priest who sacrifices himself, like Manfred or Prometheus. The analogue to Christ hovers in the Romantic background. But to what god does Manfred give himself?

Manfred's last words are a proud, naturalistic farewell to the Abbot:

Old man! 'tis not so difficult to die.

Yet even the defiance here is gracious, for the dying Manfred has previously said to the Abbot, "Give me thy hand." Byron insisted that Manfred's last words contained "the whole effect and moral of the poem." The death of Manfred is clearly a release, not a damnation, for his burden of consciousness has long been his punishment. He drives off the demons, who are not so much seeking to drag him down to an inferno of punishment as trying to compel a human will to abandon itself as being inadequate. Manfred has no assurance of oblivion as he dies, but he has the Promethean satisfaction of having asserted the supremacy of the human will over everything natural or preternatural that would oppose it. The supernatural or spiritual world does not enter into the poem; Manfred's relations, if any, with heavenly grace are necessarily a mystery. His rejection of the Abbot is merely to deny a mediator's relevance.

Cain

Byron went further, into mystery itself, in his dramatic piece *Cain* (1821). Manfred's crime of incest is paralleled by Cain's crime of murder, for Manfred's complete knowing of his sister destroyed her, and Cain's destruction of his brother completes an act of knowledge. Byron's radical conception makes Cain the direct ancestor of a tradition that has not yet exhausted itself, that of the artist not just as passive outcast but as deliberate criminal seeking the conditions for his art by violating the moral sanctions of his society.

For Byron, Cain is the first Romantic. Hazlitt best typifies the Romantic in his portrait of Rousseau: "He had the most intense consciousness of his own existence. No object that had once made an impression on him was ever effaced. Every feeling in his mind became a passion."

This is true of Byron also, and of Cain. The tragedy of Cain is that he cannot accomplish his spiritual awakening without developing an intensity of consciousness which he is ill-prepared to sustain. His imaginativeness flowers into murderousness, as it will later in the terrible protagonists of Dostoevsky. The dialectic that entraps Byron's Cain is simplistic and inexorable. Cain suspects that Jehovah is malicious, and identifies his own exclusion from Paradise with the ultimate punishment of death, which he does not feel he deserves. Lucifer presents him with evidence that an age of innocence existed even before Adam. Cain fears death, but Lucifer hints that death leads to the highest knowledge. As Northrop Frye points out, this "links itself at once with Cain's own feeling that the understanding of death is his own ultimate victory — in other words, with the converse principle that the highest knowledge leads to death." Cain is mistaken because he does not go far enough imaginatively; he moves to a mere negation of the moral law, a simple inversion of Jehovah's repressive ethic. And yet Byron gives him a capacity to have accomplished more than this. At the climactic moment, when Abel has offered up a lamb in sacrifice to Jehovah, and urges his brother to emulate him, Cain offers instead the first fruits of the earth. Abel prays, abasing himself. Cain speaks his defiance directly to Jehovah:

> If a shrine without victim,
> And altar without gore, may win thy favour,
> Look on it! and for him who dresseth it,
> He is — such as thou mad'st him; and seeks nothing
> Which must be won by kneeling: if he's evil,
> Strike him! thou art omnipotent, and may'st —
> For what can he oppose? If he be good,
> Strike him, or spare him, as thou wilt! since all
> Rests upon thee; and good and evil seem
> To have no power themselves, save in thy will;
> And whether that be good or ill I know not,
> Not being omnipotent, nor fit to judge
> Omnipotence, but merely to endure
> Its mandate; which thus far I have endured.

This powerfully ironic speech acquires, in context, the further irony of the demonic, for it precedes the sacrifice of Abel to his brother's inadequately awakened consciousness of man's freedom. God accepts Abel's lamb, and rejects the fruits of the earth. Cain overthrows his brother's altar, in the name of the creation. When Abel interposes himself and cries that he loves God far more than life, he provokes his brother to murder in the name of life and the earth. The act done, the terrible irony of having brought death into the world by his very quest for life destroys Cain's spirit:

> Oh, earth!
> For all the fruits thou hast render'd to me, I
> Give thee back this.

This is the self-imposed culmination of Byron's Prometheanism. We can leave Blake to make the apt answer, before we pass to the satiric poems in which Byron found a less arbitrary balance for his divided universe. Blake replied to *Cain* with the dramatic scene he called *The Ghost of Abel* (1822), addressed "to Lord Byron in the wilderness." Byron is in the state that precedes prophecy, an Elijah or John the Baptist prefiguring a coming of the truth, and his *Cain* prepares Blake's way before him for *The Ghost of Abel*. Byron's error, in Blake's judgment, is to have insisted that the Imagination necessarily participates in the diabolical, so that the poet must be exile, outcast, and finally criminal. This is the pattern of Byron's obsession with incest, an element present in *Cain* in the beautiful relationship between Adah and Cain, who are both sister and brother, and husband and wife. The murder of Abel, in Byron, is a crime of Imagination, not of passion or society. In Blake, as Frye says, "murder cannot be part of genius but is always part of morality," for genius breaks not only with conventional virtue but with conventional vice as well. Byron could not free himself from societal conventions, and so his Promethean poems do not show us the real man, the Imagination, fully at work within him. The digressive, satirical poems and the handful of late lyrics of personal reappraisal come closer to a full expressiveness. The values of the sequence from *Childe Harold* to *Cain* still exist, but Byron's achievement in them is dwarfed by the great Romantic poems of Titanic aspiration, the Ninth Night of *The Four Zoas* and *Prometheus Unbound*.

THE DIGRESSIVE BALANCE

Beppo

Writing to his publisher, John Murray, in October 1817, Byron expressed his admiration for a poem by John Hookham Frere published earlier in the same year. This work, under the pseudonym "Whistlecraft," is an imitation of the Italian "medley-poem," written in *ottava rima*, and inaugurated by the fifteenth-century poet Pulci in his *Morgante Maggiore*. The form is mock-heroic or satirical romance, and the style digressive, colloquial, realistic. Byron, in imitating Frere, had at first no notion that he had stumbled on what was to be his true mode of writing:

> I have written a story in eighty-nine stanzas in imitation of him, called *Beppo* (the short name for Giuseppe, that is, the *Joe* of the Italian Joseph), which I shall throw you into the balance of the fourth canto to help you round to your money; but you had perhaps better publish it anonymously.

Beppo, thus offered to Murray as a throw-in with the last canto of *Childe Harold*, is a permanent and delightful poem, and hardly one to need anonymous publication, which it received in 1818. Byron's caution and respect for convention were characteristic, but he had embarked nevertheless on the great venture of his career, for out of *Beppo* came the greater poems, *Don Juan* and *The Vision of Judgment*, in which the poet at last found aesthetic balance and an individual ethos.

The story of *Beppo*, based on an anecdote of Venetian life told to Byron by the husband of one of his Venetian mistresses, is so slight as to need only a few stanzas of narration. The final version of the poem contains ninety-nine stanzas, and could as effectively go on for ninety-nine more, for the poem's point is in its charming digressiveness. The Venice of Byron's prose (and life) suddenly flowers in his verse, and the man himself is before us, all but unconcealed.

Venice and the Carnival before Lent set the place and time:

> This feast is named the Carnival, which being
> Interpreted, implies "farewell to flesh."

As the Venetians "bid farewell to carnal dishes," to "guitars and every other sort of strumming," and to "other things which may be had for asking," Byron moves among them with an eye of kindly irony. *Beppo*, like the Carnival, is an escape into freedom. For a little while, as he thinks, Byron puts aside the world of *Childe Harold*, and the Pilgrim becomes a man who can live in the present.

After the introduction, *Beppo* digresses on the happy and parallel themes of Venetian women and gondolas, until Byron introduces his heroine, Laura, whose husband, Beppo, has sailed east on business and failed to return. After a long wait, and a little weeping, she takes a Count as protector:

> He was a lover of the good old school,
> Who still become more constant as they cool.

This leads to a digression on the amiable institution of the "Cavalier Servente," and so to Byron in Italy, who was to play that role for the Countess Teresa

Guiccioli, the great love of the poet's life after his half-sister Augusta. Praises of the Italian climate, landscape, and way of life are followed by Byron's appreciation for Italy's chief adornments, the language and the women:

> I love the language, that soft bastard Latin,
>   Which melts like kisses from a female mouth.

This provides a contrast for a backward glance at England, with its "harsh northern whistling, grunting guttural," its "cloudy climate" and "chilly women." Remembering the circumstances of his exile, Byron shrugs himself off as "a broken Dandy lately on my travels" and takes Laura and the Count, after a six-year relationship, off to a Carnival ball, where Laura encounters a Turk who is the returned Beppo. A digression on Moslem sexual ways flows into another upon authors, which includes an oblique glance at Byron's central theme of lost innocence. The ball ends; Beppo as Turk follows Laura and the Count to the stairs of their palace, and reveals the inconvenient truth. The three go within, drink coffee, and accept a return to the earlier arrangement, Beppo and the Count becoming friends. Byron's pen reaches the bottom of a page:

> Which being finish'd, here the story ends;
>   'Tis to be wish'd it had been sooner done,
> But stories somehow lengthen when begun.

Don Juan

On the back of his manuscript of Canto I of *Don Juan*, Byron scribbled an exemplary stanza:

> I would to heaven that I were so much clay,
>   As I am blood, bone, marrow, passion, feeling—
> Because at least the past were pass'd away—
>   And for the future—(but I write this reeling,
> Having got drunk exceedingly to-day,
>   So that I seem to stand upon the ceiling)
> I say—the future is a serious matter—
> And so—for God's sake—hock and soda-water!

The empirical world of *Don Juan* is typified in this stanza. The poem is identifiable with Byron's mature life, and excludes nothing vital in that life, and so could not be finished until Byron was. *Don Juan*'s extraordinary range of tone is unique in poetry, but Byron's was a unique individuality, pre-eminent even in an age of ferocious selfhood.

Don Juan began (September 1818) as what Byron called simply "a poem in the style and manner of *Beppo*, encouraged by the success of the same." But as it developed, the poem became something more ambitious, a satire of European Man and Society which attempts epic dimensions. In the end the poem became Byron's equivalent to Wordsworth's projected *Recluse*, Blake's *Milton*, Shelley's *Prometheus*, and Keats's *Hyperion*. As each of these attempts to surpass and, in Blake's and Shelley's poems, correct Milton, so Byron also creates his vision of the loss of Paradise and the tribulations of a fallen world of experience. There is no exact precedent for an epic satire of this kind. Byron's poetic idol was Pope, who kept his finest satiric strain for *The Dunciad* and wrote his theodicy, without overt satire, in the *Essay on Man*. Had Pope tried to combine the two works in the form of an Italianate medley or mock-heroic romance, something like *Don Juan* might have resulted. Byron's major work is his *Essay on Man, Dunciad, Rape of the Lock*, and a good deal more besides. Where Byron falls below his Augustan Master in aesthetic genius, he compensates by the range of his worldly knowledge, and the added complexity of bearing the burden of a Romantic Imagination he could neither trust nor eradicate. Much as he wished to emulate Pope, his epic moves in the poetic world of Wordsworth and Shelley, very nearly as much as *Childe Harold* did.

Yet he wills otherwise. The poem's most acute critic, George Ridenour, emphasizes that Byron has chosen "to introduce his longest and most ambitious work with an elaborately traditional satire in the Augustan manner." The seventeen-stanza "Dedication" savages Southey, Wordsworth, and Coleridge, and suggests that Byron is a very different kind of poet and man, whose faults "are at least those of passion and indiscretion, not of calculation, venality, self-conceit, or an impotence which manifests itself in tyranny," to quote Ridenour again. Byron is establishing his *persona* or dramatized self, the satirical mask in which he will present himself as narrator of *Don Juan*. Southey, Wordsworth, and Coleridge are renegades, revolutionary zealots who have become Tories. Southey indeed is an "Epic Renegade," both more venal than his friends (he is poet laureate) and an offender against the epic form, which he so frequently and poorly attempts. As laureate, he is "representative of all the race" of poets, and his dubious moral status is therefore an emblem of the low estate to which Byron believes poetry has fallen:

> And Coleridge, too, has lately taken wing,
>   But like a hawk encumber'd with his hood, —
> Explaining metaphysics to the nation —
> I wish he would explain his Explanation.

Coleridge's flight is genuine but blind. Southey's poetic soarings end in a "tumble downward like the flying fish gasping on deck." As for Wordsworth, his "rather long *Excursion*" gives a "new system to perplex the sages." Byron does not make the mistake of mounting so high, nor will he fall so low:

> For me, who, wandering with pedestrian Muses,
>   Contend not with you on the winged steed,
> I wish your fate may yield ye, when she chooses,
>   The fame you envy, and the skill you need.

He will not attempt the sublime, and thus he need not fall into the bathetic. From Southey he passes to the Master Tory, "the intellectual eunuch Castlereagh," a pillar of the Age of Reaction that followed Napoleon, and the master of Southey's hired song:

> Europe has slaves, allies, kings, armies still
> And Southey lives to sing them very ill.

The mock dedication concluded, the epic begins by announcing its hero:

> I want a hero: an uncommon want,
>   When every year and month sends forth a new one,
> Till, after cloying the gazettes with cant,
>   The age discovers he is not the true one:
> Of such as these I should not care to vaunt,
>   I'll therefore take our ancient friend Don Juan—
> We all have seen him, in the pantomime,
> Sent to the devil somewhat ere his time.

This last may be a reference to Mozart's *Don Giovanni*. Byron's Don Juan shares only a name with the hero of the legend or of Mozart. At the root of the poem's irony is the extraordinary passivity and innocence of its protagonist. This fits the age, Byron insists, because its overt heroes are all military butchers. The gentle Juan, acted upon and pursued, sets off the aggressiveness of society.

The plot of *Don Juan* is too extensive for summary, and the poem's digressive technique would defeat such an attempt in any case. The poem organizes itself by interlocking themes and cyclic patterns, rather than by clear narrative structure. "A deliberate rambling digressiveness," Northrop Frye observes, "is endemic in the narrative technique of satire, and so is a calculated bathos or art of sinking in its suspense." *Don Juan* parodies epic form and even its own digressiveness. Its organization centers, as Ridenour shows, on two thematic metaphors: the Fall of Man, in terms of art, nature, and the passions; and the narrator's style of presentation, in terms of his rhetoric and his *persona*. Juan's experiences tend toward a cyclic repetition of the Fall, and Byron's style as poet and man undergoes the same pattern of aspiration and descent.

Canto I deals with Juan's initial fall from sexual innocence. The tone of this canto is urbanely resigned to the necessity of such a fall, and the description of young love and of Donna Julia's beauty clearly ascribes positive qualities to them. Yet Julia is rather unpleasantly changed by her illicit love affair, and her parting letter to Juan betrays a dubious sophistication when we contrast it to her behavior earlier in the canto. As Byron says, speaking mockingly of his own digressiveness:

> The regularity of my design
> Forbids all wandering as the worst of sinning.

His quite conventional moral design condemns Julia, without assigning more than a merely technical lapse to the seduced sixteen-year-old, Juan. The self-baffled Prometheanism of *Childe Harold* manifests itself again here in *Don Juan*, but now the emphasis is rather more firmly set against it. "Perfection is insipid in this naughty world of ours," and Byron is not prepared to be even momentarily insipid, but the price of passion, with its attendant imperfections, may be damnation. And so Byron writes of "first and passionate love":

> ─ it stands alone,
> Like Adam's recollection of his fall;
>   The tree of knowledge has been pluck'd
>   ─ all's known ─
> And life yields nothing further to recall
>   Worthy of this ambrosial sin, so shown,
> No doubt in fable, as the unforgiven
> Fire which Prometheus filch'd for us from heaven.

Imaginatively this is an unfortunate passage, as it reduces both Man's crime and the Promethean theft from the level of disobedience, which is voluntaristic, to that of sexuality itself, a natural endowment. Byron's paradoxes concerning sexual love are shallow, and finally irksome. It is not enlightening to be told that "pleasure's a sin, and sometimes sin's a pleasure."

Byron does better when he finds Prometheanism dubiously at work in human inventiveness:

> One makes new noses, one a guillotine,
>   One breaks your bones, one sets them in their sockets.

In an age full of new inventions, "for killing bodies, and for saving souls," both alike made with great good will, the satirist finds a true function in exploring the ambiguities of human aspiration. When Byron merely condemns all aspiration as sinful, he repels us. Fortunately, he does not play Urizen for very long at a time. What is most moving in Canto I is the final personal focus. After extensive ridicule of Coleridge and Wordsworth, Byron nevertheless comes closest to his own deep preoccupations in two stanzas that are no more than a weaker version of the "Intimations" and "Dejection" odes:

> No more — no more — Oh! never more on me
>   The freshness of the heart can fall like dew,
> Which out of all the lovely things we see
>   Extracts emotions beautiful and new;
> Hived in our bosoms like the bag o' the bee.
>   Think'st thou the honey with those objects grew?
> Alas! 'twas not in them, but in thy power
> To double even the sweetness of a flower.

This is a very naïve version of the "Dejection" ode. What we receive is what we ourselves give. Byron's scorn of "metaphysics" and "system" in Coleridge and Wordsworth, which is actually a rather silly scorn of deep thought in poetry, betrays him into a very weak though moving performance in the mode of Romantic nostalgia for the innocent vision both of external and of human nature:

> No more — no more — Oh! never more, my heart,
>   Canst thou be my sole world, my universe!
> Once all in all, but now a thing apart,
>   Thou canst not be my blessing or my curse:
> The illusion's gone for ever, and thou art
>   Insensible, I trust, but none the worse,
> And in thy stead I've got a deal of judgment,
> Though heaven knows how it ever found a lodgment.

The last couplet helps the stanza, as an ironic equivalent to Wordsworth's "sober coloring" of mature vision, but the preceding lines are weak in that they recall *Peele Castle*, and fall far short of it. Not that Byron is thinking of either Coleridge or Wordsworth in these two stanzas; it is more to the point to note that he might have done better to think of them, and so avoid the bathos of unconsciously, and awkwardly, suggesting their major poetic concerns.

In Canto II Juan is sent on his travels, and suffers seasickness, shipwreck, and the second and greatest of his loves. The shipwreck affords Byron a gruesome opportunity to demonstrate fallen nature at its helpless worst, as the survivors turn to a cannibalism that is rather nastily portrayed. From the flood of judgment only Juan is saved, for only he refrains from tasting human flesh. He reaches shore, a new Adam, freshly baptized from the waves, to find before him a new Eve, Haidée, daughter of an absent pirate. She seems innocence personified, but for Byron no person is innocent. Though it is an "enlargement of existence" for Haidée "to partake Nature" with Juan, the enlargement carries with it the burden of man's fall. Byron himself keenly feels the lack of human justice in this association. First love, "nature's oracle," is all "which Eve has left her daughters since her fall." Yet these moments will be paid for "in an endless shower of hell-fire":

> Oh, Love! thou art the very god of evil,
> For, after all, we cannot call thee devil.

Canto III is mostly a celebration of ideal love, but its very first stanza pictures Juan as being

> loved by a young heart, too deeply blest
> To feel the poison through her spirit creeping,
>   Or know who rested there, a foe to rest,
> Had soil'd the current of her sinless years,
> And turn'd her pure heart's purest blood to tears!

This seems an equivocal deep blessing for Haidée, "Nature's bride" as she is. Yet, Byron goes on to say, they *were* happy, "happy in the illicit indulgence of their innocent desires." This phrasing takes away with one hand what it gives with the other. When, in the fourth canto, all is over, with Juan wounded and sold into slavery, and Haidée dead of a romantically broken heart, Byron gives us his most deliberate stanza of moral confusion. Haidée has just died, and her unborn child with her:

> She died, but not alone; she held within
>   A second principle of life, which might
> Have dawn'd a fair and sinless child of sin;
>   But closed its little being without light,
> And went down to the grave unborn, wherein
>   Blossom and bough lie wither'd with one blight;
> In vain the dews of Heaven descend above
> The bleeding flower and blasted fruit of love.

This is a pathetic kind of sentimental neo-Calvinism until its concluding couplet, when it becomes a statement of the inefficacy of heavenly grace in the affairs of human passion. At the start of the fourth canto Byron has modulated his tone so as to fit his style to the saddest section of his epic. If a fall is to be portrayed, then the verse too must descend:

> Nothing so difficult as a beginning
>   In poesy, unless perhaps the end;

> For oftentimes when Pegasus seems winning
>   The race, he sprains a wing, and down we tend,
> Like Lucifer when hurl'd from heaven for sinning;
>   Our sin the same, and hard as his to mend,
> Being pride, which leads the mind to soar too far,
> Till our own weakness shows us what we are.

Few stanzas in *Don Juan* or elsewhere are as calmly masterful as that. The poet attempting the high style is likely to suffer the fate of Lucifer. Pride goes before the fall of intellect, and the sudden plunge into bathos restores us to the reality we are. The movement from *Childe Harold* into *Don Juan* is caught with fine self-knowledge:

>   Imagination droops her pinion,
> And the sad truth which hovers o'er my desk
> Turns what was once romantic to burlesque.

Self-recognition leads to a gentler statement of mature awareness than Byron usually makes:

> And if I laugh at any mortal thing,
>   'Tis that I may not weep; and if I weep,
> 'Tis that our nature cannot always bring
>   Itself to apathy, for we must steep
> Our hearts first in the depths of Lethe's spring
>   Ere what we least wish to behold will sleep:
> Thetis baptized her mortal son in Styx;
> A mortal mother would on Lethe fix.

This is noble and restrained, and reveals the fundamental desperation that pervades the world of the poem, which is our world. After the death of Haidée most of the tenderness of Byron passes out of the poem, to be replaced by fiercer ironies and a reckless gaiety that can swerve into controlled hysteria. It becomes clearer that Byron's universe is neither Christian nor Romantic, nor yet the eighteenth-century cosmos he would have liked to repossess. Neither grace nor the displaced grace of the Secondary Imagination can move with freedom in this universe, and a standard of reasonableness is merely a nostalgia to be studied. What haunts Byron is the specter of meaninglessness, of pointless absurdity. He is an unwilling prophet of our sensibility. The apocalyptic desires of Blake and Shelley, the natural sacramentalism of Coleridge and Wordsworth, the humanistic naturalism of Keats, all find some parallels in Byron, but what is central in him stands apart from the other great Romantics. He lacks their confidence, as he lacks also the persuasiveness of their individual rhetorics. Too traditional to be one of them, too restless and driven to be traditional, impatient of personal myth if only because he incarnates his own too fully, he creates a poem without faith in Nature, Art, Society, or the very Imagination he so capably employs. Yet his obsessions betray his uncertainties of rejection. *Don Juan* cannot let Wordsworth alone, and cannot bring itself to mention Shelley, Byron's companion during much of the poem's composition. Until Shelley's death, Byron could not decide what to make of either the man or the poet, both of whom impressed him more than he cared to acknowledge. After Shelley's death, Byron seems to have preferred to forget him, except for one stanza of *Don Juan* where the puzzle of Shelley continues as a troubling presence:

> And that's enough, for love is vanity,
>   Selfish in its beginning as its end,
> *Except where 'tis a mere insanity,*
>   *A maddening spirit which would strive to blend*
> *Itself with beauty's frail inanity,*
>   On which the passion's self seems to depend;
> And hence some heathenish philosophers
> Make love the main-spring of the universe.

The italics are mine, and indicate the probable Shelley reference. The stanza's first two lines express the mature judgment of Byron on love, a vanity that begins and ends in selfishness, except in the case of the rare spirits who madden themselves and others by questing as though the world could contain the object of their fierce desire. The tone here is uneasy, as it is in Byron's continuous digressions on Wordsworth's *Excursion*. *The Excursion* contains just enough of Wordsworth's greatness both to influence and to repel Byron, and its emphasis on the correction of a misanthropic Solitary may have offended him directly. We cannot know, but a surmise is possible. There are moments in *Don Juan* when Byron longs to make nature his altar, and moments when he is drawn toward a desperate religion of love. His rejection of Wordsworth and evasion of Shelley have deep and mysterious roots within *Don Juan*'s underlying assumptions concerning reality.

After the love-death of Haidée, Byron moves Juan into the world of two rapacious empresses, Gulbeyaz of Turkey and the historical Catherine the Great of Russia. Between these tigresses the poem progresses by an account of a battle between Turks and Russians. After Catherine's court, *Don Juan* starts its last, most interesting and unfinished movement, a view of the English society that Byron had known before his exile. A fierce love, a faithless war, another fierce love, and a social satire of what was closest to Byron's heart form a suggestive sequence. Seduced by a young matron, shipwrecked into an idyl of natural and ideal love, wounded and sold into bondage — the passive Juan has encountered all these adventures without developing under their impact. As he falls further into experience, he does not gain in wisdom, but he does maintain a stubborn Spanish aristocratic pride and a basic disinterestedness. Turkish passion and the horror of battle do not seem to affect him directly, but the embraces of Catherine finally convert his disinterestedness into the sickness of uninterestedness. Probably, like Childe Harold and Byron, the Don begins to feel the "fulness of satiety." His diplomatic rest trip to England is a quest for a renewal of interest, and the quest's goal, Lady Adeline, becomes Byron's last vision of a possible and therefore ultimately dangerous woman. In thus patterning the course of the poem, I have moved ahead of my commentary, and return now to Juan in slavery.

The memorable elements in that episode are the digressions. With Juan pausing, involuntarily, between women, Byron is free to meditate upon the impermanence of all worldly vanities, including poetry. He is back in the mood of *Childe Harold*, from which only the therapy of his own epic can rescue him:

> Yet there will still be bards: though fame is smoke,
>   Its fumes are frankincense to human thought;
> And the unquiet feelings, which first woke
>   Song in the world, will seek what then they sought:
> As on the beach the waves at last are broke,
>   Thus to their extreme verge the passions brought
> Dash into poetry, which is but passion,
> Or at least was so ere it grew a fashion.

Poetry here is expression and catharsis, and nothing more. At most it can help keep the poet (and his readers) sane. Elsewhere in *Don Juan* Byron rates poetry as simultaneously higher and lower, when he sees it as a dangerous mode of evading the consequences of Man's Fall, an evasion that must resolve at last in the consciousness of delusion. The impermanence of poetry is related to human mortality and what lies beyond its limits. Before introducing Juan into a Turkish harem, Byron perplexes himself with the mystery of death, drawing upon "a fact, and no poetic fable." His acquaintance, the local military commandant, has been slain in the street "for some reason, surely bad." As Byron stares at the corpse, he cannot believe that this is death:

> I gazed (as oft I have gazed the same)
> To try if I could wrench aught out of death
> Which should confirm, or shake, or make a faith;

> But it was all a mystery. Here we are,
>   And there we go: — but *where?* five bits of lead,
> Or three, or two, or one, send very far!
>   And is this blood, then, form'd but to be shed?
> Can every element our element mar?
>   And air — earth — water — fire live — and we dead?
> *We*, whose minds comprehend all things. No more;
> But let us to the story as before.

What is effective here is the human attitude conveyed, but Byron's own turbulence weakens the expression. Few great poets have written quite so badly about death. The Muse of Byron was too lively to accommodate the grosser of his private apprehensions. The paradox of an all-comprehensive mind inhabiting a form vulnerable to every element is the basis of Byron's dualism, his own saddened version of "the ghost in the machine." The inevitable corruption of the body obsesses Byron, and this obsession determines his dismissal of passionate love as a value. Julia was self-corrupted, and Haidée the most natural and innocent of sinners, too harshly judged by her father, himself a great cutthroat but perfectly conventional in questions of his own family's morality. Gulbeyaz is further down in the scale of female culpability. Her features have "all the sweetness of the devil" when he played the cherub. She has the charm of her passion's intensity, but her love is a form of imperial, or imperious, bondage, her embrace a chain thrown about her lover's neck. Her love is a variation of war and preludes Byron's ferocious and very funny satire on the siege, capture, and sack of the Turkish town Ismail by the ostensibly Christian imperial Russian army of Catherine the Great, Juan's next and most consuming mistress. Byron introduces Canto VII and its slaughter by parodying Spenser, whose *Faerie Queene* sang of "fierce warres and faithful loves." For Byron, it is altogether too late in the day to sing so innocently, especially when "the fact's about the same," so his themes are "fierce loves and faithless wars":

> "Let there be light!" said God, "and there was light!"
>   "Let there be blood!" says man, and there's a sea!
> The fiat of this spoil'd child of the Night
>   (For Day ne'er saw his merits) could decree
> More evil in an hour, than thirty bright
>   Summers could renovate, though they should be
> Lovely as those which ripen'd Eden's fruit;
> For war cuts up not only branch, but root.

War completes the Fall of Man, costing us our surviving root in Eden and nullifying the renovating power of nature. This does not prevent Byron from an immense and sadistic joy in recording the butchery and rapine, but his *persona* as Promethean poet, whose every stanza heightens aspiration and deepens guilt, justifies the seeming inconsistency.

Juan has butchered freely, but refrained from ravishing, and next appears as hero at the court of Catherine the Great, where he falls, not into love, but into "that no less imperious passion," self-love. Flattered by Catherine's preference, Juan grows "a little dissipated" and becomes very much a royal favorite. As this is morally something of a further fall, Byron is inspired to reflect again upon his favorite theme:

> Man fell with apples, and with apples rose,
>   If this be true; for we must deem the mode
> In which Sir Isaac Newton could disclose
>   Through the then unpaved stars the turnpike road,
> A thing to counterbalance human woes:
>   For ever since immortal man hath glow'd
> With all kinds of mechanics, and full soon
> Steam-engines will conduct him to the moon.

The triumphs of reason are now also identified as sinfully and gloriously Promethean, and Sir Isaac observing the apple's fall is responsible for the paradox that Man's initial fall with apples was a fortunate one. The glowing of human intellect is "a thing to counterbalance human woes," and soon enough will take us to the moon. Byron quickly goes on to qualify his counterbalance as "a glorious glow," due only to his internal spirit suddenly cutting a caper. Cheerfulness thus keeps breaking in, but does not alter the fundamental vision of our world as "a waste and icy clime." That clime surrounds us, and we are "chill, and chain'd to cold earth," as our hero Prometheus was upon his icy rock. But we look up, and see the meteors of love and glory, lovely lights that flash and then die away, leaving us "on our freezing way." *Don Juan* is not only, its poet tells us, "a nondescript and ever-varying rhyme," but it is also "a versified Aurora Borealis," a northern light flashing over us.

Love and glory have flashed too often for Juan, and he begins to waste into a clime of decay just as his creator laments that Dante's "obscure wood," the mid-point of life, draws close. In "royalty's vast arms," Juan sighs for beauty, and sickens for travel. The now motherly Catherine sends her wasting lover on his last quest, a mission to England, and Byron returns in spirit to the Age of Elegance of his triumphant youth, the London of the Regency.

This, *Don Juan*'s last and unfinished movement, is its most nostalgic and chastened. Byron, once "the grand Napoleon of the realms of rhyme," revisits in vision his lost kingdom, the Babylon that sent him into exile and pilgrimage. "But I will fall at least as fell my hero," Byron cries, completing his lifelong comparison to the other Titan of the age. The poem of Juan, Byron says, is his Moscow, and he seeks in its final cantos his Waterloo. Juan has met his Moscow in Catherine, and evidently would have found a Waterloo in the Lady Adeline Amundeville, cold heroine of the final cantos and "the fair most fatal Juan ever met."

The English cantos are a litany for an eighteenth-century world, forever lost, and by Byron forever lamented. The age of reason and love is over, the poet insists, and the age of Cash has begun. The poem has seen sex displaced into war, and now sees both as displaced into money. Money and coldness dominate England, hypocritically masked as the morality that exiled Byron and now condemns his epic. There are other and deeper wounds to be revenged. The Greek and Italian women of the poet's life have given fully of their passion and spirits, and Byron has returned what he could. But England stands behind him as a sexual battlefield where he conquered all yet won nothing, and where at last he defeated himself and fled. Incest, separation, mutual betrayal of spirit are his English sexual legacy. In his sunset of poetry he returns to brood upon English womankind, products of "the English winter—ending in July, to recommence in August." Beneath the Lady Adeline's snowy surface is the proverbial *et cetera*, as Byron says, but he refuses to hunt down the tired metaphor. He throws out another figure: a bottle of champagne "frozen into a very vinous ice."

> Yet in the very centre, past all price,
>   About a liquid glassful will remain;
> And this is stronger than the strongest grape
> Could e'er express in its expanded shape.

Severity and courtliness fuse here into definitive judgment, and bring the spirit of this female archetype to a quintessence:

> And thus the chilliest aspects may concentre
> A hidden nectar under a cold presence.

Adeline is mostly a cold potential in this unfinished poem; her fatality is only barely felt when Byron breaks off, in his preparation for his final and genuinely heroic pilgrimage, to battle for the Greeks. She is Byron's "Dian of the Ephesians," but there is more flesh and activity to "her frolic Grace," the amorous Duchess of Fitz-Fulke. No personage, but an atmosphere, dominates these English cantos, with their diffused autumnal tone and their perfectly bred but desperately bored aristocrats, with whose breeding and boredom alike Byron is more than half in sympathy.

Don Juan, begun as satiric epic, ends as a remembrance of things past, with Byron's last glance at home, and the poet's last tone one of weary but loving irony. The last word in a discussion of *Don Juan* ought not to be "irony," but "mobility," one of Byron's favorite terms. Oliver Elton called Byron's two central traits his mobility and self-consciousness, and the former is emphasized in *Don Juan*. Adeline is so graceful a social performer that Juan begins to feel some doubt as to how much of her is *real*:

> So well she acted all and every part
>   By turns—with that vivacious versatility,
> Which many people take for want of heart.
>   They err—'tis merely what is call'd mobility,
> A thing of temperament and not of art,
>   Though seeming so, from its supposed facility;
> And false—though true; for surely they're sincerest
> Who are strongly acted on by what is nearest.

This is Byron's own defense against our charge that he postures, our feeling doubts as to how much of *him* is real. An abyss lies beneath mobility, but Adeline and Byron alike are too nimble to fall into it, and their deftness is more than rhetorical. The world of *Don Juan*, Byron's world, demands mobility; there is indeed no other way to meet it. Byron defines mobility in a note that has a wry quality, too sophisticated to acknowledge the tragic dimension being suggested: "It may be defined as an excessive susceptibility of immediate impressions—at the same time without *losing* the past: and is, though sometimes apparently useful to the possessor, a most painful and unhappy attribute."

This is Byron's social version of the Romantic term "Imagination," for mobility also reveals itself "in the balance or reconciliation of opposite or discordant qualities: of sameness, with difference; the individual, with the representative; the sense of novelty and freshness, with old and familiar objects." The great Romantic contraries—emotion and order, judgment and enthusiasm, steady self-possession and profound or vehement feeling—all find their social balance in the quality of mobility. Viewed thus, Byron's achievement in *Don Juan* is to have suggested the pragmatic social realization of Romantic idealism in a mode of reasonableness that no other Romantic aspired to attain.

Byron lived in the world as no other Romantic attempted to live, except Shelley, and Shelley at the last despaired more fully. *Don Juan* is, to my taste, not a poem of the eminence of *Milton* and *Jerusalem*, of *The Prelude* or *Prometheus Unbound* or the two *Hyperions*. But it is not a poem of their kind, nor ought it to be judged against them. Shelley said of *Don Juan* that "every word of it is pregnant with immortality," and again: "Nothing has ever been written like it in English, nor, if I may venture to prophesy, will there be; without carrying upon it the mark of a secondary and borrowed light." Byron despaired of apocalypse, and yet could not be content with Man or nature as given. He wrote therefore with the strategy of meeting this life with awareness, humor, and an intensity of creative aspiration, flawed necessarily at its origins. Mobility is a curious and sophisticated ideal; it attempts to meet experience with experience's own ironies of apprehension. It may be that, as Byron's best critic says, *Don Juan* offers us "a sophistication which (in a highly debased form, to be sure) we have already too much of." We have, however, so little besides that a higher kind of sophistication can only improve us. Whatever its utility, *Don Juan* is exuberant enough to be beautiful in a Blakean sense, little as Blake himself would have cared for Byron's hard-won digressive balance.

THE BYRONIC ETHOS

The Vision of Judgment

The parody poem *The Vision of Judgment* contains Byron's best work outside of *Don Juan*. It is, as Byron said, "in the Pulci style," like *Beppo* and *Juan*, but its high good nature reveals a firmer balance than Byron maintains elsewhere in his Italian mock-heroic vein. Southey, the battered poet laureate, is the scapegoat again, as he was in the "Dedication" to *Don Juan*. Byron's treatment of his victim is both more humane and more effective in the *Vision*, once the reader gets past the angry prose preface.

George III died in 1820, and poor Southey performed the laureate's task of eulogizing his late monarch in *A Vision of Judgment* (1821), a poem no better than it needed to be, and not much worse than most of Southey. The laureate's misfortune was to write a preface in which he denounced lascivious literature and attacked the "Satanic school" (Byron and Shelley) for producing it: "for though their productions breathe the spirit of Belial in their lascivious parts, and the spirit of Moloch in those loathsome images of atrocities and horrors which they delight to represent, they are more especially characterized by a satanic spirit of pride and audacious impiety, which still betrays the wretched feeling of hopelessness wherewith it is allied."

Byron was not the man to pass this by. His *Vision of Judgment* takes its occasion from Southey's and permanently fixates the laureate as a dunce. But it does something rather more vital besides. *Don Juan* has its Miltonic side, as we have seen, yet the *Vision* as it develops is even closer to *Paradise Lost* in material, though hardly in spirit or tone. Milton's anthropomorphic Heaven is sublime and also sometimes wearisome, too much like an earthly court in its servile aspects. Byron's burlesque Heaven is sublimely funny. St. Peter sits by the celestial gate

and can happily drowse, for very little goes in. The Angels are singing out of
tune and are by now hoarse, having little else to do. Down below, George III
dies, which does not disturb the yawning Peter, who has not heard of him. But
the mad old blind king arrives in the angelic caravan, and with him comes a very
great being, the patron of the "Satanic school":

> But bringing up the rear of this bright host
>   A Spirit of a different aspect waved
> His wings, like thunder-clouds above some coast
>   Whose barren beach with frequent wrecks is paved;
> His brow was like the deep when tempest-toss'd;
>   Fierce and unfathomable thoughts engraved
> Eternal wrath on his immortal face,
> And *where* he gazed a gloom pervaded space.

Those "fierce and unfathomable thoughts" remind us of Manfred, but this
is great Lucifer himself, come to claim George as his own. The gate of heaven
opens, and the archangel Michael comes forth to meet his former friend and
future foe. There is "a high immortal, proud regret" in the eyes of each immortal
being, as if destiny rather than will governs their enmity:

> Yet still between his Darkness and his Brightness
> There pass'd a mutual glance of great politeness.

Michael is a gentleman, but the Prince of Darkness has the superior hauteur
of "an old Castilian poor noble." He is not particularly proud of owning our
earth, but he does own it, in this quietly Gnostic poem. But, as befits a poor noble with hauteur, he thinks few earthlings worth damnation save their kings,
and these he takes merely as a kind of quitrent, to assert his right as lord. Indeed, he shares Byron's theory of the Fall as being perpetually renewed by Man:

> they are grown so bad,
> That hell has nothing better left to do
> Than leave them to themselves: so much more mad
> And evil by their own internal curse,
> Heaven cannot make them better, nor I worse.

Lucifer's charges against George and his calling of witnesses are nimbly
handled. Life comes exuberantly into the poem with the intrusion of Southey
upon the heavenly scene. The devil Asmodeus stumbles in, under the heavy
load of the laureate, and the poor devil is moved to lament that he has sprained
his left wing in the carry. Southey has been writing his *Vision of Judgment*, thus
daring to anticipate the eternal decision upon George. The laureate, glad to get

an audience, begins to recite, throwing everyone into a horror and even rousing the deceased King from his stupor in the horrible thought that his former laureate, the abominable Pye, has come again to plague him. After a general tumult, St. Peter

> upraised his keys,
> And at the fifth line knock'd the poet down;
> Who felt like Phaëton.

Phaëton (or Phaethon) attempted to drive the chariot of the sun across the sky, but could not control the horses, who bolted, and so Phaethon fell to his death. Southey attempts to ride in the chariot of Apollo, god of poetry, and suffers a fall into the depths, a bathetic plunge. The same imagery of falling is associated with Southey in the "Dedication" to *Don Juan*, but there it is more direct:

> He first sank to the bottom—like his works,
> But soon rose to the surface—like himself.

In the confusion, King George slips into heaven, and as Byron ends his *Vision*, the late monarch is practicing the hundredth psalm, which is only fitting, as it adjures the Lord's people to "enter into his gates with thanksgiving." The ethos of *The Vision of Judgment* is remarkably refreshing. Byron is so delighted by his fable that his good will extends even to Southey, who does not drown like Phaethon but lurks in his own den, still composing. George is in heaven, and the very dignified and high-minded Lucifer back in hell. In this one poem at least, Byron writes as a whole man, whose inner conflicts have been mastered. If the earth is the Devil's, the Devil is yet disinterested, and damnation a subject for urbane bantering. Peculiar as Byron's variety of Prometheanism was, *The Vision of Judgment* makes it clear that we err in calling the poet any genuine sort of a Calvinist:

> for not one am I
> Of those who think damnation better still:
> I hardly know too if not quite alone am I
> In this small hope of bettering future ill
> By circumscribing, with some slight restriction,
> The eternity of hell's hot jurisdiction.

If there is any mockery in the poem which is not altogether good-humored, it is in Byron's conscious "blasphemy":

> I know one may be damn'd
> For hoping no one else may e'er be so;
>   I know my catechism; I know we're cramm'd
> With the best doctrines till we quite o'erflow;
>   I know that all save England's church have shamm'd,
> And that the other twice two hundred churches
> And synagogues have made a *damn'd* bad purchase.

Religious cant was no more acceptable to Byron than the social or political varieties, however darkly and deeply his own orthodox currents ran. *The Vision of Judgment* is perhaps only a good parody of aspects of *Paradise Lost*, but few of us would prefer Milton's heaven to Byron's as a place in which to live.

"Stanzas to the Po"

Byron's lyrics are an index to his poetic development, though only a few of them are altogether adequate in the expression of his complex sensibility. The best of them include the "Stanzas to the Po" (1819), the undated "Ode to a Lady," which applies the poet's negative Prometheanism to the theme of lost human passion, and the last poems written under the shadow of death at Missolonghi. Byron's personal ethos, the dignity of disillusioned intensity and disinterested heroism, despairing of love and its human limitations but still longing for them, continued to shine out of this handful of lyrics.

The last poems have the poignancy of their occasion, but the "Stanzas to the Po" constitute Byron's finest short poem, and one perfectly revelatory of his mature spirit.

In April 1819 Byron, aged thirty-one, fell in love with the Countess Teresa Guiccioli, aged nineteen, who had been married only a little over a year to the fifty-eight-year-old Count. Byron had already lamented in *Don Juan* the cooling of his heart, now that he was past thirty, but he proved no prophet in this matter. Momentarily separated from Teresa, he wrote the first draft of his "Stanzas to the Po." The firm diction of this beautiful poem shows an Italian influence, probably that of Dante's *Canzoniere:*

> River, that rollest by the ancient walls,
>   Where dwells the Lady of my love, when she
> Walks by thy brink, and there perchance recalls
>   A faint and fleeting memory of me;
>
> What if thy deep and ample stream should be
>   A mirror of my heart, where she may read

> The thousand thoughts I now betray to thee,
>   Wild as thy wave, and headlong as thy speed!

The movement of this is large and stately, but there is a curious and deliberate reluctance in the rhythm, as if the poet wished to resist the river's swift propulsion of his thoughts toward his absent mistress. As he stares at the river he sees suddenly that it is more than a mirror of his heart. He finds not similitude but identity between the Po and his heart:

> Thou tendest wildly onwards to the main.
>   And I — to loving *one* I should not love.

He should not love only because he had said his farewell to love, and is reluctant to welcome it again. But it has come; he longs desperately for his beloved, yet he still resists the longing:

> The wave that bears my tears returns no more:
>   Will she return by whom that wave shall sweep? —
> Both tread thy banks, both wander on thy shore,
>   I by thy source, she by the dark-blue deep.

As the Po is one with the passion of Byron's heart, a love that Teresa reciprocates, the geographical position of the lovers symbolizes the extent to which they have given themselves to their love. Teresa is "by the dark-blue deep," but Byron still lingers by the source, struggling with the past:

> But that which keepeth us apart is not
>   Distance, nor depth of wave, nor space of earth,
> But the distraction of a various lot,
>   As various as the climates of our birth.

> A stranger loves the Lady of the land,
>   Born far beyond the mountains, but his blood
> Is all meridian, as if never fann'd
>   By the black wind that chills the polar flood.

His hesitation keeps them apart, and he traces it to the division within his own nature. But his blood triumphs, though in his own despite:

> My blood is all meridian; were it not;
>   I had not left my clime, nor should I be,
> In spite of tortures, ne'er to be forgot,
>   A slave again of love, — at least of thee.
> 'Tis vain to struggle — let me perish young —
>   Live as I lived, and love as I have loved;

> To dust if I return, from dust I sprung,
>   And then, at least, my heart can ne'er be moved.

Complex in attitude as these two final stanzas of the poem are, they did not satisfy Byron. As he gives himself again to love, he senses that he also gives himself to self-destruction and welcomes this as a consummation to be wished. By loving again, he is true to both his own past and his own nature, but to a past he had rejected and a nature he had sought to negate. His heart is moved again, and to have its torpor stirred is pain, but this is the pain of life.

Less than two months later, as he made his final decision and moved to join Teresa, he redrafted his poem. Characteristically, the poem is now more indecisive than the man, for he alters the final lines to a lament:

> My heart is all meridian, were it not
>   I had not suffered now, nor should I be
> Despite old tortures ne'er to be forgot
>   The slave again — Oh! Love! at least of thee!
>
> 'Tis vain to struggle, I have struggled long
>   To love again no more as once I loved,
> Oh! Time! why leave this worst of earliest
>   Passions strong?
>   To tear a heart which pants to be unmoved?

Byron was too courtly to leave the penultimate line as above, and modified it to "why leave this earliest Passion strong?" With either reading, this makes for a weaker and less controlled climax to the poem than the first version, as it denies the strength of the poet's own will. The first set of "Stanzas to the Po" makes a permanent imaginative gesture, and deserves to be read repeatedly as the universal human legacy it comes so close to being. The heart divided against itself has found few more eloquent emblems.

Last Poems

On the morning of his thirty-sixth birthday, at Missolonghi, where he was to die three months later, Byron finished the poem that is his epitaph:

> 'Tis time this heart should be unmoved,
>   Since others it hath ceased to move:
> Yet, though I cannot be beloved,
>   Still let me love!

He begins with an echo of the final line of the "Stanzas to the Po," but the emphasis is different. He now fears not that he will love again but that he cannot:

> My days are in the yellow leaf;
>   The flowers and fruits of love are gone;
> The worm, the canker, and the grief
>   Are mine alone!

The Macbeth comparison is perhaps rather too melodramatic, but the next stanza modulates to the more appropriate Promethean image of fire:

> The fire that on my bosom preys
>   Is lone as some volcanic isle;
> No torch is kindled at its blaze —
>   A funeral pile.

The fire is not yet out, the volcano not extinct, but the volcano is isolated and the fire will be consumed with the poet. He wears the chain of love (for the abandoned Teresa?) but he cannot share in its pain and power. In a recovery of great rhetorical power he turns upon his grief and delivers himself up to his destiny:

> Tread those reviving passions down,
>   Unworthy manhood! — unto thee
> Indifferent should the smile or frown
>   Of beauty be.
>
> If thou regrett'st thy youth, *why live?*
>   The land of honourable death
> Is here: — up to the field, and give
>   Away thy breath!
>
> Seek out — less often sought than found —
>   A soldier's grave, for thee the best;
> Then look around, and choose thy ground,
>   And take thy rest.

Byron seems to have intended this as his last poem, but his Muses had it otherwise, and ended him with an intense love poem for his page-boy Loukas. The suffering conveyed by this poem clearly has its sexual element, so that the complex puzzle of Byron is not exactly simplified for us, but this is a problem for his biographers, who have reached no agreement upon it. Certainly Byron had homosexual as well as incestuous experience; his questing and experimental psyche, and his conviction of necessary damnation, could have led him to no less. In his final lines he liberates himself from his last verbal inhibition and writes a very powerful homesexual love poem:

I watched thee when the foe was at our side,
  Ready to strike at him — or thee and me.
Were safety hopeless — rather than divide
  Aught with one loved save love and liberty.

I watched thee on the breakers, when the rock
  Received our prow and all was storm and fear,
And bade thee cling to me through every shock;
  This arm would be thy bark, or breast thy bier.

Love and death come dangerously close together in these tense stanzas, so much so that one can understand why Loukas was wary enough to cause Byron to lament:

And when convulsive throes denied my breath
  The faintest utterance to my fading thought,
To thee — to thee — e'en in the gasp of death
  My spirit turned, oh! oftener than it ought.

Thus much and more; and yet thou lov'st me not,
  And never wilt! Love dwells not in our will.
Nor can I blame thee, though it be my lot
  To strongly, wrongly, vainly love thee still.

It is very moving that this agonized hymn to hopeless love should be Byron's last poem. Had he been more of a Promethean he would still not have achieved a better either sexual or rhetorical balance, when one remembers the English and European society through which he had to take his way. But he might have had more faith in his own imaginings, more confidence in his own inventive power, and so have given us something larger and more relevant than *Manfred* in the Romantic mode, good as *Manfred* is. We have *Don Juan*, and the record, still incomplete, of Byron's life. Byron did not seem to regret his not having given us more, and was himself realistic enough to believe that there was no more to give.

G. WILSON KNIGHT

The Two Eternities

A poet's work may often appear to contradict his life. With Lord Byron this is not so. He is, as a man, a vital embodiment of post-Renaissance poetry: a proud individualist, asserting the primacy of instinct through an agonized self-conflict. His social sympathies are violently given to causes of liberty. He incurs charges of immorality. He lives what others so often write, leaving his native land somewhat as Timon leaves Athens. That insistent aspiration, that aristocracy of spirit, met with variously in fiction after fiction, is here incarnate: more, it is given, as in Shakespeare's plays, an outward formulation in aristocracy of birth. Such aristocracy may be used in poetry to materialize an inner, spiritual, royalty, as in *Tess of the D'Urbervilles*: and Byron is so much the more effective, as a dramatic figure, by reason of his title. In close alliance he shows an ingrained Shakespearian respect for tradition, for history, increasing the agony and tension of revolt. He has weakness, and is tortured by a sense of sexual sin. The vice, weakness, and nobility behind all high literary adventures are his, as a man. How slight some famous poets might appear should we choose to scrutinize their apparent littleness, their failure to match in life the spectacular essences of their work. A slight shift of perspective and Wordsworth looks like an old maid; Coleridge becomes a not very pleasant blend of talkative don and dope-fiend; Keats an adolescent; Shelley a seraphic blur. But Byron has warm flesh and colour. His life itself falls into poetic and tragic form. Mediterranean coasts are perennially fertilizing forces to northern poetry. Italy floods the Renaissance and particularly the Shakespearian consciousness; poets from Chaucer and Milton to Browning and Lawrence have travelled there; and many have managed to die there, or

From *The Burning Oracle: Studies in the Poetry of Action.* © 1939 by Oxford University Press. Originally entitled "The Two Eternities: An Essay on Byron."

thereabouts. But Byron does it all more superbly than any. Greece — to put a subtle matter crudely — seems for some time to have been challenging our traditional Christian culture, many poets offering an Olympian or Dionysian theology as co-partners with the Christian. Moreover, liberty — of spirit, mind, body, and community — has been for centuries a widening and pressing imaginative demand. Our dominant personal and communal poetic directions from Marlowe and Milton through Pope to Shelley, Browning, and Lawrence are, I should suppose, (i) something closely related to erotic instincts, and (ii) the cause of liberty. Byron suffers social ostracism and banishment for the one and death for the other. Incest, says Shelley, is a very poetical thing: presumably since every act of artistic creation involves a kind of incestuous union within the personality. Byron is suspected of it in actual fact. Next, he dies fighting for the perfect sacrificial cause: the liberty of Greece. He lives that eternity which is art. He is more than a writer: his virtues and vices alike are precisely those entwined at the roots of poetry. He is poetry incarnate. The others are dreamers: he is the thing itself.

His literary work (our only present concern) is continuous with these impressions. He did not at first see himself as a poet, as an early preface shows; and when he did start writing in earnest, went after stories of colour and action. His human understanding is glamorous, his incidents well costumed. Piratical adventure mixes with passionate love; there is the flash of steel and smell of powder. His is a cruel, yet romantic, world where blood flows hot. It is objectively conceived. Byron can lose himself in creation of emotional shapes outside his direct experience. He will use a reverential Christianity for his purpose; but can equally well salute a dying Moslem in *The Giaour* with the consummate technical ease of:

> But him the maids of Paradise
>   Impatient to their halls invite,
> And the dark heaven of Houris' eyes
>   On him shall glance for ever bright.

This is a truly Shakespearian power, one with the impersonal historical interest of *Childe Harold* and his love of peoples and places generally. A strong sense of a particular and honourable past lingers round each person or place he touches. He is poetically sensitive to variations in human tradition and culture. He is cosmopolitan and extraverted. And yet his tales also express a certain violent and recurring psychological experience with mysterious depths of passion and guilt variously hinted or revealed. To this I give my primary attention.

The Giaour is a powerful example. The inside of mental agony is revealed, Byron's poetry piercing and twisting into its centre:

> The mind, that broods o'er guilty woes,
>   Is like the Scorpion girt by fire;
> In circle narrowing as it glows,
> The flames around their captive close,
> Till inly search'd by thousand throes,
>   And maddening in her ire,
> One sad and sole relief she knows,
> The sting she nourish'd for her foes,
> Whose venom never yet was vain,
> Gives but one pang and cures all pain,
> And darts into her desperate brain.

The rhetorical tension is maintained with a never-failing grip. Each word is charged, each sentence tight. What universes are here housed in the tiny yet deadly form of the scorpion: its own venomous nature makes its agony the more terrifying. The little drama symbolizes the horror, which is one with the energies, of biological existence: it gets at the very nerve behind ecstasy and anguish alike. Byron's in-feeling into animal life and energy is from the start distinctive. *The Giaour* is rich with it:

> Go when the hunter's hand hath wrung
> From forest-cave her shrieking young,
> And calm the lonely lioness:
> But soothe not — mock not, my distress!

He continually attributes sensitive nerves and minds to the animal creation; or may delight in its more lyric vitalities, as when he sees a butterfly

> rising on its purple wing
> The insect queen of eastern spring

being chased by a boy, and makes subtle comparison between this and love. Either the fleeting loveliness rises far above the 'panting heart', or, if caught

> With wounded wing, or bleeding breast,
> Ah! where shall either victim rest?
> Can this with faded pinion soar
> From rose to tulip as before?

See the choice placing of a well-considered diction; also the peculiarly soft use of consonants. Stern as are his tales, Byron's poetry masters with equal ease a lyric grace and wrenching guilt: and through all burns deep sympathy for animals, often small ones (as in Pope); which is again one with his penetration to the

central energies, the springs of action, in beast or man. The two are continuous.
The hero of *The Giaour* is typical of Byron's tales, a man in hell, yet unbowed,
and with a certain obscurity as to the dark cause of his suffering:

> Wet with thine own best blood shall drip
> Thy gnashing tooth and haggard lip;
> Then stalking to thy sullen grave,
> Go—and with Ghouls and Afrits rave;
> Till these in horror shrink away
> From spectre more accursed than they!

This ends a passage of towering satanic virulence; and its compressed explosive-
ness must surely win respect even from those whose direct response will be most
impeded by the traditionally modelled—though pulsing—phraseology.
Though the hero retires to a monastery where it "soothes him to abide," for
"some dark deed without a name," he nevertheless "looks not to priesthood for
relief." The balance of some irreligious passion against orthodox Christianity approaches in tone that of "Eloisa to Abelard"; while the rejection of religious assistance as powerless to ease the dark anguish and alter an inevitable course recalls
Faustus, Wuthering Heights, and Byron's own *Manfred*. The close is subdued:

> I would not, if I might, be blest;
> I want no paradise, but rest.

He would be buried with no record but a simple cross. The Moslem's hatred for
the infidel is here burningly proud and fierce; but Christianity is also at the last
reverenced. Such opposites of pagan fire and Christian gentleness are characteristically Byronic; and they are to be in poem after poem subdued, as here, to an
eternal peace.

Perhaps Conrad in *The Corsair* is the finest of his early human studies:

> Lone, wild, and strange, he stood alike exempt
> From all affection and from all contempt. (I. 11)

The narratives revolve generally on an inward psychic, or spiritual, conflict.
Though Conrad is a pirate chief of stern and ruthless action, his is a deeply
spiritual bitterness. His anguish is almost brutally revealed:

> There is a war, a chaos of the mind,
> When all its elements convulsed, combined,
> Lie dark and jarring with perturbed force,
> And gnashing with impenitent remorse. (II. 10)

The lines suit Macbeth: and though we may be reminded of Crabbe the Byronic hero has a tragic direction not found in "Peter Grimes." He is noble and Miltonic:

> His was the lofty port, the distant mien,
> That seems to shun the sight—and awes if seen:
> The solemn aspect, and the high-born eye,
> That checks low mirth, but lacks not courtesy. (I. 16)

No captive girls ever seduce his attention from Medora. "None are all evil" (I. 12), we are told, and at the core of his personality is a love, a "softness"; this word, or "soft," recurring throughout Byron's work with the deepest central significance. In this very poem Antony is the "soft triumvir" (II. 15). Conrad is, however, a grim figure; and his endurance whilst awaiting torture is given terrible poetic disclosure. Yet he refuses to save himself by a cowardly murder and is nauseated by a woman, Gulnare, doing it for him. Indeed, all horrors of his wide piratical experience or natural imagination are shown as nothing to that arising from this desecration of feminine gentleness. From none

> So thrill'd, so shudder'd every creeping vein,
> As now they froze before that purple stain. (III. 10)

The passage is most powerful, tracing territories explored in the conception of Lady Macbeth. The hero suffers originally through determination to save women from his own piratical massacre: which, though perhaps irrational, is intensely Byronic. Frequently we come across such ruthless evil and cynical callousness enshrining a strangely soft, almost feminine, devotion. Conrad's heart "was form'd for softness, warp'd to wrong" (III. 23). The poem's conclusion holds a reserved depth of feeling reminiscent of Pope. He finds Medora dead:

> He ask'd no question—all were answered now
> By the first glance on that still, marble brow. (III. 21)

Notice how strongest emotion is uttered through a simple statement: "all were answer'd now"; and how that makes of one human death a vast eternity, almost an assurance. So

> his mother's softness crept
> To those wild eyes, which like an infant's wept. (III. 22)

Yet he is not sentimentalized. As in *Macbeth*, the poet dares to end with a condemnation, leaving the human delineation to plead its own cause:

> He left a Corsair's name to other times,
> Link'd with one virtue, and a thousand crimes. (III. 24)

From the start, the central complex of loneliness and cruelty is undefined. The same figure recurs in *Lara*. Though cold, ruthless, and with a smile "waned in its mirth and wither'd to a sneer" (I. 17) the hero is yet one "with more capacity for love than earth bestows" (I. 18) on most men. The dark mystery shrouding his past is never lifted. They are all, like Heathcliff and Captain Ahab, personalities tugged by some strange evil between time and eternity.

The poetic vigour of each narrative, depending on choice and exact statement rather than abstruse analogy or magic sound, never fails. Subtle rhythmic variation may finely realize description, as this of a floating corpse, from *The Bride of Abydos*:

> As shaken on his restless pillow
> His head heaves with the heaving billow. (II. 26)

Continually a fine thing is said as a way to realize some great feeling. Especially strong are the darkest moments, as "I want no paradise, but rest" and "This brow that then will burn no more" from *The Giaour*. The decasyllabic couplets of *The Corsair* hold an equal tragic force:

> Oh! o'er the eye Death most exerts his might,
> And hurls the spirit from her throne of light (III. 20)

Verbs play a major, often a dominating part, as in the remorseless beat of the line "Eternity forbids thee to forget" (I. 23) from *Lara*. The diction accepts personifications of a vast yet simple and un-ornate kind, and traditionally "poetic" words of various sorts. These, as in Pope, are chosen to express a ready-made fusion of the particular and general. The influence of Pope may be at times very obvious, too, in couplet-modulation, as — to take random examples from a wide field — in *The Corsair*, I. 11, and the lines beginning "No danger daunts . . ." from *The Bride of Abydos*, II. 20. As in Pope, each word is exactly used but loaded with more than its natural maximum of force. The lines cry to be uttered and can be understood, if not fully appreciated, at once. The emotional precision is unerring, defined yet never metallic: like the twang of a taut string.

However perfect the control, the energies — spiritual or physical — set in action are striking. Many fine animal creations are symptomatic of the Byronic mastery of the vital and organic, as in the wild Tartar horse of the later story *Mazeppa* with the "speed of thought" in his limbs, and the other thousand with

> Wide nostrils never stretch'd by pain,
> Mouths bloodless to the bit or rein. (XVII)

Byron feels in and with the animal. There is the "stately buffalo" with his "fiery eyes" and stamping hoofs attacked by wolves in *The Siege of Corinth* (XXIII);

the insect stinging to save its property (compare the wren in *Macbeth*) and the adder seeking vengeance when trodden on, in *The Corsair* (I. 13–14). The end of *The Prisoner of Chillon* provides perhaps the best; where the hero, after an eternity of dark imprisonment, has actually made such friends with the spiders of his dungeon and so long loved the mice at their "moonlit play" that he is reluctant to leave; and I doubt if the whole range of Byron's work provides a sweeter instance of his uncanny penetration into the most secret chambers of a mind in agony and loneliness. The moon in Byron has elsewhere such tragic associations. Continuous with these animal intuitions is the Shakespearian feeling for human personality, characterized by ability and desire to give vital action and project figures of innate dignity — quite apart from their ethical standing — and blazing courage; and women, including Gulnare in *The Corsair*, of an utterly instinctive, yet magnificent, devotion.

The tales are characterized by (i) vivid and colourful action, and (ii) a recurring psychological conflict normally related to some feminine romance-interest. You may get mainly action, as in *The Bride of Abydos* and the nightmare frenzy of the ride in *Mazeppa*; or mainly a psychological study, as in *Lara*. *The Corsair* is I think the finest in its balance of both. The atmosphere of *The Giaour* is powerfully realized, but the hero's remorse seems disproportionate to the occasion. The central guilt-complex is, of course, always best left without premature definition, as in *Hamlet* and *Macbeth*. We can feel the poet aiming at a story-action that fits his intuition. However, in the tightly woven and sustained power of *Parisina* a short plot is cleverly devised to condition logically the mind-state of the Byronic hero, the story stopping where he begins. The perfect fusion of inward experience and active plot is never perhaps quite mastered. There is no deeply significant outer conflict, no clash of universal forces, unless the balance of religions in *The Giaour* might so qualify. Profundities are found in most searching human comment continually, but the action is not by itself profound. A bridge of some sort is needed; a conduit to flood the whole setting with something of the hero's tragic power. The narratives are to this extent slightly inorganic in comparison with Shakespeare: they have a hero, but no heart. A field of dramatic meaning has not been generated — an individual psychological and spiritual study, however deep, cannot quite do this — and the incidents and persons accordingly lose generalized significance and stature: though the tragic direction generally works to create a sense of some mysterious eternity at the close. Only a judgement most insensitive to the deadly marksmanship of Byron's peculiar excellences would stigmatize them as "melodramatic."

These tales of action and geographic colour are strung together by a central, expressly personal, experience. The human penetration, the revelation of mental suffering, is always primary. But *Childe Harold* is more consistently extraverted,

though it has a similar twofold appeal, with, again, a separateness: nature-des-
criptions, however, doing something towards a fusion, as I shall show. A series of
meditations on places and events is given unity by the shadowy conception of
Harold, that is, Byron. Yet, this once forgiven, we are struck by the amazing
vitality of creation. Byron is the only poet since Shakespeare to possess one of
Shakespeare's rarest gifts: that of pure artistic joy in the annals—after searching I
can find no better word—of human action; in close association, moreover, with
places. He feels the tingling nearness of any heroic past. Gray had something of
this; so had Scott; and Hardy gets it in his *Dynasts* as a whole, perhaps, if not in
the parts. This is something quite beyond our contemporary sophistication. It is
an ability to love not mankind, as did Shelley, but men; and men—or women—
of various sorts, places, and times:

> Is it for this the Spanish maid, aroused,
> Hangs on the willow her unstrung guitar. (I. 54)

Or, of Waterloo:

> And wild and high the 'Cameron's gathering' rose!
> The war-note of Lochiel, which Albyn's hills
> Have heard, and heard too have her Saxon foes—
> How in the noon of night that pibroch thrills. (III. 26)

And this of the dying gladiator:

> He reck'd not of the life he lost nor prize,
> But where his rude hut by the Danube lay. (IV. 141)

He is fascinated with the persons of one scene or event after another. The scattered incidents are given a sincere unity by the autobiographical thread; this extraverted interest, almost love, being integral to the Byronic imagination.

But the suffering behind every glamorous association is not forgotten.
Historic excitement is often one with a condemnation of history: since a fundamental love of men is involved and history often cruel. For example:

> Ah, monarchs! Could ye taste the mirth ye mar,
> Not in the toils of glory would ye fret;
> The hoarse dull drum would sleep, and Man be happy yet! (I. 47)

There is no facile militarism: but rather an opposition to the clang and fury of
world affairs of simple—and often, as here, sensuous—joys. On the eve of Waterloo a "heavy sound" of cannon breaks short the pleasures of the dance. Then are
there

> cheeks all pale, which but an hour ago
> Blushed at the praise of their own loveliness;
> And there were sudden partings, such as press
> The life from out young hearts, and choking sighs. (III. 24)

I point not merely to verbal excellences but to the especially impersonal, yet warm, sympathy with human instincts. So from "Beauty's circle" they are shown next in "battle's magnificently proud array"; and finally hurled, horse and rider, friend and foe, "in one red burial." The fervour which so admires courage and battle-finery is one with that which pities the transition from dance to slaughter. It is a total awareness of the Shakespearian sort. Byron can start to describe a bull-fight in a glamorous stanza (I. 73) of steeds and spurs and ladies' eyes; only to give a poignant sympathy to the suffering of bull and horse in a "brutal" sport. The same sympathy is accorded the dying gladiator in Book IV butchered for Rome's enjoyment; yet this does not preclude a feeling for Rome's imperial greatness. The poet is aware of emotional opposites involving each other, or rather of a single emotion taking opposite forms of assertion and pathos: just as the agonized conflicts and evil passions of his heroes are somehow one with their instincts of chivalry and tenderness. So he lets himself be, as it were, annihilated continually before each splendour and pathos in turn.

His feeling for human nobility past and present is also one with his acceptance of a traditional poetic diction. This repays our close attention. Few poets have accomplished so much effortless force in single lines, as, for example:

> Stop! — for thy tread is on an Empire's dust! (III. 17)

Or

> The spouseless Adriatic mourns her lord. (IV. 11)

Or

> Oh Time! the beautifier of the dead. (IV. 130)

The utterance is weighty yet carried easily: the thing said seems to be all in all, with no attempt at original expression. There is a play of metaphor and often what Ruskin — in a confused and misleading essay — named the "pathetic fallacy": but such call no attention to themselves and are accompanied by no especial excitement. The style, here, as in the tales, is peculiarly assured, involving a use of words where the fusion of general and particular, philosophic meditation and objective description, has already been performed; though in *Childe Harold* both the general scheme and stanza form alike demand a more fluid and less packed and explosive language. No effort is expended on abstruse comparison

or the jerking of word or image from its habitual use or associative value. Personifications and abstractions are frequent but never cloudy, denoting concepts
generally accepted. They are always words of an adequate syllabic weight;
words, as it were, tested in the past and found to ring true; words of poetic
lineage. In the first two lines just quoted "tread," "dust," "spouse," "mourns"
all strike me as examples of what might be called a middle diction, a workman-
like poetic, but not too poetic, manner. This may rise even to

> Their praise is hymn'd by loftier harps than mine (III. 29)

without loss of sincerity. So we have strong nouns, plain, usually active, verbs,
sentences cleanly turned out, well drilled, and marching to their purpose. No
verbal magic is allowed at the expense of clarity. Similarly, Byron's religious intuitions are based on a preliminary acceptance of the conventional, seen in the
robust Johnsonian phraseology — as well as thought — of

> I speak not of men's creeds: they rest between
> Man and his Maker. (IV. 95)

As a rule every accent is poetically distinguished with none superlative: nor
meant to be. But the thing said, or the object seen, may be of superlative
grandeur, as this, of Rome:

> The Niobe of nations! There she stands,
> Childless and crownless, in her voiceless woe. (IV. 79)

The sympathy with the present pathos of ruins cannot be detached from that acceptance of the one-time historic splendour which also chooses well-worn associations such as the splendour of "nations," the awe of crowns, the traditional
poetic appeal of a word such as "woe." Byron likes, as a poet, what is already
warm with human contact. He injects into it his own vitality, whether in admiration or rebellion. He likes human society and its history: which is but a surface
effect of that deeper in-feeling into animal or human vitality that enables him to
display both convincing action and a moving pathos.

And yet again he stands outside the world he writes of, balancing human
purpose against human futility. *Childe Harold* is a lamentation in noble phrases
over the widespread ruins of a dead chivalry and a dead tyranny. Byron is superbly
conscious of the whole of Europe. But he also sees it as one vast theatre of tomb-
stones: though at his touch the dead are temporarily raised, and in the poetry
there is no futility. He ranges across the centuries accepting and cherishing a
past — or recent present — which he simultaneously repudiates and regrets. So he
hymns empires whilst hating the wrongs of tyranny; recognizes the "lion" in

Napoleon whilst decrying servility to "wolves" (III. 19); glories in patriot battlefields though attacking the iniquities of wars by which monarchs "pave their way
with human hearts" (I. 42); at the limit, he praises life whilst entranced by
death. He is a militant pacifist, exposing the fallacies of ambition (I. 42–44). The
tragic notes are his surest, the richer for the human excellences apprehended. The
whole poem is written from a vast eternity-consciousness to which historic events,
as events, are the negative symbols of its expression. There is thus a very "life" in
"despair," a mysterious "vitality of poison" (III. 34). Particulars are vivid chiefly by
reason of their felt transience. Somehow their transience *is* their eternity:

> Far other scene is Thrasimene now. (IV. 65)

Or, when we come to Rome, the mystery of time itself takes ghostly form, entwined with infinite space and natural magic:

> But when the rising moon begins to climb
> Its topmost arch, and gently pauses there;
> When the stars twinkle through the loops of time,
> And the low night-breeze waves along the air
> The garland-forest, which the gray walls wear,
> Like laurels on the bald first Caesar's head;
> When the light shines serene but doth not glare,
> Then in this magic circle raise the dead:
> Heroes have trod this spot—'tis on their dust ye tread. (IV. 144)

The grandeur of Rome lives most in its ruins. After visiting the Coliseum and
wandering through memories of a dead empire we come to St. Peter's, which
strikes from the poet both a magnificent religious fervour and subtle architectural appreciation in living terms, characteristically, of the *human* mind unable
to take in the whole splendour with a single glance, yet at last distended to eternal comprehension; and end with the great invocation to the sea, imperial
beyond all empires—

> Roll on, thou deep and dark blue Ocean—roll!
> Ten thousand fleets sweep over thee in vain. (IV. 179)

With what sureness are handled, as in Gray's *Elegy*, the noble platitudes so often
composing the greatest poetry. "Assyria, Greece, Rome, Carthage, what are
they?" he asks. Their life was conditioned by that spirit (he calls it "freedom"
but perhaps we should give it a wider name) that alone can preserve, without
which they are dust. That spirit is reflected by both (i) the poet's ranging consciousness—the "eternal spirit of the chainless mine" of his Chillon sonnet—

autobiographical soliloquy significantly alternating with the scenic progress and reaching its culmination in the great personal apologetic and satiric outburst near the close; and (ii) the sea, unfettered by temporal law.

> Time writes no wrinkle on thine azure brow:
> Such as creation's dawn beheld, thou rollest now.

This vast unfathomable interlocks itself with that humanism, that social and historic sympathy, so dearly deep in Byron; something other, drawing him near the awestruck naturalism of Wordsworth.

Childe Harold has, continually, passages of a more elemental sort, with also a continual swerve in comment from particular to general. My remarks on diction do not say the whole truth. Often a metaphor may start up with at once surface flash and revealing psychological depth, the more vivid for the generally level style:

> And how and why we know not, nor can trace
> Home to its cloud this lightning of the mind. (IV. 24)

Natural immensities fill out wide areas of the later Cantos III and IV, acting as a bridge between the hero and his world: his own consciousness is shown as, personally, more akin to them than to the human drama that was his first story. The process reflects that dissociation found first in *Timon of Athens* and urgent since: but no other poet of Byron's period shows a range of sympathy sufficient to include both sides of the opposition. So the sea is felt as a bounding freedom (as in *The Corsair*), especially freedom from stifling human contacts (III. 2, 3). He now invokes "maternal Nature" (III. 46). That other vastness of mountains so weightily insistent in the imagination of Byron's day is duly honoured:

> Not vainly did the early Persian make
> His altar the high places, and the peak
> Of earth-o'ergazing mountains. (III. 91)

Such an association may be referred back to both Wordsworth and Coleridge. But there are passages more finely detailed, more energy-striking than this: as that describing the roar and hell-cauldrons of a "Kubla Khan" mountain waterfall, the rising mist above, the ever fertilized green turf, the peaceful river of the plain; and, as we look back, an Iris rainbow shot through the dreadful waters, still and brilliant above agonized distraction, like "Love watching Madness with unalterable mien" (IV. 69–72): a line whose depth and fervency of human — or other — understanding shows the author to be, potentially, a tragic artist of Shakespearian stature. Often such a swift transition transfixes its mark with quivering intensity: Byron's nature-images are, normally, made to serve, or at least blend into, some human purpose. But they are also great in their own right: so we have "shaggy summits" (IV. 73) where, when storm and darkness riot, there are flashes lovely as — typically — a woman's "dark eye," as

> From peak to peak, the rattling crags among
> Leaps the live thunder! (III. 92)

"Live": a living ecstasy continually energizes Byron's work. But he can also treat of mighty glaciers or the placid Rhone with immediate descriptive force. All such vast natural symbols objectify that in himself that demarks him from men's society. Any man "who surpasses or subdues mankind" is as a mountain looking on the hate of those below (III. 45). Himself he is a "portion" of that nature "around" him, rejecting the agonies of human society, finding life in natural kinship with the "mountains, waves, and skies," as "part" of his soul, and looking to death for cosmic freedom (III. 71–75). He knows the secrets of "pathless woods" and "lonely shore" (IV. 178). They and their eternity are the watch-towers from which he looks down on the rise and fall of empires. But he never for long forgets man. "I love not man the less but nature more" (IV. 178) is really an over-statement. All his finest nature-impressions up-pile to blend with the supreme human grandeur of Rome. His mind outdistances his companions, that is all: if he could put all of himself into one word, that word were "lightning" (III. 97). The choice is exact: and the image can be reversed. His brow, like that of his own Azo ploughed by the "burning share" of sorrow (*Parisina*, 20), may be, metaphorically, felt kin also to that of Milton's Satan which "deep scars of thunder had intrench'd"; or the She-wolf of his own description, the "thunder-stricken nurse of Rome" whose limbs lightning has blackened (IV. 88); or, best of all, the bust of Ariosto "doubly sacred" by the thunder-flame that stripped it of its crown (IV. 41).

Few poets show so instinctive a human insight: yet he is being forced against his will into the individualism of Wordsworth and Shelley. Yet there is a difference. He assimilates, but is not subdued by, the splendours of nature. He has been blamed for lightly and theatrically making poetic gestures not deeply felt; and it is true that certain lines in *Childe Harold* appear to merit the charge. Sometimes the transition from the more Augustan diction of the tales (mostly written before the latter Cantos of *Childe Harold*) to a newly vital nature-imagery is not perfect. Byron seems to gather in his new material with something of too sweeping a gesture, too aristocratic a superiority: he takes it for his own, more human, purpose. He is not, any more than Shakespeare, subdued to nature-mysticism. Yet he can, when he cares to, turn it to a far finer, because more human, account, as in the image of love and madness recently noticed, than any poet of his day. He is always above, not below, his contemporaries. The

others rave over cataracts and mountains: and he too goes to mountains for inspiration. As it happens, they serve him magnificently: probably as a man, certainly as a poet. But they do not rank so importantly with him as that other more
Shakespearian vastness, the sea. That from *The Corsair* (which contains some
fine sea-poetry) to *The Island* and *Don Juan* is a permanent possession, whereas
mountains affect him deeply only now, in mid-career. No English poet has written more finely of the sea, as in the rolling volumes—got by "o"-sounds—of

> Thou glorious mirror, where the Almighty's form
> Glasses itself in tempests; in all time,—
> Calm or convulsed, in breeze or gale or storm,
> Icing the pole, or in the torrid clime
> Dark-heaving—boundless, endless, and sublime,
> The image of eternity, the throne
> Of the Invisible; even from out thy slime
> The monsters of the deep are made; each zone
> Obeys thee; thou goest forth, dread, fathomless, alone. (IV. 183)

"The image of eternity": the concept pulses throughout Byron's work. Contrast
this with his great denunciatory and prophetic passage (IV. 133–7) where he
piles on the heads of mankind his curse of "forgiveness"; next strikes the exact
note and manner of Pope's satiric epistles ("petty, perfidy," "the small whisper
of the as paltry few," "venom," "reptile"); and finally asserts the undying powers
("something unearthly") of his poetry to reassert his rights. You can see how the
two elements—objective human interest and lonely individualism—of the early
narratives are rending apart. He is torn between history and tragic insight,
mankind and lonely self-conflict, time and eternity. The disparity is bridged by
sea and mountains, infinite expanse and lifting mass, each at once symbols of
both the natural and the eternal.

NORTHROP FRYE

Lord Byron

The main appeal of Byron's poetry is in the fact that it is Byron's. To read
Byron's poetry is to hear all about Byron's marital difficulties, flirtations, love for
Augusta, friendships, travels, and political and social views. And Byron is a consistently interesting person to hear about, this being why Byron, even at his
worst of self-pity and egotism and blither and doggerel, is still so incredibly
readable. He proves what many critics declare to be impossible, that a poem can
make its primary impact as a historical and biographical document. The critical
problem involved here is crucial to our understanding of not only Byron but literature as a whole. Even when Byron's poetry is not objectively very good, it is
still important, because it is Byron's. But who was Byron to be so important?
Certainly not an exceptionally good or wise man. Byron is, strictly, neither a
great poet nor a great man who wrote poetry, but something in between: a tremendous cultural force that was life and literature at once. How he came to be
this is what we must try to explain as we review the four chief genres of his work:
the lyrics, the tales (including *Childe Harold*), the dramas, and the later satires.

Byron's lyrical poetry affords a good exercise in critical catholicity, because
it contains nothing that "modern" critics look for: no texture, no ambiguities,
no intellectualized ironies, no intensity, no vividness of phrasing, the words and
images being vague to the point of abstraction. The poetry seems to be a plain
man's poetry, making poetic emotion out of the worn and blunted words of ordinary speech. Yet it is not written by a plain man: it is written, as Arnold said,
with the careless ease of a man of quality, and its most striking and obvious feature is its gentlemanly amateurism. It is, to be sure, in an amateur tradition, being

From *Major British Writers*, Enlarged edition, Vol. 2, ed. G. B. Harrison. © 1959 by Harcourt Brace
Jovanovich.

a romantic, subjective, personal development of the kind of Courtly Love poetry that was written by Tudor and Cavalier noblemen in earlier ages. Byron's frequent statements in prefaces that this would be his last work to trouble the public with, his offhand deprecating comments on his work, his refusal to revise, all give a studious impression of a writer who can take poetry or leave it alone. Byron held the view that lyrical poetry was an expression of passion, and that passion was essentially fitful, and he distrusted professional poets, who pretended to be able to summon passion at will and sustain it indefinitely. Poe was later to hold much the same view of poetry, but more consistently, for he drew the inference that a continuous long poem was impossible, whereas *Childe Harold* has the stretches of perfunctory, even slapdash writing that one would expect with such a theory.

In Byron's later lyrics, especially the *Hebrew Melodies* of 1815, where he was able to add some of his Oriental technicolor to the Old Testament, more positive qualities emerge, particularly in the rhythm. "The Destruction of Sennacherib" is a good reciter's piece (though not without its difficulties, as Tom Sawyer discovered), and anticipates some of the later experiments in verbal jazz by Poe and Swinburne. Some of the best of his poems bear the title "Stanzas for Music," and they have the flat conventional diction appropriate to poems that depend partly on another art for their sound:

> One shade the more, one ray the less,
>   Had half impaired the nameless grace
> Which waves in every raven tress,
>   Or softly lightens o'er her face;
> Where thoughts serenely sweet express
>   How pure, how dear their dwelling-place.

(If the reader would like a clue to the caressing rhythm of this stanza, he should read the iambic meters so as to give the stresses twice the length of the unstressed syllables. Then the lines will fall into four bars of three-four time, beginning on the third beat, and the rhythm of a nineteenth-century waltz will emerge.) We notice that while Byron's amateur predecessors wrote in a convention and Byron from personal experience, Byron was equally conventional, because his personal experience conformed to a literary pattern. Byron's life imitated literature: this is where his unique combination of the poetic and the personal begins.

Byron was naturally an extroverted person, fond of company, of travel, of exploring new scenes, making new friends, falling in love with new women. Like Keats, in a much more direct way, he wanted a life of sensations rather than of thoughts. As he said: "I can not repent me (I try very often) so much of any thing I have done, as of anything I have left undone. Alas! I have been but idle, and have the prospect of an early decay, without having seized every available instant of our pleasurable years." In the records of his journeys in his letters and Hobhouse's diaries, it is the more introverted Hobhouse who dwells on the dirt and the fleas, and it is Hobhouse too who does the serious studying and takes an interest in archaeology. It is Byron who swims across the Hellespont, learns the songs of Albanian mountaineers, makes friends with a Moslem vizier, amuses himself with the boys in a monastery school, flirts with Greek girls, and picks up a smattering of Armenian. He was continually speculating about unknown sensations, such as how it would feel to have committed a murder, and he had the nervous dread of growing older that goes with the fear of slowing down in the rhythm of experience. His writing depends heavily on experience; he seldom describes any country that he has not seen, and for all his solitary role he shows, especially in *Don Juan*, a novelist's sense of established society.

It was an essential part of his strongly extroverted and empirical bent that he should not be a systematic thinker, nor much interested in people who were. He used his intelligence to make common-sense judgements on specific situations, and found himself unable to believe anything that he did not find confirmed in his own experience. In his numerous amours, for example, the absence of any sense of sin was as unanswerable a fact of his experience as the presence of it would have been to St. Augustine. He thought of sexual love as a product of reflex and mechanical habit, not of inner emotional drives. When he said: "I do not believe in the existence of what is called love," we are probably to take him quite literally. Nevertheless, his extroversion made him easily confused by efforts at self-analysis, and he flew into rages when he was accused of any lack of feeling. One reason why his marriage demoralized him so was that it forced such efforts on him.

Now if we look in Byron's tales and *Childe Harold* we usually find as the central character an inscrutable figure with hollow cheeks and blazing eyes, wrapped in a cloud of gloom, full of mysterious and undefined remorse, an outcast from society, a wanderer of the race of Cain. At times he suggests something demonic rather than human, a Miltonic Satan or fallen angel. He may be a sinister brigand like the Corsair, or an aloof and icily polite aristocrat like the Lucifer of *The Vision of Judgment*, but he is always haughty and somber of demeanor; his glance is difficult to meet; he will not brook questioning, though he himself questions all established social standards, and he is associated with lonely and colorful predatory animals, as ordinary society is with gregarious ones like sheep and domestic fowl. "The lion is alone, and so am I," says Manfred. The name of the Corsair is "linked with one virtue, and a thousand crimes": the virtue is manifested when he refuses, as a prisoner, to assassinate his captor to escape being impaled. Fortunately his mistress Gulnare was less scrupulous. As for Lara, who is the Corsair returned from exile to his estates:

He stood a stranger in this breathing world,
An erring spirit from another hurled.

This type of character is now known as the "Byronic hero," and wherever he has
appeared since in literature there has been the influence, direct or indirect, of
Byron. And if we ask how a witty, sociable, extroverted poet came to create such
a character, we can see that it must have arisen as what psychologists call a projection of his inner self, that inner self that was so mysterious and inscrutable even
to its owner.

It happened that this type of character had already been popularized in the
"Gothic" thrillers or "horrid stories" of Mrs. Radcliffe, M. G. Lewis (a friend of
Byron's, known as "Monk" Lewis from his violent and sadistic tale *The Monk*),
John Moore, whose *Zeluco*, a much more serious work, Byron greatly admired,
and lesser writers. The period of their greatest popularity was the last decade of the
eighteenth century, but they survived through Byron's lifetime. Jane Austen's
Northanger Abbey was written as a parody of them in 1798, but it still had a
point when it was published in 1818. These thrillers were intended for an English
Protestant middle-class reading public: consequently their horrid surroundings
were normally Continental, Catholic and upper class, though Oriental settings
also had a vogue. Into such settings stalked a character type, sometimes a villain,
sometimes presented in a more sympathetic, or more-sinned-against-than-
sinning, role, but in either case misanthropic, misunderstood, and solitary, with
strong diabolical overtones. The devil is a powerfully erotic figure, his horns and
hoofs descending from the ancient satyrs, and the various forms of sadism and
masochism glanced at in these thrillers helped to make them extremely popular,
not least with the female part of the reading public.

Childe Harold and the other lowering heroes of Byron's tales not only popularized a conventional type of hero, but popularized Byron himself in that role.
For Byron was a dark and melancholy-looking lord with a reputation for wicked-
ness and free thought; he seemed to prefer the Continent to England, and took
a detached view of middle-class and even Christian morality. He owned a
gloomy Gothic castle and spent evenings with revelers in it; he was pale and thin
with his ferocious dieting; he even had a lame foot. No wonder he said that
strangers whom he met at dinner "looked as if his Satanic Majesty had been
among them." The prince of darkness is a gentleman, and so was Byron. Again,
when a "nameless vice" was introduced into a Gothic thriller, as part of the
villain's or hero's background, it generally turned out, when named, to be incest. This theme recurs all through Romantic literature, being almost obsessive
in Shelley as well as Byron, and here again a literary convention turns up in
Byron's life. Even a smaller detail, like the disguising of the ex-Corsair's mistress

in *Lara* as the pageboy Kaled, recurs in Byron's liaison with Caroline Lamb, who looked well in a page's costume.

Byron did not find the Byronic hero as enthralling as his public did, and he made several efforts to detach his own character from Childe Harold and his other heroes, with limited success. He says of Childe Harold that he wanted to make him an objective study of gloomy misanthropy, hence he deliberately cut humor out of the poem in order to preserve a unity of tone. But Byron's most distinctive talents did not have full scope in this part of his work. Most of the Gothic thriller writers were simple-minded popular novelists, but the same convention had also been practised on a much higher level of literary intelligence. Apart from Goethe's early *Sorrows of Werther*, an extraordinarily popular tale of a solemn suicide, Addison in *The Vision of Mirza* and Johnson in *Rasselas* had used the Oriental tale for serious literary purposes. Also, Horace Walpole in *The Castle of Otranto* (1764) and William Beckford in *Vathek* (1786) had written respectively a Gothic and an Oriental romance in which melodrama and fantasy were shot through with flickering lights of irony. They were addressed to a reading public capable, to use modern phraseology, of taking their corn with a pinch of salt. It was this higher level of sophistication that Byron naturally wanted to reach, and he was oppressed by the humorless solemnity of his own creations. His sardonic and ribald wit, his sense of the concrete, his almost infallible feeling for the common-sense perspective on every situation, crackles all through his letters and journals, even through his footnotes. But it seem to be locked out of his serious poetry, and only in the very last canto of *Don Juan* did he succeed in uniting fantasy and humor.

Byron's tales are, on the whole, well-told and well-shaped stories. Perhaps he learned something from his own ridicule of Southey, who was also a popular writer of verse tales, sometimes of mammoth proportions. In any case he is well able to exploit the capacity of verse for dramatizing one or two central situations, leaving all the cumbersome apparatus of plot to be ignored or taken for granted. But he seemed unable to bring his various projections of his inner ghost to life: his heroes, like the characters of a detective story, are thin, bloodless, abstract, and popular. Nor could he seem to vary the tone, from romance to irony, from fantasy to humor, as Beckford does in *Vathek*. Byron was strongly attracted by Beckford, and is thinking of him at the very opening of *Childe Harold*, as Beckford had lived for two years in Portugal. When Byron writes:

> Deep in yon cave Honorius long did dwell,
> In hope to merit Heaven by making earth a Hell.

he obviously has in mind the demure remark in the opening of *Vathek*: "He did not think . . . that it was necessary to make a hell of this world to enjoy paradise in the next." But though Byron is the wittiest of writers, the Byronic hero cannot manage much more than a gloomy smile. Here, for instance, is Childe Harold on the "Lisbon Packet":

> The sails were filled, and fair the light winds blew,
> As glad to waft him from his native home . . .
> And then, it may be, of his wish to roam
> Repented he, but in his bosom slept
> The silent thought, nor from his lips did come
> One word of wail, whilst others sate and wept,
> And to the reckless gales unmanly moaning kept.

and here is Byron himself in the same situation:

> Hobhouse muttering fearful curses,
>   As the hatchway down he rolls,
> Now his breakfast, now his verses,
>   Vomits forth — and damns our souls . . .
> "Zounds! my liver's coming up:
> I shall not survive the racket
> Of this brutal Lisbon Packet."

The same inability to combine seriousness and humor is also to be found in the plays, where one would expect more variety of tone. The central character is usually the Byronic hero again, and again he seems to cast a spell over the whole action. Byron recognized this deficiency in his dramas, and to say that his plays were not intended for the stage would be an understatement. Byron had a positive phobia of stage production, and once tried to get an injunction issued to prevent a performance of *Marino Faliero*. "I never risk *rivalry* in anything," he wrote to Lady Melbourne, and being directly dependent on the applause or booing of a crowd (modern theaters give us no notion of what either form of demonstration was like in Byron's day) was something he could not face, even in absence. Besides, he had no professional sense, and nothing of the capacity to write for an occasion that the practising dramatist needs. Hence, with the exception of *Werner*, a lively and well-written melodrama based on a plot by somebody else, Byron's plays are so strictly closet dramas that they differ little in structure from the tales.

The establishing of the Byronic hero was a major feat of characterization, but Byron had little power of characterization apart from this figure. Like many brilliant talkers, he had not much ear for the rhythms and nuances of other people's speech. Here again we find a close affinity between Byron's personality and the conventions of his art. For instance, in his life Byron seemed to have curiously little sense of women as human beings. Except for Lady Melbourne, he addressed himself to the female in them, took a hearty-male view of their intellectual interests, and concentrated on the ritual of love-making with the devotion of what an earlier age would have called a clerk of Venus. This impersonal and ritualistic approach to women is reflected in his tales and plays, where again in fits the conventions of Byronic romance. It is difficult for a heroine of strong character to make much headway against a gloomy misanthropic hero, and Byron's heroines, like the heroines of Gothic romance in general, are insipid prodigies of neurotic devotion.

But if Byron's plays are not practicable stage plays, they are remarkable works. *Manfred*, based on what Byron had heard about Goethe's *Faust*, depicts the Byronic hero as a student of magic whose knowledge has carried him beyond the limits of human society and given him superhuman powers, but who is still held to human desire by his love for his sister (apparently) Astarte. At the moment of his death the demons he has controlled, with a sense of what is customary in stories about magicians, come to demand his soul, but Manfred, in a crisp incisive speech which retains its power to surprise through any number of rereadings, announces that he has made no bargain with them, that whatever he has done, they can go to hell, and he will not go with them. The key to this final scene is the presence of the Abbot. Manfred and the Abbot differ on all points of theory, but the Abbot is no coward and Manfred is no villain: they face the crisis together, linked in a common bond of humanity which enables Manfred to die and to triumph at the same time.

Two of Byron's plays, *Cain* and *Heaven and Earth*, are described by Byron as "mysteries," by which he meant Biblical plays like those of the Middle Ages. Wherever we turn in Byron's poetry, we meet the figure of Cain, the first man who never knew Paradise, and whose sexual love was necessarily incestuous. In Byron's "mystery" Cain is Adam's eldest son and heir, but what he really inherits is the memory of a greater dispossession. "Dost thou not live?" asks Adam helplessly. "Must I not die?" retorts Cain. Adam cannot comprehend the mentality of one who has been born with the consciousness of death. But Lucifer can, for he too has been disinherited. He comes to Cain and gives him what he gave Adam: fruit of the tree of knowledge, of a kind that Raphael, in the eighth book of *Paradise Lost*, warned Adam against: a knowledge of other worlds and other beings, a realization that the fortunes of humanity are of less account in the scheme of things than he had assumed. From such knowledge develops the resentment that leads to the murder of Abel and to Cain's exile. And just as Milton tries to show us that we in Adam's place would have committed Adam's sin, so Byron makes us feel that we all have something of Cain in us: everybody has killed something that he wishes he had kept alive, and the fullest of lives is wrapped around the taint of an inner death. As the princess says in *The Castle of Otranto*: "This can be no evil spirit: it is undoubtedly one of the family."

The other "mystery," *Heaven and Earth*, deals with the theme of the love of angels for human women recorded in some mysterious verses of Genesis, and ends with the coming of Noah's flood. Angels who fall through sexual love are obvious enough subjects for Byron, but *Heaven and Earth* lacks the clear dramatic outline of *Cain*. All Byron's plays are tragedies, and as Byron moved further away from the easy sentiment of his earlier tales he moved toward intellectual paradox rather than tragedy. It is particularly in the final scenes that we observe Byron becoming too self-conscious for the full emotional resonance of tragedy. In *Sardanapalus*, for example, we see the downfall of a king who pursued pleasure because he was too intelligent to want to keep his people plunged into warfare. His intelligence is identified by his people with weakness, and his pursuit of pleasure is inseparably attached to selfishness. What we are left with, despite his final death on a funeral pyre, is less tragedy than an irony of a kind that is very close to satire. Byron's creative powers were clearly running in the direction of satire, and it was to satire that he turned in his last and greatest period.

In *English Bards and Scotch Reviewers* Byron spoke of Wordsworth as "that mild apostate from poetic rule." This poem is early, but Byron never altered his opinion of the Lake Poets as debasers of the currency of English poetry. His own poetic idol was Pope, whom he called "the moral poet of all civilization," and he thought of himself as continuing Pope's standards of clarity, craftsmanship and contact with real life against the introverted metaphysical mumblings of Coleridge and Wordsworth. Byron's early models were standard, even old-fashioned, later eighteenth-century models. *English Bards* is in the idiom of eighteenth-century satire, less of Pope than of Pope's successors, Churchill, Wolcot, and Gifford, and the first part of *Childe Harold*, with its pointless Spenserian stanza and its semi-facetious antique diction—fortunately soon dropped by Byron—is also an eighteenth-century stock pattern. Byron was friendly with Shelley, but owes little to him technically, and in his letters he expressed a vociferous dislike for the poetry of Keats (considerably toned down in the eleventh canto of *Don Juan*). His literary friends, Sheridan, Rogers, Gifford, were of the older generation, and even Tom Moore, his biographer and by far his closest friend among his poetic contemporaries, preserved, like so many Irish writers, something of the eighteenth-century manner.

It was also an eighteenth-century model that gave him the lead for the phase of poetry that began with *Beppo* in September, 1817, and exploited the possibilities of the eight-line (*ottava rima*) stanza used there and in *Don Juan* and *The Vision of Judgment*. Byron seems to have derived this stanza from a heroi-comical poem, *Whistlecraft*, by John Hookham Frere, whom Byron had met in Spain, and which in its turn had owed something to the Italian romantic epics of the early Renaissance. Byron went on to study the Italian poems, and translated the first canto of one of the best of them, Pulci's tale of a good-natured giant, *Morgante Maggiore*. But there was one feature in Frere that he could not have found in the Italians, and that was the burlesque rhyme. In Italian the double rhyme is normal, but it is a peculiarity of English that even double rhymes have to be used with great caution in serious poetry, and that all obtrusive or in-genious rhymes belong to comic verse. This is a major principle of the wit of *Hudibras* before Byron's time, as of W. S. Gilbert and Ogden Nash since, and without it the wit of *Don Juan* is hardly conceivable:

> But—Oh! ye lords of ladies intellectual,
> Inform us truly, have they not hen-pecked you all?

Armed with this new technique, Byron was ready to tackle a narrative satire, and in narrative satire he found not only a means of exploiting all his best qual-ities, but of turning his very faults as a poet into virtues. He could digress to his heart's content, for digression is part of the fun in satire—one thinks of *Tristram Shandy* and the "Digression in Praise of Digressions" in *A Tale of a Tub*. He could write doggerel, but doggerel in satire is a sign of wit rather than incompe-tence. He could be serious if he liked, for sudden changes of mood belong to the form, and he could swing back to burlesque again as soon as he was bored with seriousness, or thought the reader might be. It is particularly the final couplet that he uses to undercut his own romantic Byronism, as in the description of Daniel Boone in Canto VIII:

> Crime came not near him—she is not the child
>   Of solitude; Health shrank not from him—for
> Her home is in the rarely trodden wild,
>   Where if men seek her not, and death be more
> Their choice than life, forgive them, as beguiled
>   By habit to what their own hearts abhor—
> In cities caged. The present case in point I
> Cite is, that Boon lived hunting up to ninety.

In the new flush of discovery, Byron wrote exultantly to his friend Douglas Kin-naird: "[*Don Juan*] is the sublime of *that there* sort of writing—it may be bawdy, but is it not good English? It may be profligate but is it not *life*, is it not *the thing*? Could any man have written it who has not lived in the world?" But even Byron was soon made aware that he was not as popular as he had been. The women who loved *The Corsair* hated *Don Juan*, for the reason that Byron gives with his usual conciseness on such subjects: "the wish of all women to exalt the *sentiment* of the passions, and to keep up the illusion which is their empire." Teresa, as soon as she understood anything of the poem, boycotted it, and forced Byron to promise not to go on with it, a promise he was able to evade only with great difficulty. His friend Harriet Wilson, significantly enough a courtesan who lived partly by blackmail, wrote him: "Dear *Adorable* Lord Byron, *don't* make a mere *coarse* old libertine of yourself."

Don Juan is traditionally the incautious amorist, the counterpart in love to Faust in knowledge, whose pursuit of women is so ruthless that he is eventually damned, as in the last scene of Mozart's opera *Don Giovanni*. Consequently he is a logical choice as a mask for Byron, but he is a mask that reveals the whole Byronic personality, instead of concealing the essence of it as Childe Harold does. The extroversion of Byron's temperament has full scope in *Don Juan*. There is hardly any characterization in the poem: even Don Juan never emerges clearly as a character. We see only what happens to him, and the other characters, even Haidée, float past as phantasmagoria of romance and adventure. What one misses in the poem is the sense of engagement or participation. Everything happens to Don Juan, but he is never an active agent, and seems to take no responsibility for his life. He drifts from one thing to the next, appears to find one kind of experience as good as another, makes no judgements and no commitments. As a result the gloom and misanthropy, the secret past sins, the gnawing remorse of the earlier heroes is finally identified as a shoddier but more terrifying evil — boredom, the sense of the inner emptiness of life that is one of Byron's most powerfully compelling moods, and has haunted literature ever since, from the *ennui* of Baudelaire to the *Angst* and *nausée* of our own day.

The episodes of the poem are all stock Byronic scenes: Spain, the pirates of the Levant, the odalisques of Turkish harems, battlefields, and finally English high society. But there is as little plot as characterization: the poem exists for the sake of its author's comment. As Byron says:

> This narrative is not meant for narration,
> But a mere airy and fantastic basis,
> To build up common things with common places.

Its wit is constantly if not continuously brilliant, and Byron's contempt of cant and prudery, his very real hatred of cruelty, his detached view of all social icons, whether conservative or popular, are well worth having. Not many poets give us as much common sense as Byron does. On the other hand the opposition to the poem made him increasingly self-conscious as he went on, and his technique of calculated bathos and his deliberate refusal to "grow metaphysical" — that is, pursue any idea beyond the stage of initial reaction — keep the poem too resolutely on one level. The larger imaginative vistas that we are promised ("a panoramic view of hell's in training") do not materialize, and by the end of the sixteenth canto we have a sense of a rich but not inexhaustible vein rapidly thinning out. As *Don Juan* is not Don Juan's poem but Byron's poem, it could hardly have been ended, but only abandoned or cut short by its author's death. The Mozartian ending of the story Byron had already handled, in his own way, in *Manfred*.

The Vision of Judgment is Byron's most original poem, and therefore his most conventional one; it is his wittiest poem, and therefore his most serious one. Southey, Byron's favorite target among the Lake poets, had become poet laureate, and his political views, like those of Coleridge and Wordsworth, had shifted from an early liberalism to a remarkably complacent Toryism. On the death of George III in 1820 he was ill-advised enough to compose, in his laureate capacity, a "Vision of Judgment" describing the apotheosis and entry into heaven of the stammering, stupid, obstinate, and finally lunatic and blind monarch whose sixty-year reign had lost America, alienated Ireland, plunged the country into the longest and bloodiest war in its history, and ended in a desolate scene of domestic misery and repression. George III was not personally responsible for all the evils of his reign, but in those days royalty was not the projection of middle-class virtue that it is now, and was consequently less popular and more open to attack. The apotheosis of a dead monarch, as a literary form, is of classical origin, and so is its parody, Byron's poem being in the tradition of Seneca's brilliant mockery of the entry into heaven of the Emperor Claudius.

Byron's religous views were certainly unusual in his day, but if we had to express them in a formula, it would be something like this: the best that we can imagine man doing is where our conception of God ought to start. Religions that foment cruelty and induce smugness, or ascribe cruelty and smugness to God, are superstitions. In *Heaven and Earth*, for example, the offstage deity who decrees the deluge at the end is clearly the moral inferior of every human creature he drowns. In *The Vision of Judgment* the sycophantic Southey is contrasted with John Wilkes, who fought King George hard all his life, but who, when encouraged to go on persecuting him after death, merely says:

> I don't like ripping up old stories, since
> His conduct was but natural in a prince.

This is a decent human attitude, consequently it must be the least we can expect from heaven, and so the poet takes leave of the poor old king "practising the hundredth Psalm."

GEORGE M. RIDENOUR

Byron in 1816:
Four Poems from Diodati

It is only lately that we have learned to trace an unbroken movement from the thought of the eighteenth century to that of what used to be called the romantic revolt. We have learned that insofar as a revolt in fact took place its program and its weapons were in large part gifts of the period under attack. And certainly some of the problems faced by the English romantic poets and some of their ways of handling them have developed from contradictions implicit in attitudes characteristic of the eighteenth century.

We have noticed first of all the role played by the eighteenth century in the development of modern individualism, and that both problems and solutions that we think of as "romantic" are developments of this new attitude toward the individual person. Both the social tendencies of the period and its understanding of human nature and the human mind were beginning to focus an attention on the individual as a separate and unique being that had not been common in other ages, though this was countered by a belief in the uniformity in operation of the separate human machines. With respect to the human mind, we could say that the eighteenth century tended both to imprison each man in an individual consciousness and to reduce everything to experience within that consciousness. Each condition can in itself induce anxiety, and the relation between them is trying. Without insisting that this is a fair statement of the case, it may still be fair to argue that poets of the early nineteenth century tried to handle problems implicit in the fundamental assumptions of the previous age without surrendering the achievements of that age. This meant especially directing the powers of the emancipated intellect toward the solution of problems involved in that emancipation.

From *From Sensibility to Romanticism: Essays Presented to Frederick A. Pottle.* © 1965 by Oxford University Press, Inc.

This description applies in any case to Byron's situation in 1816, as it appears in the third canto of *Childe Harold's Pilgrimage*. The poet speaks as a compulsory exile who is trying to take advantage of his state of deprivation — to turn exile to pilgrimage. As he recognizes, the state of affairs he finds himself in is a complex product of European history, personal temperament, and circumstance, and the poem tries to maneuver the terms into a tolerable arrangement. In his other major work of the period, the drama *Manfred*, he contends more directly with his own experience of paradoxes in the mind of the previous age. Freedom is experienced as both personal necessity and intolerable burden, determination as a necessary guarantee of the value and meaning of the individual life and as a force to be resisted in the name of the freedom which is equally indispensable. The dilemma is handled by pushing both terms as far as they can go, so that the play is an enactment of a will to radical freedom and to radical determination.

But if there is some point in suggesting a connection which cannot by its nature be proved between Byron's poems and the individualism and subjectivism initiated by the preceding century, it is more obviously useful to point out a relationship that is demonstrable historically. Ian Watt, describing the close connection between the growth of individualism and the rise of the novel in the eighteenth century, has pointed out that the novel, more than any other literary form, raises the issue of its own truth. This is strikingly the case with works in the tradition of Cervantes' *Don Quixote*, that build the question of their truth into themselves as part of their meaning. Byron has used the motif in this way in the third canto of *Childe Harold*, and it will play an important role in *Don Juan* and *The Vision of Judgment*, where a more than Humean skepticism is dealt with in ways made available by aspects of eighteenth-century thought that led to that skepticism in the first place. It was during the summer of 1816, while he was living in Switzerland at the Villa Diodati, that these forces took on much of what was to be their definitive form in Byron's poems.

These few months made up a crucial period in the development of Byron's imagination. Talk with Shelley and study of Rousseau had led him to take poetry more seriously than he had been used to do, and for all his joking on the subject, this may be the most important consequence of the period. In addition to work at the larger pieces already touched on, the summer was particularly rich in shorter experimental poems in which Byron examined aspects of his developing vision, trying out ways of stating it. I shall consider four of these poems, each something of a sport in Byron's work as a whole, but each revealing with special clarity the pressures he was working under and the ways he was learning to deal with them — which draw us then into the center of his imagining. The tendency of the readings, by helping us see Byron in relation to the preceding age, may teach us something of why he was so important to his own time.

"EPISTLE TO AUGUSTA"

Byron's imagination was "antithetical." Out of honesty, wit, and perversity, he liked to set up oppositions, in the antithetical heroes of *Childe Harold* and the early tales, in the ironies of *Don Juan*, in the oppositions of ways of living in *Beppo* and of ways of being in *The Vision of Judgment*. In the "Stanzas to the Po" an opposition is studied between the poet and the woman he loves, with the river expressing what unites and divides them. The "Epistle to Augusta" is especially interesting from this point of view because of the occasion it offers for refined connection and opposition between the poet in Switzerland and his half-sister at home in England.

The poem begins with an assertion of relationship: "My Sister! my sweet Sister!" She is valuable to him for the ways in which she is close to him and far away from him, though the emphasis is on the first:

> My Sister! my sweet Sister! if a name
> Dearer and purer were, it should be thine.
> Mountains and seas divide us, but I claim
> No tears, but tenderness to answer mine:
> Go where I will, to me thou art the same —
> A loved regret which I would not resign.
> There yet are two things in my destiny, —
> A world to roam through, and a home with thee.

For all the differences in tone, both the "Stanzas to the Po" and the "Epistle to Augusta" may be in the tradition of the "heroic epistle," a verse letter to an absent lover, offering passionate comment on the relationship from a distance. The letter is most often written by a woman whose lover has abandoned her. An example in English would be Pope's rendering of Ovid's "Sappho to Phaon" (Donna Julia's letter in the first canto of *Don Juan* is a variety of this), but Byron was more struck by Pope's own development of the tradition in his "Eloisa," where the Ovidian play with antithetical value and attitude is developed with especial boldness. Byron's antitheses are less radical than Pope's, but they are equally pervasive. If Augusta, for example, were not the kind of woman who would be faithful to commitments that separate her from him, he would not desire her to be with him, or to return his "tenderness." (The paradox recalls Donne's "Twick'nam Garden," or one of Thomas Little's [Moore's] poems "To

Rosa.") So the natural barriers are not in any case the only ones, nor are they merely barriers, as we shall see.

Augusta is a fixed point to him in his wanderings, but it is in large part negatively, as a "regret," that she fills this office. His regret for her absence and for what he has done to cause it is painful, but it is the one thing he can count on. Put positively, she is the "home" that is the antithesis to his "roam"-ing. (Byron uses sound-links a good deal in the early lines.) In the same way, his "inheritance of storms" (sts. 3 and 4) is seen as both fate and will: fated because a will such as his was given him without his asking, willed because the fate is so closely shaped to the qualities of the will. The doctrine is Greek, but not the emphasis, which falls on willful error, as in the Shakespearean couplet:

> I have been cunning in mine overthrow,
> The careful pilot of my proper woe.

The first four stanzas establish the situation, antithetically, and the remaining twelve stanzas circle around on themselves twice, defining antitheses. The first (sts. 5–9) is a movement from patience to active grief, the second (10–end) from a feeling of loss to a faith in unbroken connection. Part of the meaning here and elsewhere in Byron is that this is characteristic of him, that he is drawn irresistibly, it seems, from one point to its opposite. In *Don Juan* the effect is apt to be witty; here, as in *Childe Harold*, our feeling is one of sadness that it should be so. But we may want to notice that this movement is itself both disjunctive and connecting, alienating and reconciling.

In the course of each circling movement the poet's mind moves into the past, as he recalls his childhood. In the first instance, it is the "spirit of slight patience," the "strange quiet" brought on by his defiance and despair (and the Alpine landscape) that reminds him of his "happy childhood." But childhood reminds him of home and home of Augusta, and by the end of the ninth stanza his "philosophy" has begun to break down. The second sequence is less simple. It is now the "scenes" that remind him of a childhood spent in a similar landscape, the natural forms suggesting the natural innocence he has lost by indulging the social passions. Though it is impossible to accept Byron's analysis of his difficulty, the main point is the movement of the thought. The oppositions are passion and apathy, experience and innocence, and the poem is concerned with establishing relations among them. Out of the natural innocence suggested by the Alpine scenery he moves towards an earlier innocence associated with his sister, whose name is dear and "pure." Passion has destroyed the calm of innocence and has led to apathy. The poet's problem now is to feel without feeling too much, and to be calm without falling into apathy, thus approximating the innocence he has lost. This demands both stimulation and control. The power

of the poem is its achievement from a position (that purports to be) be
pair of a state of being that precedes despair. The circling movement
compose one circle that moves from loss to recovery of value. The poet
agonized sufferings have been caused by separation from Augusta and by the
thought of what he has done to her. But this concern for her testifies to their
closeness to each other, as the Alps are both barriers and links. The poem circles
round in this way to its beginning, enacting both will and fate:

> For thee, my own sweet sister, in thy heart
> I know myself secure, as thou in mine;
> We were and are—I am, even as thou art—
> Beings who ne'er each other can resign;
> It is the same, together or apart,
> From Life's commencement to its slow decline
> We are entwined—let Death come slow or fast,
> The tie which bound the first endures the last!

It is will since it is what he wants and is the consequence of voluntary acts; it is
fate because it was built into the structure of that will, and forms a pattern out of
the disasters brought about by the exercise of will. In Byron's way, the antitheses
are not reconciled, but they are brought into tolerable relation.

"DARKNESS"

The most immediately striking thing about "Darkness," considered as an
apocalypse, is that it is scrupulously naturalistic. There is no feeling of divine
purpose being worked out, or of any power beyond the natural energies that are
running down. It was pointed out in 1825 that the poem borrows heavily on an
early example of what we would now call science fiction, and there is an important element of detached scientific description in Byron's poem. Byron is in fact
much more secular in his approach than the anonymous author of *The Last Man,
or Omegarus and Syderia, a Romance in Futurity* (1806), who is apparently trying to be orthodox. Only apparently, because it is hard to believe that many
readers would distribute their sympathies according to the author's instructions.
The main impression is of an irresponsible God and a victimized humanity. This
may have been one thing that attracted Byron to the work.

The poem begins with the poet's dreaming of a dying earth:

> I had a dream, which was not all a dream.
> The bright sun was extinguished, and the stars
> Did wander darkling in the eternal space,

> Rayless, and pathless, and the icy Earth
> Swung blind and blackening in the moonless air;
> Morn came and went—and came, and brought no day.

The force of the poem is in its depiction of enervation, powerlessness. Exhaustion of the sun is exhaustion of all man's world, and of man himself, and exhaustion for man means loss of humanity. Parts of "Darkness" suggest Shelley, but both the radical pessimism and the unindignant way it is expressed are characteristically Byronic. This vision of human weakness in the face of unmanageable forces lies behind all of Byron's work. No power of imagination can change this, no vision can make much difference. It is the outside limiting factor, like the "fate" of the Greeks, that nothing can be done about.

"THE DREAM"

> Our life is twofold: Sleep hath its own world,
> A boundary between the things misnamed
> Death and existence: Sleep hath its own world,
> And a wide realm of wild reality,
> And dreams in their development have breath,
> And tears, and tortures, and the touch of Joy;
> They leave a weight upon our waking thoughts,
> They take a weight from off our waking toils,
> They do divide our being; they become
> A portion of ourselves as of our time,
> And look like heralds of Eternity;
> They pass like spirits of the past,—they speak
> Like Sibyls of the future; they have power—
> The tyranny of pleasure and of pain;
> They make us what we were not—what they will,
> And shake us with the vision that's gone by,
> The dread of vanished shadows—Are they so?
> Is not the past all shadow?—What are they?
> Creations of the mind?—The mind can make
> Substance, and people planets of its own
> With beings brighter than have been, and give
> A breath to forms which can outlive all flesh. (ll. 1–22)

Even among the experimental poems of the summer of 1816 "The Dream" is remarkably original. "Rousseauist" speculation on the nature of imaginative creation is combined with speculation about dreams that is perhaps closest to the

German romantics. The form is that of a series of related visions, derived largely from Old Testament prophecy, with influence perhaps from "autobiographical" poems of Ossian. But for good or ill it is really like nothing else.

"The Dream" is in fact something of a stunt; but it is an interesting stunt, one that allows Byron to exercise his imagination in valuable ways. He is playing with relations between mind and reality, and the notion of dream is helpful to him because of its equivocal middle status, between the imagined and the experienced, past and future. Here he looks at the past as if it were future, the experienced as if it were imagined, while insisting in each case on the reality of the second, "mental," term. The point of this strange maneuver, or part of it, seems to be found in the question (line 18): "Is not the past all shadow?" I take this to mean that while it is only the past, in a sense, that is wholly real, the guarantee of this reality, its pastness, is by the same token the source of its ideality. The past, being past, is as unreal, mental, ideal as the future or the imagined. This suggests an area in which mental and real, imagined and experienced, future and past are not easily separable — an area of "real" imaginings. We can see now the relation between "The Dream" and Byron's "true epics," *Childe Harold* and *Don Juan*, both of which work to transform Byron's own experience into public dream.

But the opening speculation on dream (lines 1–22) does more than provide a general focus for the sequence of visions based on Byron's relationship with Mary Chaworth. It establishes vision as a term which will be developed in the rest of the poem. Within the enclosing vision we have a series of visionary moments, each individually characterized, and each a crux in the development of the action of the poem.

The first comes after some lines of weak Wordsworthian imitation ("Tintern Abbey") showing the young pair on a hilltop. He looks at her lovingly and sees everything through her eyes:

> she was his sight,
> For his eye followed hers, and saw with hers,
> Which coloured all his objects. (ll. 53–55)

But she was looking in another direction for her lover. The gaze is not returned, and the rest of the poem grows out of this failure. The next climax of vision comes at the wedding of the dreamer to the woman he makes caddishly clear was his second choice (lines 158–65). "He could see / Not that which was, nor that which should have been," but the scene of his last interview with the woman he really loved.

The last two visions present the consequences to both persons of the original failure of vision:

> she was become
> The Queen of a fantastic realm; her thoughts

> Were combinations of disjointed things;
> And forms, impalpable and unperceived
> Of others' sight, familiar were to hers.
> And this the world calls frenzy; but the wise
> Have a far deeper madness — and the glance
> Of melancholy is a fearful gift;
> What is it but the telescope of truth?
> Which strips the distance of its fantasies,
> And brings life near in utter nakedness,
> Making the cold reality too real!   (ll. 172–83)

The vision of melancholy is a vision of reality, painfully clear and unillusioned. It is in several ways like the "philosophic mind" of Wordsworth's Intimations Ode, and one of these ways is that it is the state out of which the poem that defines it claims to be written. The cold intensity of perception formed by suffering gives access to a vision of the secrets of the nature of things (sect. viii) and makes it possible to trace the pattern of fate ("doom") acted out in two lives, a dream "Almost like a reality" (sect. ix). But of course it *is* a reality, as we are assumed to know, and what happened is visionary in its intensity, coherence, and completeness. It would be a true dream, then, in at least these ways, attempting to perceive and understand a series of events that form a period in the lives of two persons, taking account and advantage of the elements that condition all attempts at perception and understanding — a program to be carried out less pretentiously and to more effect in *Don Juan*.

"A FRAGMENT"

The poem published by Moore in 1830 as "A Fragment" ("Could I remount the river of my years") combines elements of all three poems discussed so far. It has something of the brooding tone of "Darkness," and a good deal of its unindignant pessimism. And while the point of the fragment is not wholly clear, it seems to be moving towards a statement similar to that of "The Dream" and the "Epistle."

The poet tells us that if he could return through his past life to its sources, he would not do so. He would not, at least, if that were the only way; it would be a gloomy trip. (He is not saying, "If I could live my life over again. . . .") While the passing of time and the movement of life to death are disturbing, and he would like to "get to the bottom" of them, the thought of his own past is so painful that he would let his life flow quietly into the ocean of death, where personal identity is lost, rather than explore its sources in that manner. The "nameless tides" of death, then, have at least negative value. And more kinds of value are discovered. The ocean suggests peace (line 7) and, more important, totality; it suggests "The whole of that of which we are a part" (line 8). This second notion has special plausibility, since

> Life is but a vision—what I see
> Of all which lives alone is Life to me,
> And being so—the absent are the dead,
> Who haunt us from tranquillity, and spread
> A dreary shroud around us, and invest
> With sad remembrancers our hours of rest. (ll. 9–14)

If it is true that only what is directly experienced is alive to us, those absent from us are dead to us, though for this very reason they are so intensely and painfully present—a formula which recalls especially the "Epistle." And if this is true, it does not matter whether we are separated by oceans or by the earth of the grave. The grave is in any case the final barrier.

But then the grave is finally more unifying than separating, a "dark union of insensate dust" (line 22); the final reduction is a return of all of us to the earth from which everything has developed. And separate outgrowths, such as human lives, must be less than the original rich unity, which is found again in death. We are punningly told that the grave holds the key to earth's "profundity," its depth and value. It is there "Our elements [are] resolved to things untold" (line 38). So the symbol of loss, or of only relative gain, is seen to offer possibilities. In answer to the problems posed at the beginning of the poem, life's sources are explored through death, the beginning through the end, and a new unity is attained through what has seemed to be separation. The implied "logical" formulation—that if the absent are the dead the dead are the absent, and therefore somehow accessible—makes clear the relation between the imagining here and in "The Dream," while the achievement of values of origin through the manipulation of consequence is common to both "Dream" and "Epistle." All three are maneuvers for making the most of the circumstances developed, in one form, in "Darkness."

The influence on Byron and Shelley of Rousseau, whom they read together in this summer of 1816, is unclear and should be worked out. The only study at any length on Rousseau and Byron is that by Otto Schmidt (Leipzig, 1890), and Schmidt's bad judgment has added to the conclusion. Even on the basis of his spotty and indiscriminate quotation, it can be seen that Rousseau is a main influence on Byron's comments (in his poetry) on poetic creation and the ambiguity of the imagination (mostly the *Confessions*) and on his attempts at nature mysticism (presumably the *Rêveries*). There may be some influence on his development of

the ambiguities of love, but this is less obvious. More detailed statement is difficult, since one is likely to prove only that Rousseau had developed basic forms of
romantic imagining. With regard to the poems examined in this essay, the
presence of Rousseau is most apparent in "The Dream."

> The mind can make
> Substance, and people planets of its own
> With beings brighter than have been, and give
> A breath to forms which can outlive all flesh. (ll. 19–22)

> In my continued ecstasies, I intoxicated myself with full draughts of
> the most delightful sensations that have ever entered the heart of
> man. I entirely forgot the human race, and created for myself societies
> of perfect beings, heavenly alike in their beauties and virtues; trusty,
> tender, and loyal friends such as I never found in this world below. I
> found such pleasure in soaring into the empyrean. . . .
>
> (*Confessions,* bk. ix)

The emphasis on permanence in the passage from "The Dream" may be
less Rousseauist, to be sure, than generally neoclassic, but it is at least likely that
the main source is Rousseau. In the Byron, however, the creations of the mind
are recollections of actual events in the past, as in the *Confessions* themselves.
Such self-conscious feelings of loneliness and inadequacy, such *use* of one's own
experience, deliberately setting up patterns of associations calculated to produce
the greatest possible satisfaction — these to some extent "grow out of" eighteenth-
century psychology, with its tendency both to enslave the individual mind and
to reduce everything to it, and manifest themselves in Byron's alternate cries of
helplessness and mastery, solitude and union. It is a strong element in Rousseau,
and his influence may be present directly in Byron's work at this time, in addition to the effect he had on others who influenced Byron. At the very least, he
was a striking representative of the sensibility expressed by that brooding over
circumstances and states of mind and that interplay of loss and gain apparent in
the poems examined in this essay.

LESLIE BRISMAN

Troubled Stream
from a Pure Source

The conception of a true world, *the conception of morality as the essence of the world (these two most malignant errors of all time!) were once again, thanks to a wily and shrewd skepticism, if not provable, at least no longer* refutable. *Reason, the* right *of reason, does not extend that far. Reality had been reduced to mere "appearance," and a mendaciously fabricated world, the world of being, was honored as reality.*

— NIETZSCHE, *The Antichrist*

I tell you: one must still have chaos in one, to give birth to a dancing star.
— NIETZSCHE, *Thus Spake Zarathustra*

In his 1821 diary, Byron waives questions about origins with the studied nonchalance typical of the narrator of *Don Juan*: "If, according to some speculations, you could prove the World many thousand years older than the Mosaic Chronology, or if you could knock up Adam and Eve and the Apple and Serpent, still what is to be put up in their stead? or how is the difficulty removed? Things must have had a beginning, and what matters it *when* or *how*?" To the poet concerned with history, the prehistorical *when* did matter a great deal — if not in literal, calendar chronology, at least in terms of the mythic chronology of the passions, the prohibitions, the guilt. To the poet obsessed with the divorce between the tree of knowledge and the tree of life, it mattered *how* these emblems were represented in allusion and retellings of the myth. Perhaps most of all it mattered

From *Romantic Origins*. © 1978 by Cornell University. Cornell University Press, 1978. Originally entitled "Byron: Troubled Stream from a Pure Source."

that questions of creation be deflected into awareness of the fallen world as we know it. Adam and Eve can scarcely be mentioned without a shift of interest to the apple and serpent, for the creation story remains a distant fiction while the Fall is a present truth. "With a characteristic ellipsis," writes Michael G. Cooke, "Byron blanks out the supposedly historical perfect world and shows the certified world going from bad to worse."

What Byron "blanks out" remains as much a presence in his poetry as the materials of repression are presences in the psyche generally. In *A Map of Misreading*, Harold Bloom suggests that a poet's greatest moments are related to his powers of repression, and his verse seems daemonized with special energy when presences the poet would rationally or consciously dismiss are given voice while an inner censor sleeps. Calvinist in temperament but no Christian in belief, Byron thought that an undisguised faith in a paradise was at the root of intellectual and social error. Whether out of rivalry with Shelley on the subject of evil or simply in pursuit of the satirist's antimask, Byron implies that the history of inauthentic poetry—and the progress of the world at large from bad to worse— may be the responsibility of those who have failed to forget the belief in an anterior, perfect world. No doubt he would mock the idea of deep repression as much as he did the failure to put radical innocence out of mind, for Byron makes public the gesture of assigning nostalgias about an unfallen condition their proper place. What for others are the hidden workings of the psychic defenses and tropes of representation are often for him the surface subject or plaything of his verse. Remarkable always is the way he gets us to discard commonplaces about the traumatic or scandalous stuff of repression and to see sexuality and fallen experience as what we find acceptable to expose, while innocence and its priority need to be hidden.

I

Cain, Byron's most successful reworking of Genesis myth, announces from its very title the decentering of myth or the differentiating deferral from prelapsarian origins to fallen experience. Early on, the drama also makes clear a concomitant reversal of our ordinary sense of belatedness: radical innocence, not sexuality or a fall, is what we cover. Oblivious of the loincloth of Christian theology, Cain points to what seem to him to be unaccommodated facts:

> The snake spoke *truth*: it *was* the tree of knowledge;
> It *was* the tree of life: knowledge is good,
> And life is good; and how can both be evil? (I.i. 36–38)

In hushing him, Eve asks Cain to content himself with what is, and let the innocence of his perspective be relegated back in history—and to the back of the mind. Bringing to the surface what Eve has repressed, the devil offers Cain knowledge, leading him to a different sort of statement than the one with which he confronted Eve: "It was a lying tree—for we *know* nothing" (II.ii. 366). It is hard to be a devil of stature in the devil's presence, especially when Lucifer is contriving to accentuate his epigone's sense of creatureliness. The full daemonization of Cain depends on Lucifer's being gone, and Cain seems closest to the spirit whose presence he disdains when, away from Hades, he insists grandly on his innocence of the Fall and shares Lucifer's revaluation of temporal and moral priorities.

Byron shares them too. Before the drama proper he prefaces a note that ostensibly belittles a daemonic stance: "The assertion of Lucifer, that the pre-Adamite world was also peopled by rational beings much more intelligent than man, and proportionably powerful to the mammouth, etc., etc., is, of course, a poetical fiction to help him make out his case." The particularities of this pre-existence may be a "poetical fiction," but the interest in upsetting the priority of the received account is for Byron a most authentic business of poetry. In the play proper Byron dismisses the primacy of the Genesis creation and has Lucifer present visions of anterior worlds. At the same time, he images his own belatedness by centering on a fall after the inherited one, not on Adam but on Cain. References to earlier creation seem designed not for the assertion of temporal priority by itself but for the pressures they place on Cain to bear the burden of new anteriorities, and stand as the focal point on which the turn from the received to the new myth can pivot:

> CAIN: Where dost thou lead me?
> LUCIFER: To what was before thee!
>   The phantasm of the world; of which thy world
>   Is but the wreck.
> CAIN: What! is it not then new?
> LUCIFER: No more than life is; and that was ere thou
>   Or I were, or the things which seem to us
>   Greater than either. (II.i. 151–56)

If we read just the first two sentences of this exchange, we could entertain, with justified suspicion, the notion of a time machine. And "the phantasm of the world" seems a Luciferic reduction to the level of claptrap of Shelley's magnificent fiction of a shadow world in *Prometheus Unbound*. But contempt for such machinery is undermined when the word "world" is replaced by the word "wreck." If past glories are not as such to be recaptured, ruins of the past can still be very much present; if other worlds are the business of romancers turned science-fiction visionaries, still the belatedness of this world has an authentic

ring. Thus, while we can hardly make a significant imaginative gesture toward
recapturing the purity of origins — which belong somewhere back in God's country — we can come to recognize that we stand at a significant distance from such
things, and can come to see an external Hades or a dark region of the mind
haunted by the phantasms of anterior creation.

When Lucifer tells Cain that they are on their way to view shades of pre-
Adamite beings, Cain's surprise, "What! is [the world] not then new?" presents
the newness of the world balanced, as it were, on the tenuous point of the inter-
rogative. For the moment Cain holds the world up on one questioning finger.
Lucifer's casual shrug, "No more than life is," topples that world from its fragile
axis. Though the action and reaction are verbal, "In the beginning was the
Word," and this verbal exchange seems to demand priority over what is to be
seen in space. "Language is properly the medium for this play of presence and
absence," writes Derrida: "Is it not within language — is it not language itself
that might seem to unify life and ideality?" For Lucifer and for Byron language
rather separates present life from preconceptions of ideality, and a particular
verbal exchange constitutes a particular victory over both the presence or givenness of spatial reality and the possibility of past spaces and times. At this point in
Byron's drama the verbal exchange precedes the sight of anterior creatures and
precludes the sight of alternate worlds. Lucifer does not take Cain to other
planets but passes them by: "The lights fade from me fast, / And some till now
grew larger as we approach'd / And wore the look of worlds" (II.i. 167–69).

The experience of passing by these worlds preludes the experience of confronting shadows of the past and introduces the perspective from which dismissals prove more authentic than actual confrontations with preexistents could
be. Indeed, Cain finds the trip he does take no match for his anterior and superior desires. But the attitude cultivated in outer space extends to contempt for
priority more generally. Lucifer tells Cain,

> Many things will have
> No end; and some, which would pretend to have
> Had no beginning, have had one as mean
> As thou. (II. 156–59)

Beginnings are mean things, and sublimity is to be sought not in the dawning of
days or worlds but in what Nietzsche called the twilight of the gods — in grand
dismissals of the past. Lucifer is thus educating Cain to the indifference toward
beginnings that Byron expressed in his diary entry. Or perhaps more precisely,
Lucifer is abetting the process that Byron's diary witnesses by which the sense of
creatureliness (of feeling what Milton's Adam felt when he first woke and knew

himself *made*) goes underground and is covered by indifference to origins and the posturings of a fallen angel.

Brought back to his own postlapsarian world, Cain finds the price of his proclaimed freedom from the past to be a radical naturalism, knowledge of mortal nature's nothingness regardless of (or repressing knowledge of) its Creator. When Cain's offering of fruits is scattered on the earth, he exclaims, "From earth they came, to earth let them return." This is *radical* innocence because rooted in the earth, ignorant of the fact of human death that lies hidden in the phrase as it lies hidden in Cain's effort to cast down Abel's altar and return it too to the earth. If Abel's piety leads him to acknowledge God as spiritual source, Cain's knowledge of the earth makes him stick to his earthy vision of origins.

"There may be always a time of innocence," Wallace Stevens tentatively proposes in *The Auroras of Autumn*: "There is never a place." Dismissing Jehovah as a bloodthirsty God who delights in sacrifice, Cain could be said to claim both "There never was a time of innocence" and "This must be the place." Insisting on the present time, the present place, he exclaims to Adah before Abel comes on the scene to make his sacrifice, "Why, *we* are the innocent." To make this a place innocent of sacrifice, sublimation, and all experiential orderings of the world into higher and lower, spiritual and earthy, Cain proposes leveling Abel's altar. He asks Abel to "Stand back till I have strew'd this turf along / Its native soil." The intended physical deconstruction of the altar and metaphysical deconstruction of the hierarchies it acknowledges may be taken as an emblem of Byron's lifelong efforts to reduce spiritual pretensions and fictions to their "native soil."

To challenge prevenient mythology, Byron needed to do more than inherit the dichotomies of good and evil, God and Satan, and choose the other side. Nor could he simply adapt the dual vision of man as both creation of God and creature of dust who to dust returns and create a protagonist who is wholly committed to one of these Biblical statements of origins. The conflict between Cain and Abel, while it concerns two views of man's original substance, subsumes an argument between two views of what constitutes original action. For Abel and for the Bible one discovers one's originality in relation to the Originator. For Cain and for Byron one does not discover one's originality in relationship to the Author of Evil; nothing can be thought "original" till it separates itself from relationship to sources. So Byron argues about his Cain in a letter to John Murray:

> Cain is a proud man: if Lucifer promised him kingdom, etc., it would *elate* him: the object of the Demon is to *depress* him still further in his own estimation than he was before, by showing him infinite things and his own abasement, till he falls into the frame of

mind that leads to the Catastrophe, from mere internal irritation,
not premeditation, or envy of *Abel* (which would have made him
contemptible), but from the rage and fury against the inadequacy of
his state to his conceptions.

If Cain's action is to be his own, not Satan's, it must be motivated by "internal irritation," not a larger dialectical quarrel with God in which he would be a victim, and no originator. Even envy would not have been sufficiently his own,
depending directly as it does on awareness of the priority of the envied. To the
scene of the murder Cain brings a preexistent sense of infinite things and a preexistent sense of abasement, of dust-to-dust, both of which have been abetted by
Lucifer. Impelled toward both awarenesses, he is now on his own; and if the
glory seems a vision borrowed or imposed, the naturalistic dismissal of preexistent sublimity is something experienced as original to the self.

From his flight with Lucifer, Cain returns to his natural existence, his existence as natural man—a paterfamilias, a man of the earth, one who feels his
littleness far more native to his consciousness than his memory of "extinguish'd
worlds." The glory he could call his own would come from the possibility of
transcending memory, transcending the givenness of the past, and striking (if
need be, with a deathblow) a point for the originality of the self. Writing of
Proust, Gilles Deleuze voices a kind of credo for the mind unextinguished by its
immersion in preexistent materials: "It is no longer a matter of saying: to create is to
remember—but rather, to remember is to create, to reach that point where the
associative chain breaks, leaps over the constituted individual, is transferred to
the birth of an individuating world." Blake repeatedly finds this point; Byron
repeatedly discovers it to be an illusion. His Cain is disappointed in the
possibilities of breaking the chain of the past and attending the birth of an individuating world; he is confronted instead with the natural birth of an individual—his flesh-and-blood son—a birth which, in Byron's telling revisionist
chronology, antedates the slaying of Abel. When Adah berates Cain, "Do not
whisper o'er our son / Such melancholy yearnings o'er the past," she voices the
simple demystification that would put all hankerings for romantic origins in
their place. It is the kind of rebuke Byron himself makes of Cain's weak desires,
and of his own moments of soft romanticism from the lingering over childhood
scenes in *Hours of Idleness* to the moments of innocence in the Haidée episode
of *Don Juan*. Adah continues with cheerfulness she seems to have picked up
from the end of *Paradise Lost*: "Why wilt thou always mourn for Paradise? /
Can we not make another?" But the awareness of death intervenes and keeps Cain (to
borrow Byron's own term from the letter) "depressed."

This depression is not simply sadness but the reduction of man to his earthly origins and first nothingness. Tiller of the soil, father of an earthly creature who is overshadowed by cypresses and the fact of death, Cain finds that the awareness of man's grotesque lowness is the concomitant of his sublime ambition to stand original and free. "Nota," says Stevens's rejuvenated Crispin: "His soil is man's intelligence. / That's better. That's worth crossing seas to find." Cain has crossed vast seas of space and thought with Lucifer to find this soil the sum total of his intelligence and knowledge. In a terrible irony, even the soil is alienated from Cain when it absorbs Abel's blood; as a vagabond, Cain will be estranged from the earth he had thought most truly his own.

In Genesis, Cain protests that his burden is too great and that whoever finds him will slay him. In Byron, Adah voices these objections while Cain himself asks to be allowed to die. The visual brand on the forehand is thus all the more imposed and is accompanied by a verbal brand: "Stern hast thou been and stubborn from the womb, / As the ground thou must henceforth till" (III.i. 503–04). These signs of separation magically rouse Cain into authentic voice, for he speaks now with Shakespearean power and Miltonic resonance, but comes into his own:

> After the fall too soon was I begotten;
> Ere yet my mother's mind subsided from
> The serpent, and my sire still mourn'd for Eden.
> That which I am, I am; I did not seek
> For life, nor did I make myself; but could I
> With my own death redeem him from the dust—
> And why not so? (III.i. 506–12)

Truer than the plain fact ("I did not seek / For life") is the extraordinary imaginative independence that comes precisely in the diminished idea of causality—the narrowed sense of priority that nevertheless aggrandizes the self. The opening lines of this speech are like those of Shakespeare's Edgar saving for himself what little imaginative freedom is left after the wheels of causality have rolled to this catastrophic point: "The dark and vicious place where thee he got / Cost him his eyes." Asserting the metaphor-making power (the power of localizing a symbolic topos or a time) over the catastrophe from which the need for metaphor springs, these speeches leave the imagination triumphant yet. Byron's Cain seems to surpass Edgar in moving from slender to full-fledged self-assertion: "That which I am, I am." If the power of this seems limited by our awareness that it is borrowed from Milton's Satan (Tennyson's Ulysses will be similarly threatened), it becomes all the more Cain's and Byron's own when compacted with a new, unsatanic—Indeed, Christ-like—impulse. Even if it does come from despair, the wish to redeem Abel by sacrificing himself seems to contradict everything Cain stood for in opposing Abel and the sacrifice-loving God Abel worshipped. But instead of a capitulation, these lines, so summarily dismissed by the angel, represent a final fictiveness, a last emblem of the mind's capacity to transcend its circumstances and create its own vision of things.

The power given to the branded Cain is like that Byron gives his Prometheus: "Thou art a symbol and a sign / To mortals of their fate and force." Turned into signs, Cain and Prometheus have restored to them a purity of figuration which asserts both the individual origination of their actions and their special connection with ultimate origins. One's act is divine, one's daemonic, but branded forever they share the fate of having their daemonized power abstracted from their persons and made a sign of the human condition. We do not worship, but we "read" or recognize the sign, point to it and say:

> Like thee, Man is in part divine,
> A troubled stream from a pure source;
> And Man in portions can foresee
> His own funereal destiny,
> His wretchedness, and his resistance,
> And his sad unallied existence.
> To which his Spirit may oppose
> Itself. ["Prometheus"]

II

The idea of a "pure source" can be safeguarded from both the assaults of experience and the jibes of the worldly satirist by appearing to be translated from this earth to some imaginatively anterior one. In the diary entry quoted at the beginning of this chapter, Byron speculates on an original innocence: "I sometimes think that *Man* may be the relic of some higher material being, wrecked in a former world, and degenerated in the hardships and struggle through Chaos into Conformity." The stipulation of *material* being guards the innocence of the idea of preempting the satirist's ammunition and imagining man's faded spirit to have the form, originally, of a more fulfilled natural man. In the context of his satirical poems, Byron makes the anterior world that of sexuality which, he loves to protest too much, he has long renounced. Man's "original" moments, to be recalled but not recovered, are moments of satisfied love:

> No more—no more—Oh! never more on me
> The freshness of the heart can fall like dew,
> Which out of all the lovely things we see
> Extracts emotions beautiful and new. (*Don Juan*, I.ccxiv)

As an addition to the manuscript of *Don Juan*, this little nostalgia for innocence appears mid the flamboyant posturing with something of the air of an aria mid recitatif telling the story of decay.

A similar tone is struck when Byron explains his treatment of Contessa Guiccioli to the Countess of Blessington: "I am worn out in feelings; for, though only thirty-six, I feel sixty in mind, and am less capable than ever of those nameless attentions that all women, but, above all, Italian women, require." (The man who could no more resist adding that last particularizing slur than he could resist sexual objects of any sex, any nationality, was not to be worn out.) Blessington records Byron's myth of imaginative independence as that of an antecedent world from which the imagination, like a Son of God, emerges never to be capable of feeling quite at home with a single, belated Daughter of Man:

> The way in which I account for it [my boorishness, or the "something . . . in the poetical temperament that precludes happiness"] is, that our *imaginations* being warmer than our *hearts*, and much more given to wander, the latter have not the power to control the former; hence, soon after our passions are gratified, imagination again takes wing, and finding the insufficiency of actual indulgence beyond the moment, abandons itself to wayward fancies, and during this abandonment becomes cold and insensible to the demands of affection. . . . It is as though the creatures of another sphere, not subject to the lot of mortality, formed a factitious alliance (as all alliances must be that are not in all respects equal) with the creatures of this earth, and, being exempt from its sufferings, turned their thoughts to brighter regions, leaving the partners of their earthly existence to suffer alone.

Depicting the imagination as a "creature of another sphere," he grants it priority, so that turning away from a particular alliance and letting one's fancy wander back to the brighter regions becomes a matter of visionary loyalty to the mind's original place. Whether the marriage is that of man's spirit to his natural being or more literally the entanglement of a man with an actual lady, the marriage metaphor allows for both the legitimate pull into nature and the legitimized resistance to that pull on the grounds that spirit would be pulled down into unequal alliance. The concept of "factitious alliance" provides a vehicle for the conflicting ideas of origin: spiritual preexistence and demystified naturalism.

Obviously the concept of "factitious alliance" was attractive to Byron the man, allowing him to turn biographical facts into a kind of personal fall myth. The concept also has much to do with the structure of *Don Juan* and the way originality is regained in the love encounters. But let us turn, rather, to a poem whose more muted tones give the romantic alternative to naturalistic origins a better chance.

III

The advertisement to the 1814 edition of *Lara* seems to play coyly with the nature of the "factitious alliance" of the hero and heroine of the poem: "The reader of *Lara* may probably regard it as a sequel to a poem that recently appeared: whether the cast of the hero's character, the turn of his adventures, and the general outline and colouring of the story, may not encourage such a supposition, shall be left to his determination." If we follow these suppositions, Lara and Kaled are Conrad and Gulnare of *The Corsair* now caught in the unequal alliance of preoccupied man and devoted lady. What these identifications tell us about either poem is more difficult to determine. Byron seems to be toying with the concept of origin, as though seeing *Lara* as sequel to *The Corsair* answered questions about the genesis of the poem or about the mysterious preexistence of its hero. But the plot of *Lara* seems to be neither dependent on nor significantly clarified by the story of *The Corsair*, and it is not immediately apparent what insight we gain into one dark hero by the suggestion that he is to be identified with another, equally mysterious character.

The story of *Lara* may be briefly stated. After a long absence, Lara returns to his feudal seat accompanied by his faithful page Kaled. At a party some time later, Lara is recognized by Ezzelin, who, before he can challenge Lara or reveal Lara's past identity or crimes, mysteriously disappears. Hostility to Lara grows, and in an all-out battle Lara is mortally wounded. He is attended in his dying moments by Kaled, whose grief reveals her identity as a woman.

As Byron himself commented on the tale, "it is too little narrative, and too metaphysical to please the greater number of readers." The "metaphysical" quality needs to be discussed, though we may dismiss Byron's habitual protestations that his poetry was carelessly composed and insignificant. There is too little narrative in *Lara* for the "metaphysical" cast not to be a conscious goal, and one belies the work by seeming to discover, as critics have done, the obvious clanking of gothic machinery and the overt resort to mysterious silence.

In general, Byron's fondness for mystery is almost as great as his delight in satiric demystification. The poet of *Don Juan*, for example, toys with the penchant for the secret, protesting that he will, rather, be perfectly open. Introducing Haidée and Zoe, he declares, "I'll tell you who they were," as if to forestall dark conceits about their nature. "Besides, I hate all mystery, and that air / Of clap-trap which your recent poets prize" (II.cxxiv). More than an incidental laugh at his own "clap-trap," the dismissal of mystery underlies the genuine effort at the pristine. Not simply gothic trappings but the sophisticated joking about trappings must be gotten out of the way if the Haidée episode is to glimpse an unsophisticated simplicity. Later in *Don Juan* the demystification is less gentle, and it is worth recalling the last episode of that poem to keep in mind how much of what came easiest to Byron had to be laid aside in cultivating the "metaphysical" in *Lara*.

Here is Juan reacting to sounds of the Black Friar ghost's reappearance:

> Were his eyes open?—Yes! and his mouth too.
> Surprise has this effect—to make one dumb,
> Yet leave the gate which eloquence slips through
> As wide as if a long speech were to come.
> Nigh and more nigh the awful echoes drew,
> Tremendous to a mortal tympanum:
> His eyes were open, and (as was before
> Stated) his mouth. What open'd next?—the door. (XVI.cxv)

The listing of opened apertures prepares for the openness of the full naturalistic disclosure to come: the phantom is "her frolic Grace," the very much flesh-and-blood (though not too much flesh, indulged taste makes Byron pause to note) woman. The revelation of Fitz-Fulke is a veritable apotheosis of naturalism, defeating once and for all any pretenses to possible sublimity. What is banished for good is not simply the ghost-as-mystery, but more particularly the Black Friar ghost, the ghost that recalls a lost patrimony and, by extension, betrayed spiritual paternity. It is just those suggestions that *Lara* would explore, raising the metaphysical speculation of whether "some higher material being" and not simply some natural woman may lie at the origin of the story and the center of its mystery. But let me delay our return to *Lara* a little longer to glean from the *Don Juan* stanza a symbol and theme central as well to the earlier poem.

Caught with his mouth open, unable to speak, Juan is comically but significantly restored to an innocence that would fit him not for the degenerate Fitz-Fulke but for the more primary beauty (whose very name suggests beginnings), Aurora. Throughout *Don Juan* speech is the mark of the fall, and the hero's ease at social pleasantries betrays his distance from "higher material being." Aurora disdained Juan's talk, but "approved his silence" (XIV.cvi). "The ghost at least had done him this much good / In making him as silent as a ghost" (XVI.cvii). Insofar as the ghost in this ghostly silence in man's ghost or *geist*, his spiritual nature, Juan finds revived in him "the love of higher things and better days," glimpsing thus the vision of preexistent sublimity that haunts Byron, though not usually his hero in *Don Juan*. Aurora herself seems to come from such another world, and is preserved from degeneration by the outward manifestation of spiritual quietude:

The worlds beyond this world's perplexing waste
Had more of her existence, for in her
There was a depth of feeling to embrace
Thoughts, boundless, deep, but silent too as Space. (XVI.xlviii)

From her perspective we can look back at the several ladies of the epic and find them measured by their talk. Julia, who has the priority only in terms of biography or biology in Juan's life, falls into the poem's longest speech when first discovered by Alfonso. If nature is thus victorious in Canto I, the Haidée episode images a prenatural sublimity in portraying the lady coping with the pleasing restraint of a language barrier. That Edenic possibility closed, the poem moves to a parody of the speech problem when Gulbeyaz expects Juan to melt by her "merely saying, 'Christian, canst thou love?'" (V.cxvi). From the still more depraved Catherine we get no direct words.

Keeping in mind the Haidée episode, where the language problem is recognized and valorized, we may return to *Lara*, where master and page share memories of a preexistent state under the cloak of a foreign tongue. "Cloak" belies the innocence of their speech, however, for the magic of the former language is that it is spoken not behind doors but in all openness, entrancing its uncomprehending auditors. *Lara* is perhaps Byron's most silent poem, and we stand in relation to it as do the retainers or antagonists of Lara when the communication with Kaled is not to be shared. What Byron says of his hero can thus comment on or forestall what others could say of Byron here: "His silence formed a theme for others' prate" (I.xvii). We cannot dismiss *Lara* as a simple tale overlaid with mystery, because silence is theme, story but the setting in which the central silence can be examined and admired.

As the poem opens it presents in setting what I have described in theme. Lara is returned, and "The gay retainers gather round the hearth, / With tongues all loudness and with eyes all mirth." The gathering round of loud-tongued retainers is pictorially representable as a magic circle, and it describes in social terms what Wordsworth might have called a central silence at the heart of endless agitation. The potential is all there at this point for a tale like Keats's "Eve of St. Agnes," or, a little later, "Lamia." But Byron deliberately suppresses narrative and gives mystery its barest background.

One fact seems both to call for and strangely to defeat further explanation. Since Lara is returned, he does not descend into the poem like a Christ figure into earth, trailing clouds of preexistent glory from the soul's home. The land to which he returns *is* home, and the otherworldliness has been acquired elsewhere, in a place not native to him. In a way this simple story-fact captures all that story can do to dramatize the conflicting claims of natural and supernatural origins.

The fatherland seems less one's own than some other land one has made one's own, for natural and spiritual paternities seldom correspond. The question of priority is complicated by the question of whether the fatherland is a place to live or a place to die. Corresponding to the sense that *Lara* has "too little narrative," that the story is essentially over before the poem begins, would be the hero's sense that his life has really been lived elsewhere. He is now but the shadow of himself, a death-in-life figure, or, more accurately, the remains of a figure of spiritual life returned to the death that is natural life.

The conflict between spiritual and natural paternities, or perhaps more accurately between the alternate voids of both failures of relationship, is expressed in the second stanza's description of Lara, "Left by his sire, too young such loss to know / Lord of himself—that heritage of woe." As Byron discovered biographically and dramatized in stories of absent or hostile father figures, one is not simply left to oneself by a father's death; to take the self as one's domain one must both abandon a natural patrimony and seize or create a realm elsewhere. To discover in the self a "heritage of *woe*" one needs to conceive of experiential possibilities as exhausted and one's futurity burdened by belatedness. With all but the woe spent from the self-heritage, Lara returns to the patrimonial heritage, almost knowing, perhaps, that that too will be shortly spent.

In the years away was the domain of self conquered or squandered? One could retreat to the pun on a life "spent" and say simply that the gaining is the spending. Byron gives the two actions just a little more space than they would have in a pun and depicts self-knowledge as the waking from self-indulgence. A manuscript reading, "for his feelings sought / Their refuge in intensity of thought," is corrected to read, "his feelings sought / In that intenseness an escape from thought" (I.viii). "Escape" suggests that self-consciousness surrounds indulgence, preceding and following it, and evading questions about anteriority. In lines that follow, however, experience becomes not the void between moments of heightened awareness, but the height from which awareness of the soul's home can spring: "The rapture of his heart had look'd on high, / And ask'd if greater dwelt beyond the sky." Does the question signify assurance and satisfaction, challenging heaven to provide greater pleasures than those enjoyed? Or does the question, disdaining all earthly achievement, point via the appetite's insatiableness to the soul's infinity? The glimmer of ambiguity provides a glimpse at the mystery of *Lara*, the dark relationship between past experience and the kind of alternate celestial worlds Lucifer and Cain passed by.

The mystery is intensified (one cannot really say "explored") in the stanzas that follow. In the portrait gallery, "where his fathers frown'd," Lara's attendants heard "The sound of words less earthly than his own." What or whose words these may be, if they be, "must not be known." To say that mystery here is serving

its own purposes is to be on precisely the right track, though to say that mystery
without communication is gothic claptrap seems to me to avoid both the intention and achievement of such episodes. Parody of such moments will come soon
enough in *Don Juan*; and exploitation of such moments requires more narrative—the kind of mystery that provides significant or misleading clues, not the
deliberate paucity of detail we find here. We are given simply the suggestion of
voices, "the sound of words" without the words, and the single descriptive detail—always ready, in gothic literature, to turn from adjective to verb—of
frowning fathers in the portrait gallery. If those portraits were to respond to
Lara, would their frowns or voices be the communication of dead fathers to their
heir, or would they be protesting the intrusion of another ghost, another voice
out of the past that belongs to Lara alone and not to them? The moment is too
tenuous to permit such speculation to take hold, but again a manuscript revision
points to Byron's care with suggestive ambiguity. "The sound of words less earthly
than his own" was originally written, "The sound of other voices than his own."
The original line is closer to claptrap, allowing suggestions of a general communication with the dead or, for possible naturalistic solution, voices of the living;
the revised line properly focuses the ambiguity on communication "less earthly"
because spoken by a spirit of the earth's past or a spirit from other realms and
other skies.

   A similar ambiguity attends a fearful call one night when the palace occu-
pants hear a sound that rouses them from their sleep and confronts them with
preoccupied Lara's bad dream—or what may be the pre-occupied palace's ghostly
Presences:

> 'Twas midnight—all was slumber; the lone light
> Dimm'd in the lamp, as loth to break the night.
> Hark! there be murmurs heard in Lara's hall—
> A sound—a voice—a shriek—a fearful call!
> A long, loud shriek—a silence; did they hear
> That frantic echo burst the sleeping ear?
> They heard and rose, and tremulously brave,
> Rush where the sound invoked their aid to save;
> They come with half-lit tapers in their hands,
> And snatch'd in startled haste unbelted brands. (I.xii)

As in Coleridge's "Christabel," question and answer suggest the disparity between
spiritual quest and the declarative nature of the world we know. When Lara
wakes with (or is it "to"?) a shriek and fearful call, the sound of words puzzles
his attendants, for the delirious prince speaks in what seem to be "accents of
another land" (I.xiii). Neither attendants nor readers discover what those words

are, though it is not difficult to say that they have more to do with the "sound of words less earthly" than with anything explicable in "his native tongue." At this point we are given what comes closest to being a narrative thread to seize on. Lara's words were "meant to meet an ear / That hears him not — alas, that cannot hear!" If we are tired of mystery, we can use this thread to weave the connection between *Lara* and *The Corsair*. Lara would thus have had a dream of his dead love Medora, who "cannot hear," and would be comforted by Gulnare-Kaled, who knows of Medora, can speak her language, and at least quiet the spirit of the man she cannot distract into love.

To say that such are the identifications behind the "mystery" is less to resolve than to deny the mystery and its richness. If we turn back to the dream night we can discover more from the setting, the poetry that lies just outside narrative.

> It was the night, and Lara's glassy stream
> The stars are studding, each with imaged beam;
> So calm, the waters scarcely seem to stray,
> And yet they glide like happiness away;
> Reflecting far and fairy-like from high
> The immortal lights that live along the sky. (I.x)

A small but not insignificant contribution to the air of romance may be noted in the identification of the stream as "Lara's." The country too is called "Lara's" rather than by any national name, and in general the paucity of proper names or properly externalized events makes one view what story there is as belonging more to the psyche than the person of Lara. The commerce between external and internal nature seems imaged in the lines about reflection. It is not that the mind, like the stream, receives images of external nature; rather, the stream for the moment seems to image a higher spiritual reality represented by the stars. Waters that "glide like happiness away" are easily enough separated from the human emotion they are said to represent. But "The immortal lights that live along the sky" are not so easily divorced from the anthropomorphic, the inspiriting humanization of the verb "live." The adjective "immortal" moves the description into a realm of higher being, thus insulated, as it were, from assaults of self-consciousness about such projections. The riverbed seems a little Eden, complete with flowers and waters "mazy like the snake." To Lara, who feels he is already fallen, such Eden vision is best left alone, for its unadulterated perfection but "mock'd such breast as his." This mockery takes the place of the ordinary mockery satiric naturalism directs at visions of "higher spirit," and at the myths of organized religion generally. Here, where any potential demystifying mockery would have to be spirit's scorn of flesh, "You scarce would start to meet a spirit there."

What kind of spirit? Some daughter of God come down to mingle with the sons of men? Or some ghost of a daughter of man, haunting the consciousness of Lara as fallen son of God? To rephrase, would one imagine such a spirit come from man's mythic, idyllic past, or Lara's biographical, actual past? The alternatives, for the moment, mingle. If stars in water are a visual illusion and spirits in nature a romantic fantasy, the mingling of mythic and personal past is nonetheless a real mingling. Lara is painfully reminded "of other days, / Of skies more cloudless, moons of purer blaze." By itself "other days" most properly belongs to his personal past, while the purified scene belongs to imagination's ideal or anterior world. One can neither scorn Byron's fancied "higher spiritual being" as the delusion of young love nor scorn young love as an inadequate vehicle for the sense of spiritual being. Scorn is preempted by this fallen spirit who remembers what he was yet must endure the descent into nature or the nature of loss.

In a stanza Byron added to the original manuscript, Lara's relationship to his Luciferic literary ancestry is made explicit:

> As if the worst had fallen which could befall,
> He strove a stranger in this breathing world,
> An erring spirit from another hurl'd;
> A thing of dark imaginings. (I.xviii)

Taken by themselves, either the implied satanism or the naturalistic pity for lost love would seem self-indulgent. Tenuously identified, the spiritual potential of each is given a local habitation in the other. In *The Corsair*, Conrad is a little too good to be thought capable of grand satanic crimes. *Lara* taints its hero with just a suggestion of something less than sweet. Aloof from others, his mind dwelling "in regions of her own," Lara is capable of fixing himself upon others' memory like a serpent round a tree. The detail may be there to prepare for Ezzelin's recall; more significantly, it keeps the suggestions of spirit menacing as they are attractive. Lara himself is the most menaced, victim of his own power to defy forgetfulness.

The introversion of this power is dramatized in the encounter with Ezzelin, who points to Lara at Otho's party the way Keats's Apollonius stares down the no less serpentine Lamia. These demystifiers would clear away all but memory of the actual, historical past. Yet an incomplete exposure only mystifies further, and Ezzelin leaves Lara with the cryptic warning, "O! never canst thou cancel half her debt, / Eternity forbids thee to forget" (I.xxiii). Is the debt memory's debt to Eternity or Lara's debt to a specific lady? The abstractness or absence of the antecedent for "her" only heightens the thematic mystery concerning antecedence and forgetting. Though the encounter with Ezzelin is as spare of detail and information as was Lara's dream, its very silence tells us more than details of the past could. Ezzelin's questions, "how came he thence? — what doth he here?" (I.xxii), seem not to demand an account of the slings and arrows of Lara's outrageous fortune but to strip away the accidents of fortune and confront Lara's romantic origins. Robert Gleckner calls the Ezzelin encounter "a transparent device to dramatize the presentness of all the past and the inescapability of one's self, one's inner world." Ezzelin's own mysterious disappearance, while teasing the fancy into inventing story explanations arouses the imagination to confront Ezzelin as a specter of Lara himself. Instead of asking, "What did they do with Ezzelin?" we are directed to more Wordsworthian intimations: "Whither is fled the visionary gleam? / Where is it now, the glory and the dream?" Not that Ezzelin embodies glory and dream, but his presence marked the presence of the question to Lara. As voiced by the poet, the question asked the next day about Ezzelin teases us out of thoughts about visionary gleam: "But where was he, that meteor of a night, / Who menaced but to disappear with light?" (II.vi).

At a moment of visionary failure, Wordsworth looks around him and finds "waters on a starry night / Are beautiful and fair; / . . . But yet I know, where'er I go / That there hath past away a glory from the earth." If we turn back from the night of Ezzelin's disappearance to the night of Lara's dream, we can find in the waters of the starry night reflections of glory past. Lara is a fallen star, and Ezzelin, "meteor of a night," an image of star's fall — its fading into the light of common, naturalistic day. Inasmuch as these star references are images, they suggest that an experiential loss is being treated, under the license of romantic hyperbole, as a Lucifer-like fall from heaven. But in a poem so spare, where these few images are so much the light and the life of the poem, we are thrown back into the romance element with the conviction that story details, experiential losses, can only represent the "starry connaissance" that makes metaphoric language closer to reality than narrative plain song. While the story lasts, the relative claims of starry and earthly realities, spiritual and natural origins, must be kept in balance. The ambiguity is represented, for example, by the description of Lara leaving Otho's party with Kaled. "His only follower from those climes afar, / Where the soul glows beneath a brighter star" (I.xxv). If "climes afar" describes the ordinary territory of romance, the extent to which this distance is natural or supernatural depends on whether one emphasizes "beneath" or "star." Nature lovers flourish beneath their star, but the star represents all that transcends nature and connects man to primeval glory. Love is, the poet says in *The Giaour*, "A spark of that immortal fire / With angels shared" (lines 1132–33).

Only after Lara's death does the poem return to the night of the encounter with Ezzelin, as if to record that the stars shine still though the flesh is mortal. With the death of Lara the character, the poem can dispense also with the ordinary bounds between man and man or mind and mind that keep one literary figure an antagonist rather than a projection of another. In terms of the story, the demystification of Lara — when our hero is reduced from the ambiguous element Byron elsewhere calls "fiery dust" and is returned to dust — is followed by the demystification of Ezzelin's death. But whether we are wholly in the realm of nature now remains a further mystery. The story of Ezzelin's death is separated from the main narrative by being presented as a peasant's tale. Within that tale comes the poem's most startling detail, all the more prominent if the peasant's tale is read beside Byron's source, where the detail is not to be found. The Serf watches the stream into which a body has been cast:

> He caught a glimpse, as of a floating breast,
> And something glitter'd starlike on the vest;
> But ere he well could mark the buoyant trunk,
> A massy fragment smote it, and it sunk:
> It rose again, but indistinct to view,
> And left the waters of a purple hue,
> Then deeply disappear'd. (II.xxiv)

If one wishes to see the star here merely as Ezzelin's badge of knighthood, one's desire for naturalistic reduction receives this final dousing. If one sees instead an echo of the night of Lara's dream, one finds Byron approaching, in muted tones, the kind of imaginative triumph Shelley more flamboyantly executed at the end of *Adonais*. For Shelley, the star beacons from on high, while for Byron — building into the image itself its insurance against demystification — the reflection of the star glimmers for a moment from below. If Ezzelin was a pursuing specter to Lara, his death here shadows forth the life of the hero. The mysterious Lara returned to his fatherland is the star "indistinct to view" at second and final remove from its prelapsarian state. In terms of the peasant narrative, the star sinks; in terms of romantic narrative, the star image outlasts Lara's life in nature.

The mystery of *Lara* lies in the strange relationship between narrative and preexistent sublimity revealed at the end. If one believed in the temporal priority of a prenatural state, the fall into narrative — telling the story of a man's loves and losses on earth — would be a fall into nature. In itself, the Byronic speculation about an anterior spiritual state has the same fictive status as naturalistic narrative. But a narrative true to one's sense of fall restores the spiritual sublimity that lies "behind" and thus anterior to the story. Not that romance comes first, satiric reduction next. Byron's revisions, whether on the scale of individual lines of *Lara*, the addition of the romantic stanzas at the end of Canto I of *Don Juan*, or the major reworking of Act III of *Manfred*, show that often the impulse to reduction came first and had to be purged or laid aside to allow for a possible sublimity. Within the achieved fiction, however, one can find restored the

primariness of the higher spiritual state and the belatedness of n'
count of a fall contains no assurance that the prelapsarian condition..
ingly represent a higher spiritual state; neither does satire insure the anteriority
of the serious. But if a narrative has earned its emblems of spirit, the degradation of those emblems can authenticate what they once were.

As the poem draws to a close, the very story seems a degradation of the
spiritual into the literal. It is one thing to sense that a pure adventure tale is being embroidered by sophisticated innuendos and images, or turned into em-
broidery by having narrative detail cut out to leave a delicate, lacelike story-
fabric. But it is something very different to sense that the literal level has itself
descended from the metaphysical and darkly reflects a purer literary origin.
With the battle lost, Lara's faithful soldiers see that "One hope survives, the
frontier is not far, / And thence they may escape from native war" (II.xi). To
cross that border would be (or once would have been) to become border figures
and haunt the ambiguous geographical spaces that used to be more than geographic. They would "bear within them to the neighboring state / An exile's sorrows or an outlaw's hate." These burdens are theirs proleptically, for the exile's
sorrows are the inner sorrows of alienation regardless of where one stands; and
the outlaw's hate grew from the mind's war with nature before the war became
that of Lara and Otho, or before it could become the war of outcasts and citizens.
The geographic border seems a descendant of a temporal one and reminds us of
Lara's exile from an original, *un*native home, for which a new exile could be but
a literalizing repetition.

In abstract terms the significance of such a new border crossing is figured by
Foucault, who speaks of the "recession of the origin . . . on the far side of experience." Picture the "far side of experience" literalized geographically; imagine the retreat of origins turned into a military retreat, and one sees Lara's
forces traveling backward across the border to the dynasty of archaic or arcadian
imaginings, under the government of which the mysteries of life and the simple
patterns of life peacefully coexist. But does Byron's "recession of the origin"
reach the "dynasty of its own archaism"? Lara and his men look more closely and
discover not arcadia — the mythic land of prelapsarian pastoralism — but Otho's
men, who have *preempted* the border ground and cut off Lara's forces from retreat. Byron's poised verse matches one preemption with another, first descrying
the romantic or "preposterous" perspective of Lara's men, then the realistic fact
of Otho's ambush:

> It is resolved, they march — consenting Night
> Guides with her star their dim and torchless flight.
> Already they perceive its tranquil beam
> Sleep on the surface of the barrier stream;

> Already they descry — is yon the bank?
> Away! 'tis lined with many a hostile rank.
> Return or fly! — What glitters in the rear?
> It is Otho's banner, the pursuer's spear!
> Are those the shepherds' fires upon the height?
> Alas! they blaze too widely for the flight. (II.xii)

The star misguides, the *already*s mistake, and those wonderful shepherds' fires come to be seen with greater clarity as fires from the enemy camp.

The plaintive, gentle music of the question and answers in this stanza forms an equivalent, in narrative voice, of the undertones in Shakespeare's *Antony and Cleopatra*, the sad music of the god Hercules leaving Antony before that star falls. The effect in Byron's stanza is also more particular, for the misprision in the last two lines quoted does more to create a sense of the lost pastoral than could any extended description of shepherds in the beyond-the-border land whence Lara came. These two lines express a further loss, the absence of the particularity in the lines that precede them. By themselves, the last two lines would capture ordinary delusion, the defeat of expectation when an envisioned land of escape turns out to be the enemy's camp. This is what any such loss might be. The lines before, however, depend for their resonance on all that stars and streams have come to be in this poem. The expectation that reflected starlight will appear prelapsarian tumbles when the lights are more clearly descried. Whether or not a prelapsarian state was a tenable myth, the loss of that topos, that expectation, is a real loss, authenticating the imputed anteriority of the pre-existent spiritual state. For the moment we are caught expecting stars of redemption — or at least a battle of angels in which the stars throw down their spears and become the fallen angels. But the spears are simply Otho's spears, and the war is not heavenly but corporeal. The weight of allusion is lost; simultaneously, and consequently, the anteriority of the "higher spiritual state" is assured.

As far as the narrator of *Lara* is concerned, "The secret long and yet but half conceal'd" (II.xxi) is the sex of Kaled. By itself this revelation is so meager that the aura of mystery maintained throughout the poem would be no more than what the *Quarterly Review* found the dream episode to be, "a mere useless piece of lumber." Is the secret wholly demystified one must ask, when we extrapolate from the revelation of Kaled's sex that she is Gulnare, and that Lara-Conrad has been pining over Medora (first love of the hero of *The Corsair*)? By itself the turn from one set of literary facts to another avails naught. Yet the very inadequacy of such information proves instructive and leads to the recognition that the specific identity of Kaled, like the sex of Kaled and sexuality in general, are not the secrets of poetry but the cover for the mysteries of love, of innocence, and of the priority of spiritual life.

Byron's admission that the secret of Kaled's sex has been but half concealed all along makes public the kind of half concealment characteristic of the workings of repression. In a sense Kaled's devotion to Lara is founded on forgetfulness of Lara's preoccupation with Medora, and Kaled's mystification figures that of the reader. Yet as revelation, the baring of Kaled's breast is as poor a thing as would be the baring of plain facts of past experience to one undergoing psychoanalysis. To represent the fact that nothing has really been revealed, Kaled is seen ever silent while all around demand facts: "Vain was all question ask'd her of the past, / And vain e'en menace — silent to the last." What she has to reveal is love, and that is a significance that has just found public sign, though in an important sense the signs were there all along. What she has to conceal is the daemonic or transcendent rather than purely sexual nature of love, and that is something no physical unveiling could destroy. The preexistence of this bond between Lara and Kaled preempts the status of organized religion's bond between God and man. Dismissing the special sanction of churches, Byron presents Lara resting as much at peace as man could be: "Nor is his mortal slumber less profound, / Though priest nor bless'd, nor marble deck'd the mound." Yet these lines mystify as much as they demystify, for while denying special status to church or fame, they grant special status to the emotions of Kaled, which add to the burial of Lara a special grace.

The literary kinship between *The Corsair* and *Lara* confirmed at this moment also encourages the renewed mystification. We are drawn not to the sexual facts that bind the stories but to the fact of love, which, transcending the single poem, seems to transcend natural life as well and image a source purely "literary" and therefore purely spiritual. The one-sidedness of love — Kaled-Gulnare loves Lara-Conrad who loves Medora — keeps the line of transcendence looking pure, and while ostensibly confronting the fact that Lara is really the old disappointed lover of *The Corsair*, we remember also that Conrad was as much a fallen angel there as Lara is in this poem. "The relic of some higher material being," Byron specified, "wrecked in a former world." One could say that the very entrenchment of the myth of preexistence in nature authenticates it. More accurately, the entrenchment is not in nature but in a previous poem. If Conrad is not Lara but Lara's literary precursor, then the reference *Lara* makes to a preexistent state is both natural (equal fictions represent states on the same plane) and supernatural (the reference to another fictional framework represents the movement outside nature). The preexistence is real, while the knowledge that this realm is but another fiction safeguards such poetry from further demystification.

IV

Granted Byron's enormous skepticism of any romantic assertion, some solution like that discovered in *Lara* is necessary to protect the authenticity of the representation of a higher spiritual state. Unless the poet were to undertake a more strenuous career of poetic remaking — as does Wordsworth, for example, in *The Prelude* — the technical solution found in the relationship of *Lara* to *The Corsair* is a device available only once. What are other possibilities?

Perhaps closest to the play between fictions in the *Tales* is the play with the reader's knowledge within a given fiction. Byron's dramas, in particular, catch the reader in his tendency to draw premature conclusions. When the false prematurity is exposed, one is embarrassed or persuaded into accepting some other figure or story as prelapsarian. *Werner; or The Inheritance*, in which degeneration is literalized (the son *is* more a daemon than the father) may be a successful melodramatic representation of achieved anteriority. Act III, Scene iii takes place in a "secret passage" between Werner's and Stralenheim's chambers, as though spatially representing the mysterious and morally dubious paths between the generations. We are tempted into believing the Gabor's soliloquy precedes the murder of Stralenheim. When we discover later that the murder has already been committed, that the scene of anticipation is in fact belated, the degradation of our sense of time and judgment makes us more willing, in turn, to accept glimpses of fallen angel in Gabor and Werner. Though the terms are those of melodrama, the internal argument is that of, for example, Wordsworth in *Prelude* VI, confronting the fact that he has crossed the Alps before he was aware of it and finding, retrospectively, an unfathered vapor of imagination. Perhaps *Werner* remains, ultimately, the story of a too clearly fathered heritage of woe; but perhaps the very blatancy of the family romance leaves some room for intimations of spirit redeemed from the general curse.

More thematic and less technical solutions to the problem of representing the anteriority of a higher spiritual state may be discovered in Byron's stories of individual or government tyranny. If the present state of oppression can be seen as having degenerated from a purer form of nature, then our sense that demystification would parallel or participate in the generation helps forestall demystification. In the song at Haidée's banquet in *Don Juan* III, the hypothesized poet sang — or would have sung — of past glory and past song, bemoaning how the lyre "degenerated" into hands like his. "The voices of the dead / Sound like a distant torrent fall," more a part of nature, and for the moment more real, than the artificial aestheticism of the banquet or the lighthearted attitude of the poet of the surrounding stanzas. Having stood for the moment with Lambro discovering what has happened to his island home, we extrapolate on the basis of the degeneration of this paradise from our first view of it to the larger sense of paradise lost in the degeneration of historical Greece. In *The Two Foscari*, Marina exclaims that "this crowd of palaces and prisons is not / A paradise" (III.i. 147–48), a remark that has only the pristine perspective of understatement to counter the weight of Venetian corruption and unhappiness. Less ladylike is the Doge's myth of preexistence: "Methinks we must have sinn'd in some old world / And *this* is hell" (II.i. 364–65).

Byron's grandest adaptation of imputed anteriority based on a sense of present fallenness is *Manfred*. In other dramas and the tales the myth of preexistence is generally safeguarded by being grounded thoroughly in nature, so that to the skeptical eye there are only two geographies, or two historical periods, or, at most, two poetic fictions. In *Manfred* the concept of an anterior spiritual state is further guarded by the distinction drawn between Manfred's spirit and the world of other spirits, whose authenticity is ultimately denied when their power over Manfred is denied. The kind of ambiguity about spiritual or biographical past, so necessary in *Lara*, is still there: Manfred's longed-for lady is Astarte, her very name suggesting an otherworldly attraction as much as a flesh-and-blood lure. Ultimately the drama distinguishes between Manfred's quest for spiritual originality and the questionable primariness of the supernatural personae.

In his first approach to the "mysterious agency" of spirits, Manfred conjures unsuccessfully with "written charm" and magical signs. Denying the primal quality of this writing scene, the spirits respond rather to a spell "Which had its birthplace in a star condemn'd / The burning wreck of a demolish'd world" (I.i. 44–45). The song of the Seventh Spirit would imply that this is Manfred's star, though he seems both to operate under its influence and to operate its influence. The question of whether the power to raise spirits is Manfred's own or is merely lent him, as the Seventh Spirit claims, "but to make thee mine," is one of a number of questions about the past which need to be demystified rather than simply answered. Another such question concerns forgetfulness "of what – of whom – and why?" as the First Spirit asks. To give particulars about the "what" and "who" is to answer the question – perhaps a necessary stage in the demystification, and one Byron relegates, not without tact, to the confrontation with the Witch of the Alps in Act II. Beyond answers, however, the whole concept of forgetfulness needs to be exposed and perhaps discarded.

Byron was all too fond of the stance urbanely versified in the 1805 poems "To Caroline": "Not let thy mind past joys review – Our only hope is to forget." The passion for forgetfulness marks the turn to more postured romanticism in the opening of Canto III of *Childe Harold*. Perhaps poems like *Lara* sophisticate the efforts to suppress the past or escape victimization by it. Biographically, the call for forgetfulness seems more self-indulgent. Memory had no pleasure for him, he was fond of confessing, and he expressed the wish "for insanity – anything – to quell memory, the never-dying worm that feeds on the heart, and only calls up the past to make the present more insupportable." It would be too easy to walk away from *Manfred* as from a portrait of man under the weight of his personal burden of the past. Nor can we simply say that forgetfulness is dismissed in the drama. Perhaps the desire for forgetfulness is purged, but only when it is demystified or shown to be a misdirection or a misapprehension of the object of desire.

Already in Act I, Manfred discovers the powerlessness of supernatural agency in his search for oblivion. "I lean no more on super-human aid, / It hath no power upon the past" (I.ii. 4–5). At this point the path of the superhuman and the path to power over the past divaricate. Manfred does not immediately pursue either of these paths, however. He turns instead, whether by conscious redirection or the accidents of external nature, to the scene around him, and discovers the beauty of nature. "Why are ye beautiful?" is another misleading question, however, and it takes suicidal thoughts to confront him with the importance of nature: its primariness. Part sublime, part pastoral, the scene is through both attributes primordial, in touch with the sources of power because in touch with the past in a way that has nothing to do with personal memory. "Here," Manfred notes parenthetically, "the patriarchal days are not / A pastoral fable" (I.ii. 310–11).

If it would be too radical a dismissal to say that incest is not Manfred's crime, we could at least say that incest only makes literal a perverted relation to paternity and the past. The scene on the Jungfrau mountain less indulges than purges Byron's tendency to bemoan the burden of experience, and self-dramatization as fallen angel is aborted when Manfred is rescued by the Chamois Hunter. The literalized, dramatic height of the Alps permits the momentary fiction that a suicidal plunge would be a Luciferic fall. This fiction confronts us with a greater truth, that Manfred literally unfallen cannot so melodramatically impute to himself the state of fallen angel. Literally unfallen man is also spiritually unfallen in some sense not yet fully recognized by the abortive suicide but implied in the grand injunction of the hunter: "Stain not our pure vales with thy guilty blood!" (I.ii. 372). Not acquiescing to Manfred's self-abnegation, the hunter calls Manfred's blood "guilty" only proleptically. The blood would be guilty of staining the vales which are yet pure. Just as the vales retain the stamp of the primeval, Manfred himself retains contact with the unfallen element of human nature.

"Power upon the past" was a misapprehended object of desire, and questing for it is like the child's questioning whether God could build a mountain he would be unable to move. I compare a quest to a question not for verbal play but to suggest that this is the kind of play Manfred himself is engaged in. When the Witch of the Alps retires, Manfred claims he has one resource left: "I can call the dead / And ask them what it is we dread to be" (II.ii 271–72). Has he himself confused his quest with a question? He needs to learn that the object of his own quest is not power over past or future; the real desire is to be able to approach, in the future, the power *of* the past. The mountain scene was a first contact with the primeval; the colloquy with the spirits in Act II is the second.

When the phantom of Astarte answers Manfred—and she answers only him—she gives not the information Manfred requests, but knowledge nonetheless that he will translate into power. Questions of forgiving or forgetting were misdirected questions, betraying—regardless of their answer—a subjugation to the past. With the information given by Astarte, that he will die the next day, Manfred is forced to analyze or deconstruct into its components the desire to redeem his relationship with Astarte: on the one hand, guilt at violating another can be erased only by passive resignation to the will of another; "forgive me!" is something only the *you* can do for the *me*. On the other hand, the desire to be forgiven or to forget is the desire to restore the primariness of one's own will, the desire to feel one's "original" power unburdened by the past. The component of resignation baffled, Manfred asserts the full power of original will.

The mystification dispelled by the act of will involves the relationship between the past and the supernatural. In a confusion about primariness and power, the supernatural personae had been appealed to; but if they could not dispel the past, Manfred learns that he can dispel them. His was the spell that conjured them, and his is the power to deny their primacy. One's past belongs to one's self, not to any other powers, and daemons are de-mans, spirits who come from man and not parental figures who bequeath power to students of the past. Manfred identifies his present power with his skill:

> In knowledge of our fathers when the earth
> Saw men and spirits walking side by side
> And gave ye no supremacy. (III.iv. 377–79)

In this vision of primordial times man is not degenerated from the spirits but an equal with them. Thus dispelling Byron's myth of degeneration, Manfred restores the primariness of his will and lifts the burden of the past. When the "original" in the sense of what took place originally is distinguished from the "original" in the sense of manifested originality, the original moment is no longer in the lost *then* but in the present *now*. Making an end of the daemons, Manfred stands like God in the primary act of imagination asserting "I am" and silencing the deep. The mind becomes "its own origin of ill and end."

MICHAEL G. COOKE

Don Juan: *The Obsession and Self-Discipline of Spontaneity*

*T*he Giaour, at just over 1300 short lines, and *Don Juan*, at something over 16 long cantos, have one crucial structural feature in common: both are fragments. Once this has been said, it seems necessary to ask whether they are, as fragments, similar in kind (the question of quality need not even arise). Does fragmentariness express the same boisterous self-aggrandizement in *Don Juan* as in *The Giaour*, the same difficulty with aesthetic and philosophical ordering, the same misgivings about the adequacy of what has been written and the same compensatory faith that bigger is truer, as well as better?

It would be plausible to say that Byron left *The Giaour* unfinished, whereas death left *Don Juan* unfinished. Of course Byron amused himself with the contemplation of 100 cantos of *Don Juan*, a number so magnificent as to leave scant time for Byron's daily business of war and love, which after all pursued him as ardently as he them. On the face of it the poem may have been not only unfinished in fact, but in Byron's own conception of it unfinishable, inasmuch as he meant to discourse in it "De rebus cunctis et quibusdam aliis": on everything, and more besides. Such a conclusion, though, comes too easy. It is only justice to urge that Byron not be censured for eking out with fond and wilful tongue a potentially tedious tale. He certainly knew how to abandon an unprofitable venture, leaving the pretentious Polidori to complete *The Vampire*. And as for his going on with *Don Juan* to no known end, we have perhaps been remiss in not recognizing the warrant Byron obtained from his time. The unfinishable poem stands as a signal romantic contribution to the form and vital entelechy of poetry itself; it expresses a resistance to predictability in poetry, which grows in new

From *Studies in Romanticism* 14, no. 3 (Summer 1975). © 1975 by the Trustees of Boston University. Originally entitled "Byron's *Don Juan*: The Obsession and Self-Discipline of Spontaneity."

modes, and has many fulfillments. The root problem with the long poem in romanticism lay not in the collapse of sustaining philosophical structures, but in the fact that the long poem could not, in reality or in mortality, be made long enough. Which is to say, it could not be infinite.

A link between the fragmentary and the infinite attests itself in various ways in the romantic period. The sense of incompleteness as an emblem of infinity may be derived from Keats's "On Seeing the Elgin Marbles," which seems to make the combination of art's perfection and time's depredation, a fragment in short, the "shadow of a magnitude." But in fact romantic philosophy is explicit about the symbolic value of fragmentariness. Novalis espouses it as our only means of approaching infinitude, and Friedrich Schlegel, in his uncomprisingly named *Fragments*, comes out against the principle of formal conclusion to thought on the grounds that the vital fermentation of intellectual process can only be rendered inert by artificial checks.

It is wholly in keeping with this principle that we recognize an ambition of the infinite in the way the romantic poets handle the long poem. It is clear in Blake and Shelley that the long poem (taking *Prometheus Unbound* as a poem in dramatic guise) is meant to encompass infinity, and the form of the works images this fact. *Jerusalem* ends at the 99th plate, but it makes no bones about the fact that the ending is a poetic fiction and an authorial convenience. Enitharmon advises Los that the poet, Blake, is about to wind up the project they are living, and so the action, the poem, moves into a landing pattern. Accordingly, we have not so much a conclusion as a resolution of the poem, which might have flown on forever and which conceptually does fly on forever, since the human states or Zoas with which it deals are timeless. Much the same effect is achieved in *Prometheus Unbound*, where the sober, if not somber injunction of Demogorgon to struggle against relapse suggests a perennial tension, if not an everlasting cycle.

The Prelude may also be instanced as a poem boasting a sense of resolution rather than a strict conclusion; the principles of "something evermore about to be" and the contention that "our home is with infinitude" both convey a reaching toward as governing the emergencies of the poem's action, and that action, though so lucid and so comprehensive in the Snowdon episode, still remains open and unpredictable. Assurance is given, reliably so, but how to live up to this assurance will have to be discovered. Just as in "Resolution and Independence," a given solution is perennially to be tested and challenged by some inevitable, though unnameable emergency. *The Prelude* itself constitutes a resumption and a re-cognition of its own action, with every suggestion of an everlasting cycle, in Wordsworth's mind, analogous to the everlasting cycle set up between William and Dorothy at the end of "Tintern Abbey." More than this, the poem's beginning in discrete fragments and its gradual, as well as end-lessly self-modifying crystallization in Wordsworth's mind make it resemble *Don Juan* stage for stage.

In the case of *Don Juan*, then, it would seem timely to ask: is it in the singular romantic sense an infinite poem, or did it only stand in danger of grow-ing physically interminable? First let me say there is in the abstract no reason why we should not greet an interminable poem with perfect equanimity: it is nothing to us if we choose to ignore it. But benign neglect did not seem a possi-bility with *Don Juan* in 1824, and is not now a century and a half later; the pro-jected interminability of the poem accordingly threatens us, as an extension of the fact that the poem itself threatens us, at any length. I venture to say *Don Juan* threatens the reader as no comparable poem does—*Paradise Lost* and *Jerusalem* and *The Prelude* are actually consolatory efforts, and Swinburne's *Atalanta in Calydon* and Hardy's *The Dynasts* prove, though forbidding, less than inescapable in vision.

Given that it is too much and too good to ignore, what makes *Don Juan* a threatening poem? Certainly not its theme of liberty, a very shibboleth of British self-opinion. And not the sexuality of the poem, where it falls far short of Field-ing or even in some respects Goldsmith and Gay. Nor should it have been the multifariousness of the poem; an episodic structure is characteristic of epic and picaresque forms, as well as traditional in the Don Juan stories, and Fielding and Sterne would both stand as precedents for a multifarious form; Sterne indeed amuses the reader with his projection of the *opus sine fine*:

> I am this month one whole year older than I was this time twelve-month; and yet have got, as you perceive, almost into the middle of my fourth volume—and no farther than to my first day's life—'tis demonstrative that I have three hundred and sixty-four days more life to write just now, than when I first set out; so that instead of ad-vancing, . . . on the contrary, I am just thrown so many volumes back. . . . It must follow, an' please your worships, that the more I write, the more I shall have to write—and consequently, the more your worships read, the more your worships will have to read.
> (*Tristram Shandy*, ch. 13)

And yet in a way all three factors—liberty, sexuality, and multifarious-ness—help to make *Don Juan* threatening because of the peculiar and uncon-ventional use Byron makes of them. For *Don Juan* first of all confronts us with a state of dissolutions. Within a brisk four cantos it dissolves the premier genre of Western Literature, the epic, with a few perversely dextrous, or perhaps I should say sinister strokes: the opening phrase, "I want a hero," is a scandal to the tradition and a far cry from Wordsworth's anxious reverent pondering and Milton's "long choosing and beginning late"; and by the same token the insistence on beginning at the beginning and on proceeding without a Muse, that panacea against poetic disability, helps to destroy any sense of orientation or coherence in a story whose center, the hero, is already "wanting." Here is an epic, that noble and conventional form, in which anything can happen. The extent to which Byron undoes our expectations and threatens our assurance may be inferred from the fact that his greatest epic catalogue occurs in a private letter as a litany of his recent conquests, and his finest descent into the underworld occurs on the morning when he awoke and found himself in a crimson-curtained bed with Annabella Milbanke, and gave voice to the ungallant outcry: "Good God, I am surely in Hell." Meanwhile, in his ongoing epic, he proceeds to dissolve our towering estimate of Plato ("Oh Plato! Plato! you have paved the way, / With your confounded fantasies, to more / Immoral conduct . . ."), and to dissolve the marriage of Donna Julia and Don Alfonso, Juan's ties to his homeland, our faith in the covenant of the rainbow and in man's humanity to man, and one entire Aegean island:

> That isle is now all desolate and bare,
> Its dwellings down, its tenants pass'd away;
> None but her own [Haidée's] and father's grave is there,
> And nothing outward tells of human clay;
> Ye could not know where lies a thing so fair,
> No stone is there to show, no tongue to say
> What was; no dirge, except the hollow sea's,
> Mourns o'er the beauty of the Cyclades.

And having as it were immersed us in the mourning of the sea, while disingenuously denying the existence of any elegy, he is off again ad lib: "But let me change this theme which grows too sad."

The fact is that, as much as Keats would oppose this, Byron is his consummate Chameleon poet, changing themes and schemes quicker than the mind, let alone the eye, can follow. And this is what poses a threat. Byron strips us of all forms of assurance, from the generic to the linguistic to the religious, offering us in place of this slavery of custom a freedom of the moment that is inseparable from its perils. He, however, having voluntarily cast off form and custom, proceeds effortlessly on his way ("Carelessly I sing"); we struggle up behind. He keeps his footing wherever he goes, even into the pitfalls of skepticism; we do not and cannot. In short, *Don Juan* threatens us because it does not lend itself to plotting and bounding, and as we trail after it we experience not only the exhilaration of its freedom, but also the embarrassment of its unfamiliar power and ways. We might delight in its unplotted ease, indeed we do so, until there comes home to us a sense of its unboundedness. It is hard not to pull back at the intersection of spontaneity and infinity.

It has been observed that every risk entails an opportunity; no doubt every threat also disguises an invitation, It seems to me that *Don Juan* poses an invitation to explore the problem of spontaneity in romanticism; it is only the most vivid instance of a phenomenon we can recognize in poems as diverse as *The Prelude* and *The Fall of Hyperion*, namely, a structure of collision and surprise experienced by writer and reader alike. Such a structure exhibits the kind of development where a ride in a rowboat, an all-night party, reading a book by Cervantes, or climbing the Alps or Mt. Snowdon will lead to effects entirely unforeseen and unforeseeable. Significantly, this structure affects both the speaker and the reader; the poet who, say, enjoys a draught of vintage, is as subject to collision, as taken by surprise as we. Perhaps Byron for his part displaces his surprise, but he does not dissimulate his vulnerability:

> But let me change this theme which grows too sad,
> And lay this sheet of sorrows on the shelf;
> I don't much like describing people mad,
> For fear of seeming rather touch'd myself.

Or again we have his avowal that, strive as he may to become a stoic, sage, "The wind shifts, and [he flies] into a rage."

On the strength of such indications let me suggest that spontaneity is not all freedom and arbitrary lines. At bottom, indeed, spontaneity and a fatalistic tendency or bent run together, as do spontaneity and sheer local reaction. The things we describe as spontaneous, as opposed to laborious, are the things that coincide with our preferences, which after all constitute limitations as much as strengths; what the Spaniards call a "querencia" nicely suggests the rigid and bovine quality of a preference. Furthermore, we need to recall that the art of improvisation, which Byron so admired, is a highly trained art, and that, within the realm of conventional literary expression, romance flourishes on the art of *divagation*, of taking off in unforeseen directions. Allowing for the charm of a variegated energy, then, we must note that incoherence is anathema to the human mind. Closely looked at, how spontaneous is spontaneity? It seems crucial to stress the peculiarly romantic practise of clinging to random incidents as though for dear life, and of finding in them a cumulative pattern of meaning and value. For this becomes the basis and the purpose of the long unfinished or, as we may say, the infinite poem in the romantic scheme: to go over, and over and over, some material that we cannot let go, and to go into, and even further into the possibilities of that material, which becomes at once obsession and careful choice, fixation and source of revelation.

What I am proposing boils down to this: *Don Juan* builds itself on the pattern of repetition and reflection and variation, of subtle repetiton and oblique reflection and intricate variation, of the simple single action of the initial Juan-Julia episode. This multiform episode becomes the poem's central figure, or at least configuration: *Don Juan* revolves around a complex of human behavior rather than an individual character, and the poem's beginning becomes at once perpetual and final—if we knew enough of the exfoliating form of this episode, we would have to go on no further. Of this, more anon. It is well here to recall the positive implications of the avowal: "I want a hero," which advises us of a need and active desire, as well as a brute deficiency. In other words there is an affirmative thrust toward reconstitution underlying the overt dissolution of the hero in the poem. In this dispensation Juan must choose to be a hero, and of what stripe; he will not find hero status thrust upon him.

The factor of choice in *Don Juan* is easy to overlook, but it is pervasive and can readily be invoked to show the reflexive complexity of the poem's design. Let us first recall its pervasive presence; Juan must choose, that is, he cannot if he is to survive choose but choose how to respond vis-à-vis Alfonso and Lambro; it is fight or die. I would refrain from praising him merely for fighting here, especially since he does not do it well, and that only for the simplest sort of survival. But his fighting seems to anticipate and to be consonant with two other choices Juan does *not* have to make, in the shipwreck and the harem episodes. The latter choices, not impetuous but deliberate, not convenient but contradictory to survival, seem to me to enunciate a standard and principle of human dignity that the hullaballoo with Alfonso and Lambro somewhat beclouds. To choose not to die drunk and not to eat human flesh as a means of staying alive, and to declare to the smitten and nervous Gulbeyaz, "love is for the free": these are not the marks of a sensual or indifferent nature. Not that Byron goes overboard and sacrifices Juan's human plausibility to the pieties of heroism; the lad does at last, and despite "some remorse," allow himself a paw of his father's spaniel, and does treat himself to an incipient dalliance with Dudú. In a sense Byron seems to say that his heroism, if it is to come about, must come from a personal and moral act of his nature rather than from an aesthetic definition of character established by genre or authorial fiat. Thus the choices he continues to be faced with convey intuitions or intimations of deeper being; the act of saving Leila momentarily stems the tide of his commitment to the inhuman seige; the choice of becoming the Empress Catherine's plaything—a far cry from defiance of the more sympathetic Gulbeyaz—proves a choice of spiritual and physical dissipation.

The final choice of the poem as we have it involves a recapitulation of the individual moments we have seen Juan in before: the bossy Lady Adeline Amundeville, the sensual Duchess of Fitz-Fulke and the refined and lovely Aurora bring back Gulbeyaz-Catherine, Julia, and Haidée respectively. Juan has a second chance, with the intensities and precipitancies of first experience now tempered by reflection and comparison, to choose what kind of man he will be, in terms of what kind of woman he will identify himself with. Such a choice has been adumbrated in the harem episode, where Lolah, Katinka, and Dudú lend themselves to distinction, *mutatis mutandis*, according to degree of bossiness, sensuality, and serene loveliness (see esp. Canto VI, sts. xl–liv).

I would go so far as to suggest that the strategic placement of the female trios in *Don Juan* symbolizes the three modes of relationship that the protagonist may experience with women and through them with the world. Depending on the choice he makes, women (and his life) may become for him an experience of the graces, of the fates, or of the furies. In more abstract terms, Haidée-Aurora, suggesting the graces, would represent a timeless world formed of compassion, candor and love; Julia-Fitz-Fulke, suggesting the fates, would represent a sensual world marked by brute repetition and monotony; and Gulbeyaz-Catherine-Lady Adeline, suggesting the furies, would represent an unfeeling but insatiable world characterized by exhausting duty and punishment. There is some indication that Juan feels he is put to choosing among the three women at Norman Abbey, and there is every indication that the narrator has a stake in the choice Juan makes; "I want a hero" is a tacit threat, though not a threat of force. Certainly the narrator chides Juan for finally choosing war over compassionate love, and slights him as the Empress Catherine's love-object, and confronts him with an explicit and unprecedented social-moral disapprobation after his sleeping in with the opportunistic Duchess.

This last episode generates a veritable hubbab of resonances. It not only shows Don Juan falling into the casual ways of the flesh, but shows this in the midst of one of his battles against superstition and terror (shades of the shipwreck episode). Where he should be wrestling with spirits, if not angels, he gets entangled in flesh. He is left unfit to meet the new day (Aurora) or even the ordinary world (A-munde-ville), having quite spent himself on the false spirit of darkness and concealed indulgence, and having left himself, as the poem observes with a telling Spenserian resonance, with "eyes that hardly brook'd / The light. . . ." The "air rebuk'd" in which the Duchess is seen also picks up the vocabulary of "virtue" and "vice" which Byron resorts to in this scene; its evaluative tone emerges markedly where Byron calls it an occasion for "Man to show his strength / Moral or physical." It is striking that where imagery of the Fall abounds in all previous love episodes, it is actually withheld and even opposed at this stage. For Byron carefully associates Aurora with a seraphic state and a possible recovery of Eden: "She look'd as if she sat at Eden's door. / And griev'd for those who could return no more." It need not surprise us that she induces in Juan an unwonted "contemplation." She is, if Byron's pun may be spelled out, a cultivated Aurora who restores Haidée in a viable social mode, and not an idyllic, and perhaps idolatrous isolation. She affords Juan the chance of a full new beginning, bringing to the poem "an ideal of womanhood attainable *within* society, though free from all its vices and illusions."

The points may be brought into focus here. The first is what I would call the realistic humanism of this singular "non-epic" epic, which cannot consummate itself without a hero but whose hero, given opportunity and choice, seems to balk at a systematic heroism. Occasional heroism he is capable of, but he is betrayed into realism by his very capacity for heroism. To grapple with the Friar is to fall into the clutches of the Duchess of Fitz-Fulke. And we must observe that the narrator, though seeming to hope for more of his protagonist, knows human failing at first hand:

> If such doom [to be thought "Bores"] waits each intellectual Giant,
> We little people in our lesser way,
> In Life's small rubs should surely be more pliant,
> And so for one will I — as well I may —
> Would that I were less bilious — but, oh, fie on't!
> Just as I make my mind up every day
> To be a '*totus, teres,*' Stoic, Sage,
> The wind shifts and I fly into a rage.

Narrator and protagonist are not just separate figures in *Don Juan*, they are set at odds, one aspiring to stoicism and the other wavering between Aurora's purity ("beyond this world's perplexing waste") and the availability of her Frolic Grace, Fitz-Fulke. But both come together in being tripped out of the ideal. The "I want" which begins *Don Juan*, and whose epic resonances may echo in the *cri de coeur* of Saul Bellow's Henderson, finally means both "I fail to discover, anywhere," and "I fail to become, anyhow," a hero. But it also means we are made to encounter, instead of the lyrical epic of Wordsworth's *The Prelude*, another innovation taking the form of an epical elegy tinged with a mythical or translunary vision. As Haidée and the Tartar Khan and even Aurora Raby show, we may not realistically expect a relation of more than nostalgia with that high world, of love and sacrifice and "a depth of feeling to embrace / thoughts, boundless, deep, but silent too as Space." A shy leitmotif of elegy sets one of the amplitudes of *Don Juan*. The poem can make comedy of Gothic terror, as in the Black Friar episode. But Byron is not kidding when he says that he laughs in order not to weep. The realistic humanism the poem displays is in this sense an achievement, not a dubious compromise. The poem constitutes the only place, between the procrustean magnitudes of traditional heroism and the procrustean diminishments of industrialism and imperialism, where mortal individualism has any play. "Between two worlds," Byron anticipates Arnold in saying

> man hovers like a star,
> 'Twixt night and morn, upon the horizon's verge.
> How little do we know that which we are!
> How less what we may be! The eternal surge
> Of time and tide rolls on, and bears afar
> Our bubbles. . . .

To stay afloat is credit in itself, and in successive moments to defy the demon rum and deny a cannibalistic definition of human survival, and then to meet and mate Haidée constitute a life's achievement not to be sneered at. After this, of course, much is forgotten, even lost, and elegy supervenes on aspiration; but elegy, after all, is the tribute that mortality pays to the immortals of the erstwhile epic. And besides, it remains consolingly possible, with a sly shift of emphasis, "to laugh and make laugh."

The second point to focus on, in connection with the twofold pressure *Don Juan* exerts toward Man's showing his strength, moral or physical, and his showing in the field of idealism and heroism, concerns less the tone of the poem than Byron's apparent freedom from formal or conventional constraints within it. I'd like to suggest that every way he turns Byron manages to go in one direction. The way and the destination become, with each succeeding episode, increasingly difficult to sum up in a nutshell, but variations on the theme of physical and moral strength appear throughout. With this explicit theme, and with the narrator's infiltration into the poem's action, *Don Juan* becomes a generic hybrid of confession and satire, in epic guise. Confession and satire muffle each other, but both are based on a common preoccupation with the shortcomings of heroism. The play and the interplay of war and love, tyranny and individual fulfillment become the root concerns of the poem — its variety is tonal and modal, rather than substantial. Things and people do not stay long enough in the poem to change, it is true; instead they become one another, as war and love do in the person of the Empress Catherine, as Spanish, Turkish, Russian and English worlds become versions of one another, as love becomes the god of evil, as Donna Inez becomes Lambro becomes Gulbeyaz becomes Suwarrow becomes the Empress Catherine becomes Lady Adeline Amundeville, or as the fall becomes a matter of Newtonian physics and humbler physiology and sexual rhythm (see Canto IX, sts. xxii, vl, lv) as well as wry allusion and social fortune and undifferentiated theology. And linking and imaging all this Don Juan becomes a part of all he sees and encounters.

In light of this mutual presence of classifiably separate things in each other,

we may see a principle of association or ramification within the surface spontaneity and versatility of *Don Juan*. In fact we may argue a principle of unity based
on obsession: Byron keeps coming back to one issue in various guises. The idea
of obsession, startling though it may seem, does help to account for the reflexive
repetitiousness of the poem, and may be necessary to account for any form of
spontaneity, which after all expresses the unlabored capacity of a finite organism
for response and action. One does most freely what one most fundamentally is
bent to do. In literary terms we may see this also in Wordsworth's "spontaneous
overflow of powerful feelings" that are carefully cultivated and also strongly, in-
dependently resurgent.

But the psychology of spontaneity and the quality of *Don Juan* require that
more than this be said. The recurrency of obsession comes out here without its
stagnancy and arrest. We can identify a pattern of enclosures in the poem and
see that Don Juan falls deeper and deeper into prison or rather a realization of
prison; his position changes though his situation remains roughly similar from
his mother's house to Julia's tumbling bedroom to the ship *Trinidada* to Haidée's
cave and Haidée's luxurious bedroom and the slave ship and the harem. Even
this cursory catalogue makes it clear that Byron does more than repeat a certain
setting and situation; he explores its forms and implications, and makes it into
an instrument for apprehending and elucidating a human motif. In other
words, as he goes back to it obsessively, he goes into it creatively; setting becomes an evolutionary symbol. Thus we can appreciate the irony of Juan's defy-
ing Gulbeyaz with his profession that love is for the free, and then literally fighting his way into the moral and physical subjection and exhaustion of the Empress
Catherine's boudoir. The text moves from action to reflection to abstraction,
though the protagonist may fail to keep pace.

In connection with this pattern of unfolding, enlarging, and altering identity in *Don Juan*, it should be of advantage to recall two cathedrals that figure
prominently in the architectural symbolism of the romantic period: Wordsworth's
Gothic Cathedral and Byron's St. Peter's Church. The metaphor of his entire
work as a Gothic Cathedral conveys, beyond the immediate occasion of The
Preface to *The Excursion* (1814), Wordsworth's conception of all things as part of
one; this is the conception that makes beginnings so difficult for Wordsworth
("Who knows the individual hour in which / His habits were first sown, even as a
seed . . . ," when the mind, in "The words of Reason deeply weighed, / Hath
no beginning"?). It also makes ends chancy and imprecise for Wordsworth; the
contribution any part makes to the whole stands beyond dispute, but the
vagueness or failure of every guide in *The Prelude* leaves every end in doubt and
makes the poem nothing better than an exercise in frustrated theology.

The metaphorization of St. Peter's Church in *Childe Harold* IV also serves
to reveal, for the mind as well as for poetry, a process of indefinite epistemolog-
ical development; like Zeno's traveller, one gets closer to a total comprehension
of things met piecemeal, without ever quite getting there. "Thou movest,"
Byron writes of the reverent visitor whose mind "Has grown colossal":

>   —but increasing with the advance,
> Like climbing some great Alp, which still doth rise,
> Deceived by its gigantic elegance;
> Vastness which grows, but grows to harmonise —
> All musical in its immensities;
> Rich marbles, richer painting, shrines where flame
> The lamps of gold, and haughty dome which vies
> In air with Earth's chief structures, though their frame
> Sits on the firm-set ground — and this the clouds must claim.
>
> Thou seest not all; but piecemeal thou must break
> To separate contemplation the great whole;
> And as the ocean many bays will make,
> That ask the eye — so here condense thy soul
> To more immediate objects, and control
> Thy thoughts until thy mind hath got by heart
> Its eloquent proportions, and unroll
> In mighty graduations, part by part,
> The glory which at once upon thee did not dart,
>
> Not by its fault — but thine. Our outward sense
> Is but of gradual grasp: and as it is
> That what we have of feeling most intense
> Outstrips our faint expression; even so this
> Outshining and o'erwhelming edifice
> Fools our fond gaze, and greatest of the great
> Defies at first our Nature's littleness,
> Till, growing with its growth, we thus dilate
> Our spirits to the size of that they contemplate.

It would seem fair to infer, on the strength of these two cathedral metaphors, that the character of infinity does not belong to the poem as physical object, but rather to the pursuit of the object — the world and our experience of
it — which the poem embodies. And it is important to acknowledge the obverse
of the ever-expanding circuit of Byron's interest, namely, his own awareness of

the tremendous intricacy of what seems small. Such intricacy results in a kind of expansion inward; as Byron writes in "The Dream," "in itself a thought, / A slumbering thought is capable of years, / And curdles a long life into one hour." This principle of immense miniaturization is illustrated in *Don Juan*, Canto VIII, sts. lvi–lix, where Lascy and Juan reenact the Tower of Babel; Byron summarizes the episode as follows:

> And therefore all we have related in
> Two long octaves, pass'd in a little minute;
> But in the same small minute, every sin
> Contrived to get itself comprised within it.
> The very cannon, deafen'd by the din,
> Grew dumb, for you might almost hear a linnet,
> As soon as thunder, 'midst the general noise
> Of Human Nature's agonizing voice!

The passage has a severely cryptic quality, and is full of images yearning to be heard, like Juan or a linnet; but we may note that a cannon and an agonizing voice, though these are at top decibel, also fail to be heard, indicating a moral rather than an acoustical problem. The little minute contains more than every sin; it contains everything by implication, and it would seem that the poem gets larger, as by authorial commentary, not only to encompass a polyglot universe in a single aesthetic space, but also to enunciate the wealth of implication in that universe's single objects. The use of allusion, so prevalent in the poem, thus deserves special notice as a form of bringing various worlds, of time and thought and value, into concert around a given, ostensibly isolated moment.

The mode of development of *Don Juan* — "now and then narrating, / Now pondering" — clearly reinforces the techniques of turning obsession into a disciplined instrument of creative insight. The action themes of war and love consort with the contemplative motifs of skepticism and humanism. In short the poem is thinking its way through its action, through itself, fusing obsession and philosophy, incident and teleology. We should note that, after the adventitiousness of the shipwreck and arrival on Haidée's island, the sequence of incidents right up to the landing in England is very closely linked together, almost becoming a causal chain in the teeth of the casual emergency system that seems to prevail.

It is necessary to go beyond the patterning of moments and characters if we are to realize the full aesthetic discipline and shapeliness underlying the free play of *Don Juan*. There operates in the poem an idiocratic (or self-determining) action and rhythm, whereby it becomes remarkably consistent and lucid and weighty and significant in form. This action and rhythm may well derive from Byron's life, and to that extent may resemble a helpless or mechanically obsessive occurrence, but it is generalized and abstracted to meet extra-biographical, catholic needs, and so must be taken as a matter of artistic choice and deployment.

This is, of course, the action and rhythm that we recognize in all the major episodes of *Don Juan*; it first appears in the Juan-Julia episode, which I have accordingly signalized as prototypal, and it comprises five main elements:

1. an authority figure (Donna Inez, Lambro, Gulbeyaz, the Empress Catherine, Lady Adeline Amundeville) who more or less directly contributes to the development of a profane or wrong action;
2. initial passivity or dependency on the protagonist's part, though he exerts a powerful attraction and possesses great potential energy;
3. a clandestine affair of love softly, almost inadvertently begun, and with strong hints of exaltation;
4. a realistic redefinition of that love, with a burst of violence and a threat to the protagonist's life;
5. the protagonist's renewed subjugation, to force rather than authority, and his ensuing exile, a period of reflection and evaluation.

The elaboration of this idiocratic structure in *Don Juan* affords a sense of stability in the poem, but would be harmful if it implied any sort of stagnation. Rather the dynamism of the poem is invested in this structure, which grows increasingly subtle and reverberative and revelatory of the poem's values. Thus, for example, the exile from Haidée's island constitutes more of a spiritual loss than the initial exile from Spain, though Spain is technically home (the homelessness and nostalgia running through the poem are not geographical but spiritual); the superior value of Haidée's world to Julia's is manifest in Juan's naturally and nobly remembering Haidée's, as opposed to the fate of the missive with which Julia pursues him.

In short the contours, the textures, the values of the elements in the idiocratic structure of *Don Juan* significantly alter as we proceed. Perhaps the most elusive and most complicated instance occurs at the Russian court, which will repay a closer scrutiny. There is some justice in beginning at the end of Canto VIII, where Juan makes a vow "which," Byron emphasizes, "he kept," to shield the Moslem orphan, Leila. She, like Aurora to come, is one of the homeless in the text, but we may see more significance in the ways she calls Haidée back to mind; for, like Haidée's, Leila's entire world, her family and her very place of birth, have "perished." But she survives, and Juan, albeit purblindly, may be regarded here as preserving something which the poem at any rate associates with Haidée. It is an authentic act, but it continues to exist in the framework of Byron's earlier question: "What's this in one annihilated city?" The dominant energy resides with war, not compassion, and Juan approaches the Empress Catherine's court as a man capable of occasional good but, as Vergil says, intoxicated with blood.

It is ominous that Donna Inez reenters the poem here for the first and only time, to give her maternal sanction to the "maternal affection" the Empress Catherine bears Don Juan, just as she had earlier fostered Donna Julia's "platonic" affection for him. In fact the confusion of love and bad poetry and humor and war that exists in Catherine's soul (and which stands embodied in Juan artificially accoutred as "Love turned a Lieutenant of Artillery"), this confusion is compounded by the identification of the domestic and political power and by the disguise of raw impervious lust in the cloak of benevolence. A kind of metaphysical chaos is dissimulated by the splendor of the court and the recent victory, but its perversity finally appears in the very form of its disguise — if the Empress Catherine is maternal, she is the mother who consumes her own children, and consumes them incestuously. This, of course, focuses her in opposition to Haidée, the "mother" who saves Juan and whose dreams, however harrowing to herself, imply an infinite capacity for saving, if not giving, life. A further sign of chaos resides in the fact that when all is said and done, the Empress Catherine functions at once as Donna Inez, as Donna Julia, as Don Alfonso — as instigator, paramour, and punisher in this escapade. The height of Juan's reputation becomes the height of confusion and, indeed, of degradation. It is not surprising that "he grew sick," in body and spirit. Catherine of course tries to save him, and we have the final irony and confusion of the entire episode, namely that the purported cure is designed to prolong the disease and may endanger his life. A gracious but effectual exile ensues.

Juan here reaches the nadir of his career. But there are good, or at least hopeful signs. Leila, with all the benevolence that she attracts, firmly frames the episode at the Russian court, and as she heads for England over land and sea with Juan a significant positive temper springs up in him. I have suggested above that the exile scenes serve as intervals of reflection and evaluation. In each Juan has one main companion: Pedrillo, the tutor manqué; Johnson, the wordly-wise man whose wisdom is not à propos and whose skin is really saved by Juan, and now Leila. With Leila there is no uncertainty as to who is protecting whom. Juan, coming off his worst subjugation and most essential defeat in the poem, begins to recover himself as a magnanimous man. Clear and viable relationships begin to crystallize again, and even as the English scene looms ahead, wheeling like swords about his so-called "virgin face," it seems to me that in Aurora Raby he can find the three crucial relationships Comte says man bears to woman: that of veneration, as for a mother, of attachment, as for a wife, of benevolence, as for a child. Here is the relationship of wholeness that opposes the relationship of chaos we have seen in the case of the Empress Catherine. These relationships have partially existed, or perversely appeared before. Now, having gone through them, however imperfectly, and having reflected on them, however incidentally, he is in a position to commit himself and satisfy the soul of the man who cannot but "want a hero."

It is only by the structure of the poem, with its discovery of the critical value of obsession and of self-discipline in an unconventional spontaneity, that such a position has been reached. And it is in turn what I have called the realistic humanism of the poem — a compound of plangent skepticism and sardonic merriment and undying dreams of human magnificence — that makes this position so hard to resolve. The poem falls somewhere between the picaresque and the *Bildungsroman*, and so, perhaps, Don Juan becomes, more even than Wordsworth, the romantic hero of everyday, whose occasions and whose aspirations lead him to a transcendental Haidée and Aurora, while yet his occasions and his impulses involve him with hoary Empresses who stand for old Glory and indiscriminate primitive modes of love.

SHEILA EMERSON

Byron's "one word": The Language of Self-Expression in Childe Harold III

In Canto III of *Childe Harold's Pilgrimage*, just after the Alpine storm is hushed into a background music of "departing voices" (96), Byron raises his own in an apparent assault on self-expression:

> Could I embody and unbosom now
> That which is most within me, — could I wreak
> My thoughts upon expression, and thus throw
> Soul, heart, mind, passions, feelings, strong or weak,
> All that I would have sought, and all I seek,
> Bear, know, feel, and yet breathe — into *one* word,
> And that one word were Lightning, I would speak;
> But as it is, I live and die unheard,
> With a most voiceless thought, sheathing it as a sword. (97)

Thus it is that "what we have of feeling most intense / Outstrips our faint expression" (IV. 158); but even so it does not get away without leaving behind some "faint expression" of itself. Byron's feeling becomes increasingly intense between stanzas 92 and 97, as his attention moves from a natural scene to its viewer's reach for self-expression and relief from self, to return again to the landscape. This movement and the gesture of dismissal which concludes it are recurrent in *Childe Harold*; and when studied in the context of similar actions, Byron's taking leave of his stormy mood appears to be complexly politic and by no means out of order, just as phrases like "and yet breathe" or "And that one word were

From *Studies in Romanticism* 20, no. 3 (Fall 1981). © 1980 by the Trustees of Boston University.

Lightning" seem less melodramatic than they have to many readers and more appropriate to the dramatic hazards of the moment. Byron's moment in III. 97 is frustrated by the combination of self-reference and self-concealment, and so is the reader, but these impulses to describe himself and to declare himself indescribable work together again and again in Canto III. One way to approach both this collaboration, and the series of engagements between Byron and the landscape, is to look into and behind the recounted career of Byron's self-consciousness, to see exactly how reflexive attitudes and attitudes towards reflexiveness express themselves in his language.

For there is a workable analogy between the figure Byron cuts as he regards himself in the world, and the configuration of his reflexive language — language that often is, or is used to explore, the maneuver of an imagination that reflects on itself. In the following essay I will apply the term "reflexive" to images in which something is presented in terms of itself ("Vice, that digs her own voluptuous tomb," I. 83) and to syntactical movements which turn back on themselves ("to be trodden like the grass / Which now beneath them, but above shall grow," III. 27), as well as to the way such figures may ultimately refer to the speaker who makes them. Before Canto III was published Shelley wrote poetry in which these references are ambivalently positive and negative, suggesting a kinship between the creativity of the reflexive imagination and its self-destructive solipsism. And like Shelley, Byron was of course familiar with the connotations of Milton's reflexive imagery and imagery of recoil, both of which are powerfully infused with the experience of a being whose mind is its own place. Although criticism has dwelt on Byron's celebrated way with the Satanic persona, very little has been said about his grasp, in *Childe Harold*, of the way Milton's imagery evokes the closed circuit of self-projection, the enlarging yet confining continuum of inner and outer landscapes.

In fact Byron's positions and movements are far more often tracked in the criticism of Canto III than is the language in which he makes them known. And yet the remarkable persistence of reflexive imagery and syntax is a material witness of particular value in the case of a poet who is himself his own material. Of course this fact does not settle the question of premeditation — always a tricky one with Byron. I will pursue his meditations in the order and in the language in which he presents them, for his language gathers meaning episodically, as does much else that accumulates in *Childe Harold*. By the time Byron reaches stanza 97 the pattern of his self-expression is fully articulated. And the relationship between his verbal strategy and his verbalized experience suggests an important point of negotiation, a promising means of coming to terms with a poet who says repeatedly what he will not say.

Images like these help explain why Byron gives two different reasons in stanzas 4 and 6 for writing Canto III. He wants to forget all "agitation," but without any real or imagined "high adventure" (III. 42) the cure of quiet will prove as fatal as the disease: the "intense" existence he creates keeps Byron from being "Even as a flame unfed, which runs to waste / With its own flickering, or a sword laid by / Which eats into itself, and rusts ingloriously" (III. 44). As for the actual life of high adventure, Byron banishes those struggles which can neither attain the "sun of glory" nor evade "Contending tempests" (III. 45). His declaration that "true Wisdom's world will be / Within its own creation" (III. 46) recalls the impulse of Harold's proud desolation to "find / A life within itself" (III. 12).

These descriptions of self-sufficiency are, like Byron's rationale for writing, far less ominous than the kind of preying on oneself he describes in stanza 42. But the likeness is troubling regardless of what Byron intends, and the likeness only deepens when he turns back again to the world of "Maternal Nature" (III. 46). He now associates "the mountain-majesty of worth" with "immortality" (III. 67), and it is fitting that when Lake Leman "woos" him "with its crystal face," there are stars mirrored in the water among the mountains:

> The mirror where the stars and mountains view
> The stillness of their aspect in each trace
> Its clear depth yields of their far height and hue: (III. 68)

But once he has been brought to the water, Byron's own reflection may be what gets in his way; he at once protests that "There is too much of man here, to look through / With a fit mind the might which I behold." The reflection of man's image, displacing that of nature, makes way for the reflexive language of Byron's formula for a life that would be the "survivor of its woe" (III. 67):

> keep the mind
> Deep in its fountain, lest it overboil
> In the hot throng, where we become the spoil
> Of our infection. . . . (III. 69)

Thus the mountains become volcanic and may either implode or explode; under the circumstances it may be "better, then, to be alone" (III. 71). The solitary bird to which he likens himself two stanzas later may spurn "the clay-cold bonds which round our being cling," but it takes off into some circular syntax—"waxing vigorous, as the blast / Which it would cope with"—that recalls those ill-fated voyagers whose "breath is agitation, and their life / A storm whereon they ride" (III. 44). Without access to "the immortal lot" (III. 74), these flights, like the mingling in stanza 72, might be "in vain."

It is as a sharer in "the immortal lot" that Byron later celebrates the author of *La Nouvelle Héloïse*, but Rousseau's love of "ideal beauty, which became / In him existence" (III. 78) recalls not only the enlivening life Byron breathes into Harold but also the troubling reflexiveness of that creation, "which could find / A life within itself, to breathe without mankind" (III. 12). At first the creation of Harold promises to take Byron where he wants to go, but it delivers no more completely than do those Napoleonic figures whose "breath is agitation." The reflexive agitation of Rousseau is mingled with the breath of his inspiration, much as they are in Byron's verse, so that the "breath which made him wretched" (III. 77) also "breathed itself to life in Julie" (III. 79). But Byron's telling note to stanza 79 lets some of the air out of this mouth-to-mouth resuscitation: he extols Rousseau's description of a kiss, then denies the adequacy of even this superlative expression — and he does it, characteristically, because such words "must be felt, from their very force, to be inadequate to the delineation." As in stanza 97, Byron's dismissal of mere language helps substantiate emotion that is said to be ineffable; but for Byron's Rousseau, the imperfect fit of words and feeling offers no escape from reflexive interchange, which is sustained in hope and frustrated in fact. And if this form of self-expression may bring no relief from self, it may also shorten the lives of those who have mastered it. Although his words start innocently enough as "sunbeams" (III. 77), Rousseau is soon said to be "Kindled . . . and blasted" by the "ethereal flame" which, in turn, "teems / Along his burning page" (III. 78).

Byron eventually turns back from these to nature's pages as reflected in the purity and stillness of "Clear, placid Leman" (III. 85). But the contemplation of nature again comes around to a circular pattern of thought. Glittering in the dark on a hillside, the star-reflecting dews (like the drop that reflexively weeps its own tear in Marvell's "On a Drop of Dew") "All silently their tears of love instil, / Weeping themselves away, till they infuse" — very much in the Shelleyan spirit of *Epipsychidion* (lines 465-69) — "Deep into Nature's breast the spirit of her hues" (III. 87). There is something comparable to this kind of interaction in the next stanza, in which man seeks to "read" his fate in the stars to which he has already claimed kinship and after which earthly fortune, fame, power, and life have already "named" themselves. Given the number of stanzas Byron has devoted to the vanity of glory-seeking, this sort of nomenclature may sound a troubling hint of the spells that Rousseau cast. "'Tis to be forgiven," Byron says, that "in our aspirations to be great, / Our destinies o'erleap their mortal state" (III. 88), although he once found it hard to forgive the fiery souls who "aspire / Beyond the fitting medium of desire" (III. 42). The point is not that Byron is carried away by the "poetry of heaven," but that he carries himself away. And in so doing he brings home to the reader the dangerous glamour of Rousseau, who is very much in Byron's mind when he confronts the storm on the lake where Julie once drew breath.

II

In stanza 89 Byron expands his involvement with the stars into a vision of the involvement of all creation in a single "life intense." Stanza 85 makes way for this imagery of nature "Mellowed and mingling" (III. 86), as he sails into Lake Leman and so into the night when heaven and earth are silent as "we" are in "thoughts too deep" to express (III. 89). The "feeling infinite" at once "purifies" Byron from self and keeps him company when he is by himself—both soundlessly; for its "tone" is not the familiar harmony of music but its "Eternal" soul and source, a tone which, like "the fabled Cytherea's zone," is impalpable except to the imagination (III. 90). But when the sky changes and thunder sounds among "the rattling crags" (III. 92), Byron's simile for the scene is suddenly more discordant. In this image—which is glimpsed while the mountains echo and "the lit lake shines" with reflected lightning, "a phosphoric sea" (III. 93)—the banks of the Rhone are seen to answer to each other across the water, or rather, it is seen that they once did, for they are

> Heights which appear as lovers who have parted
> In hate, whose mining depths so intervene,
> That they can meet no more, though broken-hearted; (III. 94)

The image recalls those desolate souls Byron thought of as he sailed through Calpe's straits with Europe and Africa on either side (II. 22); and like those mourners, these banks seem to be turned back on themselves, left alone, as Byron puts it, "war within themselves to wage" (III. 94).

Byron's earlier use of images of reflection makes this cluster of them seem portentous; and the portents do not diminish when a distinction between man and nature develops with the storm, leaving Byron silent in his thoughtfulness while "every mountain now hath found a tongue" (III. 92). Now that it is neither moonbeams nor sunbeams that glass nature's image on the lake, Byron seems less fluent in the "mutual language" (III. 13) he and Harold share with her. This is perhaps why, although they are already intimate, Byron begs the night to let him be "A sharer in thy fierce and far delight" (III. 93). When she expresses herself "With night, and clouds, and thunder" (III. 96), nature is personified as a man who behaves "as if he did understand, / That in such gaps as desolation work'd, / There the hot shaft should blast whatever therin lurk'd." These gaps bring to mind not only the so-called desolation of Harold but also the fact that his creator may be "here" in his boat at the cleavage of the banks, where "The mightiest of the storms hath ta'en his stand" (III. 95). But even if Byron (who does not choose to specify his whereabouts) is watching the storm from a distance, the dangers the scene presents to its would-be participant are more than theoretical: Byron has already shown how those who climb too high, like Napoleon, are exposed to "The avalanche — the thunderbolt of snow" (III. 62), or how those like Rousseau are "On fire by lightning; with ethereal flame / Kindled . . . and blasted" (III. 78).

In the stanza between the outbreak of the tempest and the momentous stillness that precedes it, Byron refers to the various ways that men have expressed their emotions in "Nature's realms of worship, earth and air" (III. 91). But only "now" (III. 97) that the storm is nearly out of earshot does he speak of giving vent to his own feelings. He has staged a confrontation between himself and nature when she is the way he likes her best, "in her features wild" (II. 37); and the result — which follows a series of reflexive actions and images — is the climax of the relationship between Byron's attitudes towards self-description and self-control, and that pattern of circular reflections which is both an instance of and a comment on the way he has found to express himself in Canto III.

The force and suddenness of his outburst in stanza 97 imply not only that this impulse has been strong (and perhaps growing) since stanza 93, but also that his desire to be part of the storm has brought him neither direct nor vicarious relief. Meanwhile, the desire itself has been conditioned by Byron's response to the storm, so that it persists only as ambivalence within the conditional mood of stanza 97. This ambivalence informs his choice of words between "Could I" and "I would speak," although his opening verb indicates that under the circumstances Byron's experience (of history, of the scene, of himself) will control his ambition. "Embody" recalls his scheme to "endow / With form our fancy" (III. 6), but also the almost palpable way that the night has made itself felt. "Unbosom" relates both to his rationale for writing in stanza 4 and to the uneasy questions which conclude stanza 96. That Byron wants to express his thoughts is nothing new, but his striking use of the verb "wreak" corresponds to the violent self-indulgence — the "fierce and far delight" — with which the tempest "unbosoms" itself. "Throw" in the third line likewise answers to the way the storms "fling their thunderbolts" (III. 95). Since Byron rarely feels anything mildly, "strong or weak" probably refers to the quality rather than the intensity of his emotions, and thereby draws attention to the mixed character of "all I seek." "And yet breathe" may refer to his usual way of surviving his feelings, as in stanza 32; but the words may also function in relation to "could I wreak" in the same way that "into *one* word" relates to "Could I embody."

So Byron may be implying that he will not wreak his thoughts upon expression because he cannot do it "and yet breathe." That this is not his primary emphasis is clear from his placement of italics, but the phrase does contribute to a sense of hazardous extremity, as if Byron were as imperiled by a potential decision as Rousseau was by his overboiling passions. The seemingly perverse insistence on *"one* word" forces the reader back on Byron's previous usage and forward to the conclusion that it was loaded on the negative side. If he had simply wanted to foreclose his option, the *"one* word" would have been enough. But he adds the further condition that "that one word were Lightning," which complicates the case past immediate dismissal. After all, in the implicit parallel between nature's "Sky, mountains, river, winds, lake" (III. 96) and Byron's "Soul, heart, mind, passions, feelings" (III. 97), the "lightnings" correspond in position to the alternatively "strong or weak." Lightning has the power and beauty to which Byron is drawn in stanza 88; but it is also associated with the image of Rousseau as a tree on fire (III. 78). Even this ambivalence would be relatively simple if Byron were not so dazzled by the brilliance of Rousseau's writing, or if he did not think at times of human life as a tree which can only bear "detested fruit" (III. 34). The apples on the Dead Sea's shore suggest that man and nature are in a similarly fallen condition, and this is ultimately why Rousseau's outbursts may be related to a storm's. In stanza 96 Byron questions the tempest about the goal of its "departing voices," which he supposes might either return unquietably on the being which produced them, "like those within the human breast," or else might find such respite as eagles do. But this image conjures up both the eagles which fly "unutterably high" around Parnassus (IV. 74) and — from much less far afield — the self-consuming "eagle" Napoleon (III. 18).

It is the reduced potential of man and nature that reduces Byron to an unsatisfying choice of the lesser of two evils: "as it is" he avoids the physical and spiritual dangers of lightning, but stanza 97 still seems to fall into silence as stanza 96 fell into doubt. Once again, it is important to note that Byron's gesture of dismissal does not alter his sense of likeness to the storm. As he discovers or details this likeness his wish to participate does not so much diminish as it becomes superfluous, redundant. This is why he denies neither his wish of stanza 93 nor the storm itself but only the lightning-like outbursts of which he may or may not be capable. In refusing, at least poetically, to authorize this ultimate parallel between his own self-expression and the storm's, Byron criticizes a way of life and of writing which would provide him with no escape from his tempestuous emotions. This much may seem simple; but as has already been suggested, the conditional mood of stanza 97 contains both Byron's reservations about the storm and his onrushing impulse to explode. The dramatic result seems to be at once a natural culmination of his uneasiness and an unnaturally strained attempt to deflect the course of impulse.

It is possible that Byron deliberately represents rather than resolves this conflict, deploying italics and punctuation which give weight to the fast-moving lines and put a sort of drag on their meaning. Six nouns and five commas draw out the first line of stanza 96, and it seems appropriate to take in slowly the accumulating subject of the verb "be." But in the next stanza, Byron's "Soul, heart, mind, passions, feelings, strong or weak" are all objects of the verb "throw," which they follow at a surprisingly even pace, so that the syntax which does so much to create the momentum of stanza 97 also slows the speed with which it may be pronounced. The argument and meter of line 6 would have passed more inconspicuously through the narrow space of "a" word; instead both come up against the *"one"* italicized by Byron. But regardless of how long it takes to reach the seventh line, his requirement that his word literally be lightning rather than lightning-like suggests how far out of his way he feels he must go to make the anticlimax seem inevitable.

The same sort of pressure is behind his insisting on just *"one"* word." He does not reject all self-expression but refers instead to one particularly explosive mode which he fabricates into what seems to be a highly specific impossibility — which he accordingly finds impossible. This process would loosen logic far enough to draw attention even if it did not end in a non sequitur. But the conclusion that he will "live and die unheard" because he cannot or will not say everything in one word cannot be imputed to petulance. It amounts either to an admission that he cannot do the impossible — which may be reason for self-complacency; or it amounts, metaphorically speaking, to preferring torture by suffocation to torture by inflammation, which is not very far removed from the choice he makes in stanza 69. To put it another way, Byron's blanket statement in the last two lines may be proof that he still has energies that need to be stifled: his decisively ambiguous announcement leaves him with the same problem as before, and no further solution.

Unlike the Byron of stanza 93, the Byron of the end of 97 is sobered rather than exhilarated by nature: his likeness to the world around him no longer seems to constitute a license for flights of the spirit but rather the grounds for self-control. As so often in Canto III, Byron turns from his life among others to his kinship with nature; and — like many people who return with mixed feelings from abroad — he is reminded of himself where he is most at home. But in stanza 97 the pattern of circular returns comes to an almost operatic crisis. The familiar experience of running into himself is sharpened by a sense of dramatic danger, which is part of the role not only of the storm but also of Napoleon and Rousseau, whom its imagery recalls. With "the far roll / Of your departing voices" (III. 96), Byron seems to give himself the cue for a solo. But what happens instead is that he drops the voice that rises to a pitch in 97, which accounts for the paradox of his audibly announcing that he is now "unheard." The impression that he has forced himself up to a kind of falsetto suggests that Byron may have conjured up the storm with the purpose of compelling this voice to break. As an attempt at self-definition, stanza 97 operates by contradistinction to the careers of Napoleon and Rousseau. The crescendo of emotion which begins with nightfall involves a Napoleonic reach for the sky as well as a Rousseauan dalliance with lightning. By rehearsing their ascents Byron puts himself in a position to undergo a rhetorical fall which escapes the more fatal falls of his models. Insofar as his leap is a trial run, it is not clear whether Byron is trying to school himself or his readers or both. But if things seem to settle all too soon into their denouement, one of the points of stanza 97 is that a gentle decline is the safer way to go.

So the excess of stanza 97 may be another typically Byronic desperation measure: that is, it may be an instance of Byron's carefully measured use of desperation. Certainly he elaborates his intention in a way that compromises his innocence of self-conscious and even premeditated motives. Regardless of whether Byron means for the reader to associate this "sheathing" with Harold's in stanzas 10 and 15 or the "sword" with Napoleon's in stanza 44, and regardless of whether he assumes that no one will expect him to be "voiceless" for long, his metaphorical resignation seems almost mock-heroic. It is not surprising that Shelley uses the same imagery to make the opposite, dashingly heroic point: "Poetry is a sword of lightning, ever unsheathed, which consumes the scabbard that would contain it." But stanza 97 has its triumph too, and it is more than a matter of getting the last words in. Byron makes a gesture of triumphant self-expression out of the very boundaries that he senses in reflexive thoughts of nature, and out of the very limits that he sets to his speaking of himself. For if "sheathing it as a sword" is an act of self-defense, it is also a form of self-assertion. The life in the poetry unmistakably proclaims that he has got something to sheathe.

III

On the morning after the night before, Byron turns from the "mining depths" of the Rhone to the spot where the river has "spread himself a couch" on which Byron can now muse in peace (III. 104). He sees no more or less of himself in the scene than ever, but he sees it somewhat differently. Like Voltaire's, Byron's is a "various" wit, and his having "multiplied himself among mankind" (III. 106)—like the "broken mirror" that makes "A thousand images of one that was, / The same" (III. 33)—may contain a clue to the riddle of how a man could hypothetically say everything he thinks in "*one* word." But this is no more than a hint, and Byron once more takes leave to "quit man's works, again to read / His Maker's" (III. 109)—which he soon turns from in order to read his own.

Byron's reading of *Childe Harold* III is presented in a coda that summarizes important aspects not only of its "theme" but also of its strategy of self-expression. In stanza III, the patterns of self-concealment and self-reflexiveness converge in a recital of what "we" have been "taught":

> to steel
> The heart against itself; and to conceal,
> With a proud caution, love, or hate, or aught, —
> Passion or feeling, purpose, grief or zeal, —
> Which is the tyrant spirit of our thought,

The rhyme words "feel," "steel," "conceal," "zeal," sound a reminder of elements in stanza 97 which they draw together in ringing affirmation that "We are not what we have been." Although he has repeatedly turned away from the returns of language on its creators, although he has repeatedly given notice that his words may be no more than a "harmless wile" (III. 112), still his language of self-protection is a mode of self-confinement, and still this is deliberate. If he is no longer a man "in a shroud" of his own thoughts, he has since "filed" his mind, "which thus itself subdued" (III. 113).

But with the reflexive language a belief also persists to which he has not given voice before. "I do believe, / Though I have found them not, that there may be / Words which are things . . ." — words that do not circle him with echoes that enclose him and then fade, words that do not "weave / Snares for the failing" like the "virtues" he suspects (III. 114), words that do not just express him but go on — as he means them, and as he means them to — without him. As in stanza 97, Byron's mood is conditional, subjunctive, and as in stanza 97, his language describes the possibility of a condition of language which it denies having discovered. But what Byron gives credence to here are "Words," not "*one* word," "things," not one thing, like lightning. Although the plurals may suggest a way out of the singular rhetorical trap of stanza 97, in the present tense of Canto III it may be that words are things only in a "dream."

And it seems to be from out of a dream, or in waking from a dream, that Byron — who proudly denied that he had "cried aloud / In worship of an echo" (III. 113) — now cries aloud to his unseen daughter. The section devoted to Ada dwells on a different sort of offspring from Childe Harold or *Childe Harold's Pilgrimage*; but whatever else she means to him, Ada is also involved in Byron's hope to extend himself beyond his own lifetime. As in the case of his literary hopes in Canto IV (9–10), his confidence in his daughter will (or will not) be realized because she is his daughter and because of self-discipline. His prediction about her is shaped by the same patterns of self-reflexiveness and self-constraint as are his predictions about himself: "of thy sire / These were the elements, — and thine no less. / . . . but thy fire / Shall be more tempered, and thy hope far higher" (III. 118). This reference to fire looks back to the untamed lightning bolt of III. 97 and forward to the Apollo Belvedere which is informed rather than consumed by flame (IV. 163).

Byron concludes with a sigh over the distance that separates him from his daughter. But it is important to remember that like the "voiceless thought" which may be imagined but not heard in stanza 97, even "as it is" (III. 97 and III. 116) the voice of her father will somehow blend with Ada's "future visions" — a "token and a tone" (III. 115), something "more than life" that will persist when his is over (III. 117). She may never be what she "might'st have been" to him; but in declaring what he plans to be to *her*, Ada's unseen, unheard father makes us ponder the words which alone can reach her.

IV

The best commentary on the implications of Byron's "*one* word" is Byron's, and it comes, indirectly, in Canto IV: "History, with all her volumes vast, / Hath but *one* page" in stone or in ink (108). The words which disclose "all human tales" are likewise involved in a continuum within which they may refer to themselves or to each other, and may be envisaged as part of a single meaning, or a single meaninglessness. This reunion of far-flung multitudes has about it the spirit of Byron's repeated dismissals of the circlings of language rather than the air of any celebration; but the stanza also points to the coalescence of many words into something which is the opposite of what he mistrusts, something substantial, irreducible, invariable. The alternative Byron proposes to repeating "the same rehearsal of the past" is not no rehearsal but instead "*one*" which is "better written here" and can be recognized anywhere, any time. "Here," as elsewhere in *Childe Harold*, refers to the poem that is written as well as to the place it is written about; and Byron's swift passage between Rome and the page written in Rome presages his equally fluent translations back and forth between audible and legible words, between words which need not be written to be apprehended, and the visible words which he says he can speak on without. And thus, like the "voiceless thought" which is unsounded in Canto III, the one page which is "better written here" is, by a seeming sleight of mind, suddenly unworded, unread: "Away with words! draw near, / Admire, exult — despise — laugh, weep, — for here / There is such matter for all feeling" (IV. 108–9). In the retrospect of Canto IV, it takes no sleight of mind to see how one word which is written for the future — for Ada, for posterity — may be voiceless, and yet taken to heart: "Something unearthly, which they deem not of, / Like the remembered tone of a mute lyre . . ." (IV. 137).

In the meantime, the "clay-cold bonds" (III. 73) which encumbered him

before are galvanized into an "electric chain wherewith we are darkly bound," as
Byron associates, more generally than in Canto III, the "lightning of the mind"
with the reflexive action of "things which bring / Back on the heart the weight
which it would fling / Aside for ever" (IV. 23–24). But near the end of Canto IV
he "steal[s]" from what he may be or has been in order "To mingle with the
Universe, and feel / What I can ne'er express, yet can not all conceal" (178).
Unlike in III. 111, it is now "steal" not "steel" that rhymes with "feel" and "conceal," and the word evokes the Promethean theft which is repaid by the sculptor
of the Apollo Belvedere in stanza 163. The "blight and blackening" effects of the
"lightning of the mind" (IV. 24) are countered by the afterglow of "an eternal
glory" which "breathes the flame with which 'twas wrought" (IV. 163), as Byron
develops his ideas about "A being more intense" (III. 6) into a theory or hypo-
thesis of salvation by art in its various forms — including the form that is taken by
a poem. The "poetic marble" which is "not of human thought" (IV. 163) is opposed to the "false creation" of the self-projective imagination, which fondly
pursues outside itself the ideal "forms the sculptor's soul hath seized" (IV. 122).
Yet even while Byron describes the unearthly inspiration of the statue, a "solitary nymph" appears who has "madden'd in that vision" (IV. 162), and if only for
a moment her figure touches on the connection between the god who glances
"lightnings" (IV. 161) and the "nympholepsy of some fond despair" (IV. 115).
In thinking of the dreams which mortals entertain, Byron still cannot disown
that configuration of exhibition and inhibition, of self-projection and self-
restraint, by means of which he expresses himself in Canto III. However partial,
however fitful, the glimpse of other possibilities comes through his sense of self-
imprisonment, in terms of it, as the scent of the ocean comes to a man who feels
landlocked:

> Though from our birth the faculty divine
> Is chain'd and tortured — cabin'd, cribb'd, confined,
> And bred in darkness, lest the truth should shine
> Too brightly on the unprepared mind,
> The beam pours in, for time and skill will couch the blind. (IV. 127)

Byron moves towards the discriminations on which this outlook is based in
III. 97 and 104 when he implies that only certain kinds of "beings" of the mind
will serve his purpose: they must be disciplined, "purified," tempered by "time
and skill" into something timeless, like the ocean. In this long perspective, the
"one word" of III. 97 comes to suggest not only a kind of writing which does not
solve his problems but also a redeeming work of art of which he may not yet be
capable. These two readings are not mutually exclusive because the artist who
does not control his potential is ultimately in the same boat as the artist who

prematurely exploits it: in neither case does the end justify the dangerous means. But when he writes his way into Canto IV, Byron reverses the persistent moods of stanza 97, making declarative his intention to be heard and leaving conditional his suspicion that he might not be. Although twined with longer-winded doubts, a new note of confidence is sounded that recasts Harold's motive to forsake "his land's tongue" (III. 13): "I twine / My hopes of being remembered in my line / With my land's language" (IV. 9). When he later invokes what has been most within him, it is "a far hour" that "shall wreak" the fulness of his verse rather than his own unmediated impulse that would "wreak / My thoughts upon expression" (III. 97). Again rhyming "weak" and "seek," he now denies any implication of weakness if his "voice break forth" and declares that he means to seek "in this page a record" (IV. 134). Regardless of its intended meaning or effect — and readers have had reason to question both — it is by "Forgiveness" (IV. 135) that Byron seeks to break free of the vicious circle of his circumstances — the very "Torture and Time" which he says his words, if not his life, will outlast: "But there is that within me which shall tire / Torture and Time, and breathe when I expire" (IV. 137).

Much as Byron's "one word" eventually compresses a variety of experience and may be read in a variety of ways, a single artifact expresses the variety of the author of *Childe Harold* or *Don Juan*. The words which only "may" be things in *Childe Harold* III. 114 most emphatically "are" things in *Don Juan*:

> But words are things, and a small drop of ink,
>   Falling like dew, upon a thought, produces
> That which makes thousands, perhaps millions, think.

The enormity of its spread is all the more impressive as the markedly small drop of "ink" extends itself into "think" with the help of nothing more than the first two letters that spell out a "thought" — a cunning literalization of Byron's next remark:

> 'Tis strange, the shortest letter which man uses
> Instead of speech, may form a lasting link
>   Of ages. (III. 88)

Chosen out of the whole expanse of written language, "the shortest letter" is the most swiftly scanned link between a man and those who come after him, and the link that makes the "ages" look most expansive by contrast. Yet "the shortest letter" is not a *trompe-l'oeil* but a thing like the "one word" that is lightning "Instead of speech" in *Childe Harold*: a striking yet potentially silent thing that is taken in, as it is put out, in almost no time, and whose recurrently visible design outlasts the lifetimes of men.

So Byron's final return to the immutable ocean may suggest the access he has found through art to another "image of Eternity" (IV. 183), and artfulness — his own if not other men's — also helps rescue him from foundering in his own time-bound reflections. But before he returns to the "glorious mirror" where it is the Almighty's form that "Glasses itself in tempests" (IV. 183), Byron pauses for a stanza at a spot which lacks the glitter of Lake Leman, but which persists in the memory of *Childe Harold's Pilgrimage* — as a reminder not only of Byron's self-entrapment, but also of the strategies of self-expression by which he made his escape:

> Lo, Nemi! navelled in the woody hills
> So far, that the uprooting wind which tears
> The oak from his foundation, and which spills
> The ocean o'er its boundary, and bears
> Its foam against the skies, reluctant spares
> The oval mirror of thy glassy lake;
> And, calm as cherish'd hate, its surface wears
> A deep cold settled aspect nought can shake,
> All coiled into itself and round, as sleeps the snake. (173)

This passage begins just after Byron refers once more to "the electric chain" of a despair "Whose shock was as an earthquake's" (IV. 172) — a reference which circuitously involves Byron's allusions to lightning and his vision of "the long envenomed chain" of the asp that winds around Laocoön (IV. 160). So it may come as no surprise that the description of the volcanic Lake Nemi seems to shuffle and reuse the volcanic imagery Byron applies to himself in III. 69, or that it recalls the image of Milton's Serpent which Satan finds "fast sleeping . . . / In Labyrinth of many a round self-roll'd." But the Serpent is not harmful at this point in *Paradise Lost*, for Satan has not entered into the shape which he beholds. And at this point in *Childe Harold* the infinite regress of reflexive imagery has been worked into another kind of pattern, as the snake with its Old Testament associations of coldness and hate is wreathed into the tail-eating serpent whose figure is the emblem of eternity. Byron's art may free expression from the circle of mortality, but it leaves the sting in language that recoils upon itself.

PETER J. MANNING

The Hone-ing of Byron's Corsair

*Attention to the technology of reproduction reveals, as does scarcely any
other line of inquiry, the decisive importance of reception; it thereby
allows the correction, within limits, of the process of reification
undergone by the work of art. Consideration of mass art leads to a
revision of the concept of genius; it is a reminder not to overlook the
invoice which alone allows the inspiration involved in the genius of a
work of art to become fruitful.*

—WALTER BENJAMIN, "Edward Fuchs,
Collector and Historian"

"You should not let those fellows publish false 'Don Juans,'" Byron pro-
tested to his publisher, John Murray, on learning that William Hone had brought
out a spurious third canto of his poem. Hone's connection with the publication
of *Don Juan* is a comparatively well-studied affair, but it was not the first occasion on which the names of the poor, dissenting radical publisher and the aristocratic poet were linked. In April 1816, Byron's "Fare Thee Well" and "A Sketch
from Private Life," originally set up in an edition of fifty copies for private
circulation, had been reprinted in John Scott's *Champion*, and then repeatedly
pirated. The most widely known of these editions of Byron were assembled by
Hone, who entitled them *Poems on His Domestic Circumstances*. His first edition also contained "Napoleon's Farewell," the ode on Waterloo, putatively "from
the French," "On the Star of the Legion of Honor," and two spurious poems, an
ode ("Oh Shame on thee"), and "Madame Lavallette." By Hone's sixth edition,
still in 1816, the total had grown to nine poems by the addition of Byron's
"Adieu to Malta" and one-hundred-twelve lines of *The Curse of Minerva*.

From *Textual Criticism and Literary Interpretation.* © 1985 by the University of Chicago. The University of Chicago Press, 1985.

These pirated editions have a twofold significance: most of the poems are not domestic but political, marks of Byron's sympathy with Napoleon as against the reactionary monarchies that had defeated him. The juxtaposition of the two kinds of poems points up the degree to which Byron's separation from Annabella became a political issue; criticism of the private morality of the Regent formed a large part of the Whig attack on him, and the Tories were only too ready to reciprocate by exploiting the scandals now surrounding one of his prominent opponents. Both admires and detractors of Byron were fascinated by the *Poems on His Domestic Circumstances*, and Hone's compilations alone, moderately priced at one shilling, reached a twenty-third edition by 1817. These sales are the second important feature, because they show, in the words of Graham Pollard, that the works, which "in Byron's lifetime . . . had a vastly greater circulation than anything else he wrote," owed much of their fame to Hone and other pirates.

Between his publication of these poems in 1816 and his responses to *Don Juan* in 1819, Hone brought out an unauthorized adaptation of Byron's *Corsair* (1817). This text is noted in Samuel Chew's *Byron in England* and the bibliographies, but it has never attracted attention: not surprising, perhaps, because in strictly literary terms it is not very good, but it throws into relief facets of Byron's original volume otherwise less visible. The appearance of Byron's work under Hone's imprint, moreover, precisely focuses aspects of Byron's contemporary reputation obscured by the merely internal relations of the accepted canon of English literature, and these in turn suggest some larger questions about the modes of existence of literary works in their own time.

The first question Hone's adaptation raises is why it should have appeared in 1817. After the immense success of *The Corsair* in 1814, seven editions totaling tens of thousands of copies, sales of the poem naturally slowed; an eighth and a ninth edition appeared in 1815, from which point the poem was also available in Murray's collected editions. There had been no separate issue of the poem for at least a year, therefore, when Hone's adaptation appeared, and it was followed in 1818 by a reset version from Murray, the tenth edition. Although I cannot offer a certain explanation for this renewed interest in *The Corsair*, some evidence of what the poem may have meant to its audience in 1817 and of the activities of William Hone in that year may illuminate the subject.

On 28 January 1817, the Regent's carriage was surrounded by a hostile crowd and stoned as he returned from the opening of Parliament. The government, alarmed, or at least seizing upon the incident to fabricate an alarm, pushed through the so-called Gagging Acts and eventually obtained the suspension of habeas corpus. Hone, since 1796 a member of the London Corresponding Society, the working-class wing of the reform movement, replied by founding a twopenny weekly journal, the *Reformists' Register*, in which he was aided first

by Francis Place, the radical tailor, and then by Jeremy Bentham. Modeled upon
Cobbett's famed "twopenny trash," the *Political Register*, Hone's paper took up
some of the slack created when Cobbett, afraid like other radicals of arrest, fled
to America.

The *Reformists' Register* did not encompass all Hone's radical publishing
in 1817, and I pass over his numerous satiric pamphlets to concentrate upon
the main events. On 13 February 1817, Sherwood, Neely, and Jones published
for the first time Southey's youthful drama *Wat Tyler* (1794). Embarrassed by
the sudden unauthorized appearance of this memento of his Jacobinical sympathies, Southey sought an injunction to halt publication. The decision of the
Lord Chancellor was a landmark in the tangled history of copyright, to which I
will return: Lord Eldon ruled that according to precedent, "a person cannot
recover in damages for a work which is, in its nature, calculated to do injury to
the public." Precisely because *Wat Tyler* was seditious, therefore, the Court of
Chancery could not stop its distribution, a paradoxical conclusion that Eldon
adhered to in full recognition that its effect might be "to multiply copies of
mischievous publications." Sherwood, Neely, and Jones nonetheless withdrew
their edition, perhaps, as they said, "in deference to the Lord Chancellor's opinion of its mischievous tendency," perhaps because they feared the opinion left
them vulnerable to the graver charge of seditious libel. Hone stepped into the
breach, quickly bringing out an edition of *Wat Tyler* at the same price of three
shillings, sixpence, and adding a preface attacking Southey as an apostate to
liberty, charges that were to receive their most damning expression in Byron's
Vision of Judgment (1822). The radical campaign to discomfit the laureate and
the ministers for whom he spoke continued with ever cheaper editions, some of
which sold for as little as twopence. Sales were rumored to have reached as high
as sixty thousand copies, far exceeding the success of any of Southey's legitimate
poems.

In February 1817, Hone also published the works with which his name has
ever since been associated, *The Late John Wilkes's Catechism of a Ministerial
Member, The Political Litany*, and *The Sinecurist's Creed*. These twopenny
pamphlets put crude parodies of the liturgy to forceful satiric use, as a sample of
the *Catechism* demonstrates:

Q. Rehearse the Articles of thy Belief.
A. I believe in George, the Regent Almighty, Maker of New Streets,
and Knights of the Bath.
    And in the present Ministry, his only choice, who were conceived
of Toryism, brought forth of William Pitt, suffered loss of place
under Charles James Fox, were execrated, dead, and buried. In a few

> months they rose again from their minority: they re-ascended to the
> Treasury benches, and sit at the right hand of a little man with a
> large wig; from whence they laugh at the Petitions of the People who
> may pray for Reform, and that the sweat of this brow may procure
> them Bread.

Hone issued the parodies on 14 February: informed that they had been found
blasphemous, he stopped their sale on 22 February. In that week, they sold over
three thousand copies, and their notoriety was such that the still more radical
publisher Richard Carlile soon released another edition of them. Despite his
having withdrawn the pamphlets, Hone found himself the target of three ex of-
ficio informations filed by the attorney general, each charging him with blasphemous libel. Such an instrument enabled the attorney general to file a com-
plaint without convening a grand jury and thus operated as a general weapon of
intimidation. On 3 May Hone was arrested; unable to post bond and sureties, he
remained until 5 July in prison, whence he edited the *Reformists' Register.*

The first case, that of the *Catechism*, came to trial in the Court of King's
Bench on 18 December. The impoverished Hone elected to defend himself, ru-
butting charges of blasphemy by courageously insisting upon his true intentions: "From the beginning to the end of the production in question," he asserted, "the subject and the object were political." "It was essential to him that
the jury should also understand," he reiterated, "that had he been a publisher of
Ministerial parodies, he should not now be defending himself on the floor of the
Court." To prove his point, Hone read one after another a series of parodies that
had never been prosecuted, including some by Canning, currently a cabinet
minister, in the *Anti-Jacobin Review*, others from *Blackwood's*, and going back
through his wonderfully eclectic reading to Martin Luther and several eminent
churchmen. Hone read for hours, his comic materials regularly producing bursts
of laughter in the courtroom. In less than a quarter of an hour he was acquitted.
The anomaly of English law that permitted the very pamphlets the government
was trying to suppress to be reproduced in the transcripts and newspaper accounts of the trials once they had been entered in testimony exposed the prosecution to ridicule.

The reverse only increased the government's determination. Though ill,
Lord Chief Justice Ellenborough replaced Justice Abbott as the presiding judge
at the next trial. The second day was much like the first, but one aspect of the
bill against Hone deserves to be stressed. The attorney general had argued that
the low price of the pamphlets placed them in the hands of "the lower classes of
society, which are not fit to cope with the sort of topics which are artfully raised
for them" and had inveighed against "such publications [being] cheaply thrown

among this class of people." Hone now replied that twopence was merely the customary price for half a sheet, on which he could make an adequate profit, and that he knew that the wealthy as well as the poor had purchased the pamphlets. A day's fencing between Hone and Ellenborough, greatly displeased by the amusement provoked by Hone's selections, ended as before with Hone's acquittal. It was widely expected that the government would abandon its course: an editorial in the *Times* warned that the verdicts indicated the temper of the people. Ellenborough, however, persisted, and on 20 December, Hone was acquitted for the third time, in twenty minutes.

It was a humiliating setback for Ellenborough, who soon retired, dying shortly afterward, and for Tory prestige. The Wordsworths, deeply committed to the "House of Lonsdale," were in London at the time of the trial, and Dorothy no doubt conveyed her brother's sentiments when she wrote Thomas Monkhouse: "The acquittal of Hone is enough to make one out of love with English Juries." To others the verdicts were a landmark in the fight for freedom of the press: twenty thousand people cheered Hone outside the hall on the third day, and an ample subscription was raised on his behalf. He quickly published the three trials, which were available separately at one shilling each or together with additional materials at four shillings, and they ran into many editions. Buyers of these documents of radical triumph would have found Byron's *Poems on His Domestic Circumstances* and a shilling portrait of the poet listed among Hone's publications, which included such titles as the *Addresses* of Charles Phillips, a flamboyant Irish radical, and the *Letters to the Lord Mayor* by Major Cartwright, whose petition for reform Byron had presented at his last speech in Parliament in 1813.

One other important perspective needs to be outlined in order to suggest the aura of an edition of *The Corsair* from Hone in 1817. In June, there had been an uprising at Pentridge, fomented in part by government *agents provocateurs* and quickly crushed. The leaders, respectable workingmen, were harshly indicted for high treason in July and brought to trial at the Derby Assizes in the middle of October. Jeremiah Brandreth, the "Nottingham Captain," who had in the course of the rising killed a man, was found guilty on the eighteenth, as was William Turner on the twenty-first. Faced with these convictions, the defense sought to exonerate the third man charged, Isaac Ludlam, by arguing that he had only "Yielded to the overpowering force of their extraordinary leader." No doubt remembering Byron's maiden speech in Parliament in 1812 against the death penalty for this very same class of rioting Nottingham weavers, Denman, a Whig, attempted to establish the irresistible magnetism of Brandreth by comparing him to Byron's Corsair. "I may spare the Court the trouble of hearing a second time, my own observations upon him," Denman began, "because I have since found him so wonderfully depicted by a noble poet of our own time, and one of the greatest geniuses of any age, that I shall take the liberty of now reading that prophetic description. It will perfectly bring before you his character, and even his appearance, the commanding qualities of his powerful but uncultivated mind, and the nature of his influence over those that he seduced to outrage." Denman then read some thirty lines of *The Corsair* including the famous description of Conrad's mysterious power:

> What is that spell that thus his lawless train
> Confess and envy, yet oppose in vain:
> What should it be, that thus their faith can bind,
> The power, the nerve, the magic of the mind.

Unfortunately, Denman's exculpatory tactic failed, and Ludlam too was found guilty. The moment is nonetheless provocative, for if it shows Byron's poem invoked in an effort to shape history, it also shows how history shaped the significance of Byron's poem. It was one thing for Jeffrey to find *The Corsair* in 1814 the epitome of an age of "visionary reform" and "boundless ambition," of "the era of revolutions and projects," it was another to have Conrad seemingly made actual in a native insurrection: the poem acquired a meaning not referable solely to Byron. Brandreth became a radical martyr, and his name carried far beyond radical circles.

The interweaving of the names discussed in this essay would have been apparent to any Londoner reading the newspapers at the end of 1817. From mid-October on, the *Times* was filled with the trials of Brandreth and his associates; Denman's quotation from *The Corsair* and his reported statement that "the noble poet could not have drawn a truer picture if he had actually contemplated Jeremiah Brandreth" appeared on the front page on 27 October. The prisoners were executed on 7 November, the day after the death of Princess Charlotte, a rallying point of the Whigs to whom Byron had addressed his celebrated "To a Lady Weeping," and particulars of their last days continued to appear until 10 November. On 14 November, the *Times* printed an account of the prosecution of Carlile for the publishing of Hone's parodies, and on the same day, a transcript of Brandreth's trials was advertised. On the twenty-second, the trial of T. J. Wooler, the publisher of the radical *Black Dwarf*, was reported, and on the twenty-fifth there was a summary of the case of another bookseller charged with selling the parodies. These matters extended into December, when the trial of Hone himself filled the paper.

These links between Hone, Byron, and Brandreth enable us to see some of the context of Hone's adaptation of *The Corsair*. If Denman's quotation was not in itself the occasion for its appearance — and I have thus far been unable to fix the exact date of publication — still this network of radical connections best discloses the implications of Hone's title page:

Hone's
Lord Byron's Corsair
Conrad,
The Corsair:
or,
The Pirate's Isle.
A Tale.
Adapted as a Romance
London:
Printed By and For William Hone,
Reformists' Register Office, 67, Old Bailey.
1817.
Price Four-pence.

Hone's proud advertisement of his address attests the co-opting of Byron, long since departed from England, by the radical cause: an adaptation of *The Corsair* emanating from the *Reformists' Register* office stands in quite another light than did the original, issued by the Tory John Murray from Albemarle Street. The price is no less significant: as the testimony in Hone's trials reveals, the authorities were fearful of the dissemination of potentially inflammatory literature among the lower classes. At Murray's price of five shillings, sixpence, a standard figure for volumes of poetry from the established houses, *The Corsair* was well beyond the reach of most readers: at fourpence, less than a sixteenth the cost, it became available for a new and different audience. When in 1816 Cobbett had dropped the price of his *Political Register* to twopence and thus raised its circulation to forty thousand copies, he commented: "Two or three journeymen or labourers cannot spare a shilling and a halfpenny [the former price] a week; but they can spare a halfpenny or three farthings each, which is what they pay for a good large quid of tobacco." Hone brought Byron, or at least his version of Byron, to this working-class but literate populace.

Fully a third of Hone's title page is taken up with a picture of the dramatic incident in *The Corsair* when Conrad throws off his disguise as a dervish and stands revealed in Seyd's palace. The picture is unsigned, but the Harvard copy, from which I am working, bears a laconic inscription by George Cruikshank: "Badly engraved from a drawing by me." The prominent illustration seems consonant with the popular audience Hone wooed, for it certainly makes a more immediate and sensational appeal than did Murray's volume, which had no plates.

Hone's daughter remembered that Cruikshank had first come to Hone's attention when recommended by Sherwood (of the Sherwood, Neely, and Jones who pirated *Wat Tyler*) to touch up a plate of either "Napoleon or Byron." *The Corsair* is a relatively early instance of the collaboration that was to produce the brilliant and enormously popular satires on the Regent and his ministers, the pamphlets running from *The Political House That Jack Built* (1819) through the racy commentaries on the trial of Caroline to *The Political Showman — at Home*! (1821).

Hone described his adaptation of *The Corsair* as "a romance." Whether the term had exact generic connotations for Hone's audience I doubt, but it does point to two characteristics of the text. Byron's narrative is not firmly placed in time, and the indefiniteness brings its turbulence closer to the reader. From the outset, Hone locates his story in a comfortably distant past: "In the beginning of the seventeenth century, a powerful band of Italian pirates seized upon one of the small rocky but beautiful islands of the Grecian Archipelago, and made it their headquarters and home." This flat opening gives Hone's version that remote quality suggested in Johnson's definition of romance as "a military fable of the middle ages"; it contrasts strongly with the original, in which Byron plunges the reader directly into the pirates' celebration of the superiority of their free life to the existence of the "luxurious slave" and the "vain Lord of wantonness and ease." A large measure of Byron's appeal for his middle-class and aristocratic readers stemmed from the fascination that the exotic holds for the perhaps overcivilized: words like "ease" and "luxury" would have been irrelevant to the audience at whom Hone aimed, but in adapting Byron to his circumstances, Hone lost the paradoxical qualities that held Byron's readers.

The most important characteristic of Hone's transformation of *The Corsair* into "romance" is already apparent in the excerpt just quoted: except for a few lines from the original at the head of each of the four chapters into which Hone divides the story and two verses of Medora's song, his adaptation is in prose. This too seems a sign of Hone's assessment of his market, for not only does he sacrifice the rapidity and variety of Byron's couplets, he makes some predictable lexical alterations as well. To a query from Murray about the propriety of putting the name of Cain in the mouth of a Moslem in *The Bride of Abydos*, Byron had angrily replied: "I don't care one lump of Sugar for my *poetry* — but for my *costume* — and my *correctness* on those points . . . I will combat lustily." As one might expect, Hone eliminates most (but not all) of the exotic words that gave Byron's poems their air of authenticity. "Sirocco," "capote," "pilaff," "almah," "saick," "afrit," and "serai" all disappear from his text, although most of these would have been familiar to educated English readers from the vogue of Orientalism begun by Beckford's *Vathek* (1786) and reinforced by the popularity of travel literature. Hone's Conrad speaks like a bluff Englishman; it is somewhat disappointing to find the gloomy, commanding Byronic hero asking his companions for assistance in accents like these:

> Friends and fellow-warriors, you are aware that I am not a man of words; and you will acquit me of unmeaning vanity, when I ask you to say if you regard me as an able and disinterested leader?

This speech arises from one of the changes Hone makes in the structure of *The Corsair*. His additions to the plot help to define by contrast the disjunctive qualities from which Byron's narratives gain power. Hone recognizes, for example, that the secret past of the Byronic hero is intrinsic to his effect, and so he writes that "of the origin of this their commander, none of the pirates knew anything." Yet Hone cannot resist filling in the gaps that Byron tantalizingly leaves in his poem and so invents a prehistory that has no warrant in the original. Conrad is made "by birth . . . a noble Venetian" who "had fallen in love, during his prosperity, with the young and beautiful daughter of another magnifico of Venice, who had encouraged his addresses until the result of his imprudence became apparent, when he abruptly dismissed him." Conrad persuades his beloved to elope with him, but they are discovered, and Conrad is banished. "From this moment, the character of Conrad was determined; and he solemnly dedicated himself to a life of rapine and revenge." Hone seems to have cribbed this twist from *The Siege of Corinth* (1816), of which the hero, Alp, is a Venetian who turns renegade when her stern father denies him the hand of Francesca.

The conflation of two of Byron's tales suggests that the Byronic hero is no mere product of later criticism: Byron and his heroes formed one composite myth, overstepping the particularities of any one tale. Hone thus tells the reader what the pirates don't know, and this all too conventional story strips the glamor from the Byronic hero, replacing the artful vagueness that stimulates the imagination with a reductive explanation of Conrad's character. "My narration may have suggested," to use the phrase Byron employs in *Don Juan* (line 59) to mock just such expectations as Hone patly fulfills, that Conrad's beloved is Medora. In *The Corsair*, Conrad's love for Medora is a given of the text: Byron offers no account of its beginning or development, and the reader accepts her presence in the story without inquiring further. Hone diminishes the absolute primacy of Conrad's passion for Medora by the very details he adds in order to establish it.

I have argued elsewhere that the plot of *The Corsair* is founded on the splitting and duplication of the heroine in Medora and Gulnare, and Hone responds to this logic of repetition by generating a structure still more schematic than Byron's own. As in the second part of the tale, Conrad, disguised as a dervish, raids Seyd's palace and attempts to rescue Gulnare, so in the new materials added before the commencement of the story proper, Conrad, disguised as a Turk, raids the convent in which Medora has been immured by her father, rescues her, and brings her to the pirates' island. I expected when first taking up his adaptation that Hone would have deepened the radical emphases of the original, but this denunciation of "parental tyranny" and brief glimpse of antimonasticism is the only instance in which Hone might be said to exceed Byron. In fact, Hone moralizes relentlessly, and his desire to compass Byron's tale within the bounds of decency leads him into some unintentionally funny contradictions. "Nature triumphed," Hone proclaims when Medora agrees to leave the convent with her lover, but Nature is not permitted to rule alone:

> Conrad and Medora were united by a captive friar the moment they reached the island, but some time elasped before Medora clearly comprehended the lawless occupation of her husband. When gradually informed of the fatal truth, her heart died within her; and though nothing could estrange her affections from her lord, a secret consciousness of their mutual degradation continually haunted her.

The narrow morality of Hone's *Corsair* highlights the equivocation in Byron's portrait of his dazzling hero. Hone came from a strict Nonconformist family and ended a member of the Congregational chapel; a radical he may be, but he sees the pirates only as "ruthless spoilers," never as champions of liberty. Though Byron's Conrad, exhorting his comrades to free the woman trapped in Seyd's burning seraglio, lectures them "wrong not on your lives / One female form — remember — *we* have wives" (2:202–3), Hone's depiction of the marriage of Conrad and Medora bespeaks an even greater propriety and indicates the distance between Byron's aristocratic nonchalance about sexual matters and the mores of the working-class radicals with whom he shared common political ground.

Hone's unwillingness to palliate Conrad's reputation is visible in the conclusion of his adaptation. Byron's poem closes with the death of Medora and the disappearance of Conrad:

> Long mourned his band whom none could mourn beside;
> And fair the monument they gave his bride;
> For him they raise not the recording stone —
> His death yet dubious, deeds too widely known:
> He left a Corsair's name to other times,
> Linked with one virtue, and a thousand crimes.

Although in Hone's version the original rhymes are still disconcertingly audible beneath the prose, the detail of the prolonged mourning and the final epigrammatic summary of the Corsair's fame have been omitted:

> The band raised a fair tomb to Medora: but the death of Conrad
> dubious, and his exploits too well known, they forebore to record
> them on perishable stone. The fate of Gulnare remains in obscurity.

The sentence about Gulnare that Hone substitutes for the most memorable
couplet of Byron's poem witnesses a need to tie up every thread of a story, even
when there is nothing to be said, and this merely conventional closure under-
scores Byron's experiments with narrative form in the tales.

Thus far I have been proceeding from Hone's adaptation: it is perhaps even
more instructive to examine Byron's work from the perspective of its bastard offspring. To turn from Hone's closely printed sixteen-page pamphlet to Murray's
fine paper and generous margins is to encounter a conception of the book as a
handsome cultural artifact rather than merely a means of cheap mechanical reproduction. The exalted cultural position occupied by *The Corsair* is displayed
in several signs of the original editions dropped by Hone. The title page, for example, contains a motto from "Tasso, Canto decimo, Gerusalemma Liberata,"
and each canto of the poem is headed by similarly untranslated epigraphs from
Dante's *Inferno*. Within the poem itself, there are allusions to Ariadne and
Cleopatra, and, in the lines on Athens that Byron took from his unpublished
Curse of Minerva to open canto 3, to Socrates and to Greek place-names known
from myth and history. This presumption of a traditionally educated audience is
apparent in the notes as well, where Byron refers the reader to *Orlando Furioso*
and supports the verisimilitude of Conrad's entering Seyd's palace in disguise by
citing analogies from Gibbon and from Sismondi (in French and Latin). All
these are cut by Hone, no doubt as not germane to the story and inappropriate
for his audience, but it is these markets that together define the milieu of
Byron's work.

As the notes are not integrally part of *The Corsair*, it might seem that lop-
ping them off would be a trivial matter, but they contribute surprisingly to the
overall effect of the poem. The notes establish the presence of Byron himself,
whether in the knowledgeable glosses on the poem's esoteric vocabulary and the
length of Greek twilights; the irony with which he dismisses his own sensationalism as in the blasé remark upon Seyd's tearing his beard that it is "a common and
not very novel effect of Musselman anger"; or the worldly observation on gallows
humor that "during one part of the French Revolution, it became a fashion to
leave some 'mot' as a legacy; and the quantity of facetious last words spoken during that period would form a melancholy jest-book of considerable size."
Byron's lordly insouciance stands out most vividly in the paragraph he appended
to the passage from *The Curse of Minerva*:

> The opening lines as far as Section II have, perhaps, little business
> here, and were annexed to an unpublished (though printed) poem;
> but they were written on the spot in the Spring of 1811, and—I scarce
> know why—the reader must excuse their appearance here if he can.

The careless and negligent ease of a man of quality could scarcely be carried
further.

The witty authorial figure of the notes nicely offsets the melodramatic intensity of *The Corsair* itself, and this speaker is the one initially heard in the volume. The reader first meets a seven-page dedication to Thomas Moore, printed
in larger type than the following poem, which from its opening "My dear
Moore" establishes a tone of gentlemanly intercourse. The Byron who modestly
asks "May I add a few words on a subject on which all men are supposed to be
fluent, and none agreeable?—Self," who discourses on the heroic couplet and
Spenser, Scott, Milton, and Thomson, and who good-naturedly agrees that
Childe Harold is "a very repulsive personage," is not finally to be confused with
his wild Giaours and Corsairs.

The urbane frame on the notes and dedication subtly influences our perception of *The Corsair*. In its flatness, Hone's adaptation has virtually no narrator: nothing in the text tempts the reader to speculate about a personal source
for the story. A reader of the original editions of *The Corsair*, in contrast, strongly
feels the personality of Byron in the volume, and consequently refers the unidenti-
fied narrative of the poem to him. Consider, for example, the following generali-
zations of a sort that stud the texture of *The Corsair*:

> There is a war, a chaos of the mind,
> When all its elements convulsed—combined—
> Lie dark and jarring with perturbed force,
> And gnashing with impenitent Remorse;
> That juggling fiend—who never spake before—
> But cries, "I warned thee!" when the deed is o'er. (2.328-33)

> Strange though it seem—yet with extremest grief
> Is linked a mirth—it does not bring relief—
> That playfulness of Sorrow ne'er beguiles,
> And smiles in bitterness—but still it smiles;
> And sometimes with the wisest and the best,
> Till even the scaffold echoes with their jest! (2.446-51)

Or this last, rather different from the rebelliousness usually thought to typify
The Corsair:

Oh! what can sanctify the joys of home,
Like Hope's gay glance from Ocean's troubled foam! (3.565–66)

Such sentiments are what Barthes called *doxa*, unexamined commonplaces
about human behavior, tacitly ideological assumptions. Their expression forms
an unspoken bond between the poet and his reader, reassuring him that however anarchic the Byronic hero may be, he and Byron inhabit the same moral
universe.

The comforting familiarity of moments like these is extended in the six supple-
mentary poems that compose the remainder of the early editions of *The Corsair*,
also disregarded by Hone. The first of these, "To a Lady Weeping," originally
printed in 1812, locates the volume within the world of recent domestic politics:
scandalous though the verses were, they grew from Byron's life as a Whig favorite
and point to an area of experience as immediate for the contemporary reader as
the *venue* of the tale is remote. The beautiful lyric entitled "From the Turkish"
and the two rather pallid sonnets "To Ginevra" pose no challenges to the tastes
and habits of a Regency audience. These are followed by "Inscription on the
Monument of a Newfoundland Dog," a eulogy on Byron's cherished Boatswain
in a common eighteenth-century mode, as Leslie Marchand observes. These
verses are dated from Newstead Abbey, and thus attest the status as well as the
sympathetic spirit of the author. The volume ends fittingly with a passionate but
conventional lyric, "Farewell! if ever fondest prayer."

Taken as a whole then, the *Corsair* volume does not stray far from the
decorum of genteel poetry of the day. The ensemble creates an untroubling impression that contains the more daring sallies Byron makes within it: the reprint-
ing of "To a Lady Weeping" that acknowledged the verses as his and the notes
that suggest an archbishop of York might once have been a pirate and comparing Conrad to a "brother buccaneer," Jean Lafitte, who was then playing a major
role in the British defeat at the Battle of New Orleans. These gestures gave
Byron's volume contemporary political applications that Hone's adaptation
lacks, but the timing of Hone's publication and the announcements of his title
page chimed with the radical resonances of *The Corsair*, whereas the cumulative
effect of Byron's collection was to damp them.

In the imaginary dialogue between Byron and "Odoherty" that constitutes
the fourth of the "Noctes Ambrosianae," "Christopher North" makes the poet
remark: "But I do confess—for I was born an aristocrat—that I was a good deal
pained when I saw my books, in consequence of [Eldon's] decree, degraded to
be published in sixpenny numbers by Benbow, with Lawrence's Lectures—
Southey's Wat Tyler—Paine's Age of Reason—and the Chevalier de Faublas."
This presumably double objection suggests the conclusions of this essay. The

first concerns price, or rather, price and class. For the noble poet who gave away his copyrights, it was essential that relations with his publisher should seem an affair of gentlemen rather than a business proposition. Murray, who Hone declared was "known to be the most loyal and . . . reported to be the most opulent bookseller in the United Kingdom," calculated his sales shrewdly, and both he and Byron did well from their partnership. As Thilo von Bremen has suggested, however, Murray may not fully have realized the possibility of increasing sales — and hence profits — by lowering the prices of his editions. To do so, however, would have meant forsaking the respectable book trade for the popular market, and Byron, as John Wilson saw, would have keenly regretted the loss of cachet. His mockery of Hobhouse for having gone beyond the gentlemen reformers, his contempt for lower-class radicals like Carlile, and his ambivalence at finding himself engaged with Cockneys like Leigh and John Hunt show the gulf Byron's consciousness of his rank put between himself and those who claimed him as an ally. I do not know the sales of Hone's adaptation of *The Corsair,* but in 1821 Byron might still have found it among the advertisements in Hone's *The Political Showman — at Home!* in what to him would have been the uncongenial company of Hazlitt's *Political Essays* (a volume initiated as well as published by Hone). It was not until the outcries caused by *Don Juan, Cain,* and *The Vision of Judgment* that Byron was to abandon Murray's elegant editions for the cheap printings of John Hunt.

The second aspect is the nature of piratical publication itself. The entwining of Byron's career with Hone culminated with the anonymous publication of *Don Juan* (1819), in an expensive quarto format designed to forestall prosecution for libel. Within four days of the appearance of Byron's poem, Hone produced *Don Juan; or, Don Juan Unmasked,* a pamphlet in which he noted with heavy irony that Murray, "Publisher to the Board of Longitude, and of the Quarterly Review — the Bookseller to the Admiralty, and a strenuous supporter of orthodoxy and the Bible Society," was shielded by his respectability from the reprisals Hone had incurred by his parodies. Murray, Hone charged, "actually publishes a Parody on the Ten Commandments of God [*Don Juan* 1. 205–06], whilst this prosecution is pending against Russell, for a Parody on the Litany, which is entirely a human composition." Hone concluded the pamphlet with a fine rhetorical flourish:

> Q. Why did not Mr. Murray suppress Lord Byron's *Parody* on the Ten Commandments?
> A. Because it contains nothing in ridicule of Ministers, and therefore nothing that *they* could suppose, would be to the displeasure of Almighty God.

The accusations were not confined to Hone's pamphlet. Aspland, the editor of the Unitarian magazine the *Monthly Repository*, had helped Hone during this trial, and the journal broadcast his contentions:

> If parodies of Scripture, *as well as of the Liturgy*, be blasphemous, even-handed justice requires that poor parodists alone should not be punished. The grossest parody of modern times is one upon the Ten Commandments in Lord Byron's *Don Juan*, published and republished within a few months, by *Murray*, of Albemarle Street, the publisher of the *Quarterly Review*, and of other "orthodox" and "loyal" works. In truth the offence is not turning the Scriptures into ridicule, but making ministers of state ridiculous.

Shortly afterward, Hone came out with his spurious third canto of *Don Juan*, in which Byron's hero is metamorphosed into a radical publisher.

This controversy had its effect on Byron, who was carefully watching the fortunes of his poem from Italy. Mindful that it was likely to fall under Eldon's decree that seditious and blasphemous works could not be protected by copyright, he wrote Murray on 4 December: "The third Canto of 'Don Juan' is completed in about two hundred stanzas — very decent — I believe — but do not know — it is useless to discuss it until it can be ascertained if [it] may or may not be a property." Whether and in what sense an author's work was his property was precisely what was at stake: the terms of Eldon's decision made clear that the connection of author and work was not a natural one of producer and product, but a complex issue involving the reigning values of society. What was not a property if it offended prevailing norms became one if judged differently.

Three years before, when James Johnston published spurious poems under his name, Byron had sought to establish his texts by fixing their publisher as the badge of authenticity. He had written Murray: "To prevent the recurrence of similar falsifications you may state — that I consider myself responsible for no publication from the year 1812 up to the present date which is not from your press." A similar attempt to limit Hone's *Poems on His Domestic Circumstances*, however, was met by a cheeky reply:

> A paragraph in the Morning Papers notices W. Hone's Advertisement of all Lord Byron's New Poems being published by him, and concludes by declaring that no Poems are "*to be considered*" as Lord Byron's or as "*being sanctioned*" by him, unless published by his Lordship's Bookseller, Mr. Murray, Albemarlestreet. W. Hone thinks Mr. Murray must be aware, that though it may be quite expeditious that the Poems published by W. Hone should not be "considered" as

> Lord Byron's, or as being "sanctioned" by Lord Byron, yet that the
> public, without any effort of logic, will still inquire — if they are not
> Lord Byron's? W. Hone therefore presents his respectful compli-
> ments to Mr. Murray, and will thank him to oblige the public by
> stating which of the Seven Poems on his Domestic Circumstances, in
> Mr. Hone's Publication is not written by Lord Byron.

As Hugh J. Luke remarks, Murray might well have answered that two of the
poems in the collection were not in fact by Byron, but there is no evidence that
he did so, and Hone continued to publish. Authentic texts could not be re-
stricted to those issued by the officially sanctioned publisher.

Hone's piracies thus bring into prominence the ways in which a text, once
written, separates from its author and enters an economy of production and distribution, to be acted upon by forces beyond the writer's prevision or control.
Byron might well have wished to explain *The Corsair* by the poetics of Romantic
genius, but comprehension of it requires that we take into account the mundane
matters of circumstance and presentation, price and surrounding materials. It
was by altering these as much as his clumsy refitting of the text itself that Hone
made *The Corsair* suit his readers as it had suited Murray's very different ones.
The current standard editions of Byron disperse the poems that once apeared together and so mask important elements of the impression the *Corsair* volume
originally made. For example, though most of the poems may be found in
volume 3 of the E. H. Coleridge edition (the "Inscription" is in volume 1), the
format separates the tale from the "Poems 1809–1813," where the shorter pieces
are located. The single-volume editions by Houghton Mifflin and in the Oxford
Standard Authors series follow generic principles that similarly break up the
contiguity of the poems, and even the admirable new Oxford edition by Jerome
J. McGann is forced by its chronological ordering to place "To a Lady Weeping"
in volume 1 and *The Corsair* in volume 3.

The honing of *The Corsair* is an amusing anecdote of literary history, but it
has the larger merit of directing attention to the influences that shape the significance of a poem, inviting us to reconsider our notions of what constitutes a text
and how it should be preserved.

JEROME CHRISTENSEN

Marino Faliero *and the Fault*
of Byron's Satire

> *But words are things, and a small drop of ink,*
>   *Falling like dew, upon a thought, produces*
> *That which makes thousands, perhaps millions, think;*
>   *'T is strange, the shortest letter which man uses*
> *Instead of speech, may form a lasting link*
>   *Of Ages.*
> —Don Juan, III, 792–98

> *Do those theorists . . . mean to attaint and disable backwards all the kings*
> *that have reigned before the Revolution, and consequently to stain the*
> *Throne of England with the blot of a continual usurpation?*
> —EDMUND BURKE, Reflections on the French Revolution

Ordinarily, when one thinks of Byron's satire it is *Don Juan* and not *Marino Faliero* that comes to mind. The horizon of my interest, to which this essay aspires, is *Don Juan*. But although I will attempt to characterize the satire of *Don Juan*, I will do so without proposing a reading of any particular canto or passage and with scant attention to the anatomical peculiarities of that protean beast. Instead I intend to be more specific about both fault and satire than about *Juan* itself. I shall try to demonstrate that *Marino Faliero*, a play written during the composition of *Juan* and situated within its generous precincts, is the best

---

From *Studies in Romanticism* 24, no. 3 (1986). © 1985 by the Trustees of Boston University.

approach to Byron's most powerful poem because *Faliero* represents, with all its
faults, a poetics of Byron's satire.

As license for this eccentric procedure I appeal to a line from *Juan*, which I
take as my subject and text: "If I have any fault, it is digression" (III, 858). The
line represents Byron in what may be called his mock confessional vein. It is hard
to decide whether this speaking to the point is a true confession or is, after all, a
digression wandering away from the poet's "people" who, he says, are "left to
proceed alone," and is therefore no efficacious confession at all—hard to decide,
that is, whether the statement purges or instances the fault that it announces. It
is as if a penitent were to confess to taking illicit pleasure in the act of confessing.
And just who *is* confessing? Is this faulty "I" the "I" of the poet *qua* poet or the
"I" of the notoriously sinful lord of regency gossip? It might be claimed that digression is a peculiarly literary failing that can be only confessed by a poet. But if
Juan is about anything it is about the impossibility of such a restriction: the
poem habitually exploits the traditional association of wandering with sinning,
and surely digression is, if nothing else, a form of wandering. Whether digression refers to poet or man, it seems disingenuous of Byron blandly to condense
his dirty laundry list of moral and artistic failings into the single fault of digression. Are sins only formal lapses or are formal lapses really sins? Perhaps digression is not the problem; perhaps there is something faulty in the notion of fault
that allows us to shift so easily between regions of morality and poetic form, as
well as between an intentional subject and a contingent personality. Is there truly
a fault? If someone *is* at fault, who is it? And what is to be done about it?

Such are the questions that give rise to satire, which stands in a special relation to fault. Fault brings satire into being, and satire punishes the faults that
make it possible. Now, we know that faults or sins or crimes or illegalities do not
grow on trees but are determined along with their punishments by historically
specific discursive formations. Or at least such is the claim of Michel Foucault. I
shall rely on Foucault's concept of discursive formation as a related group of
statements, formed by rules, and systematically dispersed in order to prosecute
two mutually implicated lines of argument. First, I shall connect the decline in
the status and the modification of the practice of satire that occurred in the
passage from the eighteenth to the nineteenth century with an epochal transformation of the discourse of punishment. Second, I shall characterize the unpar-
alleled strength of Byron's crucially digressive satire by working through a can-
tilevered interpretation of his dramatic poem and poetics of satire *Marino
Faliero, Doge of Venice.*

In *Discipline and Punish* Foucault identifies three successive punitive
regimes: the monarchic, the generalized, and the disciplinary. The monarchic
mode of punishment was to stage a spectacle of torture which publicly displayed

on the body of the accused a vengeance that both vindicated the absolute power of the sovereign and furnished an opportunity for the mass participation of the populace in the imposition of justice. The eighteenth century eliminated the dangerous excesses attendant on monarchic spectacle by redirecting the end of criminal justice from ceremonial revenge to economical punishment. If the exemplary crime for the monarch was a murder to be revenged by torture and execution, the definitive crime for the eighteenth century was fraud (theft of property by false representation) to be punished by bringing the occluded causal agent to light and assigning him his proper penalty through the exercise of the common law aims of detection and reformation. Punishment, according to Foucault, thus becomes generalized, a matter of adjusting "the two series that follow from the crime: its own effects and those of the penalty." It is designed as an example, "a sign that serves as an obstacle" to a repetition of the crime by the criminal and to emulation of the crime by others. The aim, in sum, is to construct a "punitive city" cemented by an "aesthetic of punishment." Hence if the eighteenth century defined its illegalities as the circulation of fraudulent signs of property, punishment of these crimes was legitimated by an appeal to a duly constituted, completely intelligible, ostensibly natural organization of signs. In other words, like illegality punishment exploits the circulation of signs; "the publicity of punishment must not have the physical effect of terror; it must open up a book to be read." Underline "book," which is a literal implement of punishment.

Foucault's analysis seems to me to offer the best explanation of why satire was the most forceful kind of literary discourse in the eighteenth century. If, as Defoe claimed, "the end of satyr is reformation," in the eighteenth century that end was identical with the general aim of the civil judiciary. If reformation can be espoused as a completely reasonable aim within a social field conceived of as a determinate array of representations, the artfully managed representations of the satirist are as effective instruments of punishment as any other. And if the power of generalized punishment is owed to its capacity to deploy an "aesthetic of punishment" in a "punitive city" that is also an "open book," the exemplary satire in that period of English history in which satire enjoyed unique power and authority is Pope's *Dunciad Variorum*.

The Dunciad displaces the precedent of monarchic spectacle by including it as a precinct within its own discursive space. The action that the poem imitates, "the removal of the Imperial seat of Dulness from the City to the polite world," depicts the incapacity of older, ceremonial forms of justice to control literary illegalities such as piracy, pornography, and especially slander. The ability of the Dunces to organize their own procession, to move freely through the capital, and to install their own monarch displays the emasculation of the *ancien regime* and supplies the pretext for Pope's own system of justice, which mounts no spectacle but instead bookishly assigns to "nameless somethings sleeping in their causes" the names they deserve.

Pope's satire extends the reach of the law beyond overt and justiciable acts to the furtive intentions and acts of those whose very "obscurity renders them more dangerous, as less thought of . . . . Law can pronounce judgment on open Facts, Morality alone can pass censure on Intentions of mischief; so that for secret calumny or the arrow flying in the dark, there is no publick punishment left, but what a good writer inflicts." The law is incapable of reaching a whole class of illegalities which the law would, however, punish if it could. Such mischief makers can be brought to public punishment because a secret calumny, though its cause be occluded, exists as an expression of faith in the coercive power of publicity. Pope's satire redresses the malign "imposition" on the "honest unwriting subject" by setting "the force that drove the criminal to the crime against itself," giving publicity to those who were willing to slander in order to obtain it. The most transparent, gentle, *natural* punishment of these "authors without names," authors whose anonymity is the condition of their criminality, is to acknowledge and reform them simultaneously by "assigning to each some *proper name* or other, such as he [the satirist] cou'd find." To be named in a book is the proper and punitive effect of an anonymous literary crime — a consequence which is an obstacle to any further criminality. Hence what Pat Rogers calls the "feedback effect" of *The Dunciad*, which he illustrates by the tale of the fate of Edward Oldmixion: "Oldmixion was presented as a needy hack, surrounded by dissolute and groveling creatures who were terrorised by their master Curll. The picture took on life; and Oldmixion found his reputation lowered, not only with the reading public, but also among his potential employers, the bookselling trade. . . . He was, so to speak, the victim of Pope's self-fulfilling prophecy." Let us cancel the "so to speak." Indeed, let us cancel the anecdote, for it is no accident that the picture took on life, since the life of Oldmixion, or that generalization of life, his livelihood, consisted wholly in a picture which Pope merely reformed and over which he assumed proprietarial rights and punitive authority.

Byron's stubborn adherence to the observant Pope makes just as good sense as Wordsworth's commitment to the blind Milton. Pope, *the* strong English poet in the traditon of civic humanism, practiced a poetry of tactical statement deployed within the ongoing business of the world. What capacitated Pope was the historically specific symmetry between the generic code of satire and the modality of punishment in the state. Satire, which had been there all along, suddenly in the eighteenth century found itself in a central position, the place of the general, perfectly accommodated to the discourse of power. All of Byron's polemics about Pope's propriety are less important than the insight informing *English Bards and Scotch Reviewers* that Pope was a poet who both judged and *enforced*. Pope was not a poet like Swift, who, having written in the service of the Tory state, found himself after 1714 occupying "no place except as outsider to the Whigs' monolithic machine," but a poet who, like a magistrate, continually executed public policy—and was a stronger poet than Swift because he could accomplish his ends in spite of the emergent Whig hegemony. In a century of extraordinary reverence toward the law of genre Pope most powerfully exercised the genre of the law.

Byron's practice could not be Pope's. History had intervened between an Augustan "then" and a postrevolutionary "now." The shift from what Foucault calls a discourse of generalized punishment to a panoptic disciplinary society destroyed the perfect fit between the satirist and the dominant modality of punishment. The decline in the confidence and force of satire after the eighteenth century is not to be attributed to the absence of any norm which would allow the satirist the ethical assurance necessary to his undertaking; on the contrary, normality emerged as the great index of behavior in the nineteenth century. The norm, however, was no longer a general principle of consistent application that could be elucidated in a single book. Normality having become absolute, norms were endlessly diversified and analyzed, allotted to and defined by various institutions and professional groups: penologists, critics, physicians. Satire was displaced from its privileged position by the coalescence of a political technology that acted through concrete institutions directly on the docile bodies of its subjects. Mightier than the sword, the pen of the poet had nothing like the power of the prison, the school, or the hospital.

English Bards and Scotch Reviewers is embarrassing evidence of the new order. The very title announces a polarity that was unknown to Pope—a polarity that was actually a new hierarchy: Lord Byron's feeble attempts to invoke a papal authority against the squabbling critical sectarians of his day attests to the plenary sway of the organs of opinion which he affected to disdain. The establishment of literary norms was the business of the reviews, which were one organ for a discipline that was practiced in a variety of outlets in a variety of ways. *The Edinburgh Review* spoke for and to the Whig opposition headquartered at Holland House. John Murray, publisher of Byron and *The Quarterly Review*, had intimate political and financial connections with the Tory ministry. Lord Byron's dual affiliations (he would spend the afternoon in Murray's upper room at Albemarle Street and the evening with Lord Holland) gave him considerable latitude within this system. But the freedom of his movement was politically insignificant: he ran on a leash that confined him within a well-tended consensus. Within that consensus the cheek of *English Bards* could be only a functional delinquency, one which salutes the discourse it professes to satirize. Juvenile as well as juvenalian, *English Bards* was the sort of spirited behavior by a young aristocratic poet that might be not only tolerated but indirectly rewarded. Henceforth the reviews would keep their collective eye on Byron. Indeed, the phenomenon of "Byron" would be dramatic testimony of a fundamental British agreement, a moral and political certainty elastic enough to weather even a volcanic prodigy; Byron's aberrations would serve the socially useful purpose of defining a normality to which there was no opposition, only different measures of adjustment.

The defects of *English Bards* are to be attributed to its status as a poem of Byron's minority, which was, of course, not his fault. The strength of *Don Juan*, however, *is* his fault. In order to specify better the force of the fault within Byron's poetry I would like to extend further my line on digression.

The irregularly digressive character of *Juan* makes it difficult to say what, exactly, is a digression *in Juan*. In a text that consistently refers to the process of its composition, that perversely profits from the contingency of that composition, and that flaunts its capacity both to bring anything imagined as outside inside and to disorder the hierarchy between central and peripheral, any of the various interruptions that divert the poet from narrative progress, such as the publicized interdiction supposedly imposed on Byron by the decorous Teresa Guiccioli, can be read as elaborations of the text they ostensibly interrupt. All Byron's interruptions of the "epic" project, such as the sallies into love or politics or commerce, though they are pursued as diversions from *Juan*, appear, from the vantage of the poem, as wanderings within *Juan*. All of Byron's antics, deals, and imbroglios embellish the discourse named "Byron" that continually replenishes that equivocal "I" which wanders through the poem. This Don Juanism of *Don Juan* aggrandizes as well those other texts that appear during its composition, including the dramas, which have been regarded as distinct intentional entities, appearing within the composition of *Juan* as digressions, interludic moves that show the kinds of things that a faulty *Juan* does not or cannot do, that thematically and rhetorically test the possibility of escaping the elastic matrix of *Juan*, but whose doings come to signify as items in the catlog of faults which is the parodic conquest of the poem.

Marino Faliero, Doge of Venice, a work wherein romantic ambition labors in a theater of baroque inconsequence, was the first play to be written under the general dispensation of *Juan*. The action begins in abeyance as Faliero awaits the verdict of the Forty (the patrician ruling elite) on Michael Steno for scrawling on the ducal throne a charge of infidelity against the Doge's wife Angiolina. When to the offense of Steno is added the insult of a lenient punishment by his peers, the Doge, inflamed with resentment, lends his ear to the seditious plot of the discontented plebeians, becomes convinced they have a common cause, and assumes leadership of the incipient rebellion. The Doge persuades his followers to strike quickly, and they agree to converge at St. Mark's on the sunrise signal of the bell. The plot, however, is betrayed, the uprising quelled, and Faliero and his lieutenants apprehended. Faliero is tried and executed within the palace, where there is no possibility that his words or demeanour could incite the volatile populace; after his death his engraved name in the gallery of the doges is covered by a black veil, eternal mark of this treason.

Marino Faliero both represents and enacts Byron's ambivalence about his own social status and about the possibility for effective political action in contemporary England. Faliero's gray-headed uselessness within a society that, secure from foreign threat, is intent on routinizing charisma reflects both the post-Napoleonic dejection of a man who had once aspired to noble deeds and who now is convinced that in Wellington the English have gotten the hero they deserve, and the post-*Childe Harold* cynicism of a poet who appreciates that the charismatic quality of his previously published poetry was only the trumpery of the marketplace. Faliero's biography also telescopes Byron's own idealization of his family history. In *Hours of Idleness* Byron had exposed himself to Henry Brougham's ridicule by his jejune celebration of his nobility; Brougham mockingly exposed not only the poet's graceless boastfulness but more tellingly Byron's insecurity about his aristocratic status, which emerged in the poet's Ossianic exertions to concoct and retail a past that proved his nobility was not only ancient but *earned* in glamorous Highland skirmishes. The aged bitterness of the Doge is not simply another trope of Byronic world-weariness, but, as a scene in his ancestral mausoleum makes clear, a vehicle to render the return of the fathers in the son: they are at once addressed and impersonated that they might see and suffer the disgrace administered by time and men. Moreover, the plot of *Faliero* shows Byron working out in dramatic form some of the political preoccupations that circulate throughout his correspondence.

Having become financially solvent enough to worry about *keeping* rather than *finding* money, Byron shifted his financial anxiety from moneylenders to investments. His letters are studded with queries about the current state of "the funds," imperious instructions about the management of his interest in them, and dire predictions of financial collapse. Indeed, forecasting catastrophe became something of a hobby for Byron; it allowed him to indulge the fantasy that he might return to England during the ensuing chaos as the man on the horse who would command the rebellious masses and shape a new social and economic order—a fantasy in which it is typically difficult to disentangle the purely personal motive from the more generally political one. Again, however, that tangle imitates the doubleness of the motives of Faliero: he is offended in his person but takes that offense as an insult to the sovereignty of an office which is the only guarantor of the legitimacy of the state; he allies himself with republicans but only as a supervisory mind might condescend to act through the soiled instrument of the body. In that light the plot represents both a skeptical view of the possibility of success for such a mobilization and an opportunity to endow what might be a rather messy adventure with tragic dimensions, thereby substituting vicarious experience for the effort of action.

The vacillations in Byron's exchanges with John Murray about the possible staging of *Marino Faliero* enact the ambivalence he represents. Scholars disagree about Byron's intentions. Some argue that despite his vehement protests he really wanted *Marino Faliero* to be staged and denied that aim in full confidence (justified by events) that Murray would go ahead and arrange for its production anyway, thereby enabling Byron to deny his interest in the performance should it fail or, in case of triumph, to receive the plaudits like a champion who conquers offhandedly. I do not intend to enter that dispute. What is important here is to note that in the failure of the funds to fail, and in the absence of any other pretext for Byron's physical return to England (the indefatigably drab Southey could not be provoked into a duel), the theater represented the next best thing, a symbolic return made as good as real by its occurrence in a space where symbols have a virtual life. It is crucial to realize, however, that the next best thing would, in this case, also have been the worst. Such a triumph would be poisoned at its heart, since it would merely replay the ironic relation between sovereignty and theatricality that Byron had already exposed in the Bonaparte stanzas of *Childe Harold* III. What triumph Byron could have achieved would have had its transitory reality only in the effervescent admiration of a tyrannous audience and would in any case not have been fully *Byron*'s triumph, since Byron was experienced enough in the practices of Murray and the management of Drury Lane to be certain that in the passage to the stage the text would fall under various hands which would prune his drama to customize its force. "Byron" could only appear in London as a lame monarch, one whose sovereignty was conditioned by its self-evident theatricality, one who was hedged about by a peremptory administrative machinery, and one whose acts would only be dim imitations of executive actions occurring in a real world elsewhere. Byron's irresolute management of *Marino Faliero* dramatizes the ironic thesis common to that play and to the later *Sardanapalus*: sovereignty can only exert its authority through a self-imaging, but that staging submits that authority to potential humiliation. Sovereignty cannot survive what Byron called its "cursed attempt at representation."

Nothing I have said about the relations between representation and enactment challenge the conventional reading of *Marino Faliero* as a historical tragedy about a grand risk and a glorious failure. And it is surely the case that it was as a piece of tragic sensationalism à la mode that *Faliero* appealed to Murray and his colleagues. Actually, however, the play is not about failure but about success or, to be precise, about the social machinery for transforming failure into success.

Faliero's ascendancy to the dogeship was the direct result of his heroic salvation of the state from its foreign enemies. Far from demonstrating that such heroism is irrelevant in an age of impersonal bureaucratic efficiency, the play dramatizes the ritual advantages the hero-king provides for the modern state: Faliero's action in the play neatly repeats the service by which he was originally exalted. Crucial to this interpretation is Faliero's acknowledgment prior to his meeting with the plebeian conspirators, "I am before the hour" (III, i, 1). This indication of prematurity is reinforced by the conspirators' expressions of surprise at Faliero's indignant impatience with any counsel of delay. Whatever Faliero's intentions, the effect of his leadership is to precipitate rebellion prematurely, to practice a kind of political homeopathy, infecting the state with a discord of such weakness that it could be localized and contained, thus allowing the germs of civil conflict to exhaust their malignancy before they could fester into a mortal illness. In this schematically Girardian reading, the execution of the Doge is a scapegoating which does not deny his sovereignty but decisively consummates it. He has rescued the state from civil war, and his service is sealed by his identification as the monstrous double who is beheaded and forever marked as unique by the covering of his engraved name in the gallery of the doges. That black veil puts an endstop to all the emulous strife that unsettles the established order. It naturalizes order by attributing strife not to, say, an irreconcilable class conflict, but to the anarchic passion of a prodigy of nature. The king who betrays the state saves it — such is the plaguey paradox kept under quarantine by the black veil, so that the deep truth may remain nameless.

If we can agree that the secret stratagem of Faliero's revolt is to induce homeopathically what he calls this "game of mutual homicides" in order that his sacrificial death can bring the game to a close, we may have resolved most of the effects of the play, but we are still left without any grasp of the causes. We could, of course, pursue a Girardian reading further and argue that the effect is fundamentally the *same* as the cause: that all the actions of Faliero are governed by the final cause of the preservation of hierarchial stability, that his drama is a ritual enactment of ostensible rivalry and civil war performed in order to provide the scapegoat whose succinct execution defuses a divisiveness (represented by the doublings that propagate throughout the play) that might otherwise explode into anarchy and promiscuous bloodshed. In other words, the full-scale Girardian reading would require us to interpret *Marino Faliero* as theatrical all the way down: a play about the essentially dissimulative character of a politics solely designed to satisfy symbolically the demands of a brute nature that can only be imagined as a chaos of blood and poison.

Such attention to the final cause, whether we find it reassuringly orderly or tyrannously preemptive, has the tendency to efface the potency of Steno's lampoon.

That tendency conforms to an implicit convention observed by all parties. Patriarch, patrician, and plebe all deny that the scrawl has any consequences. No cause in itself, Steno's lampoon is merely the pretext for an action proceeding from a source of more gravity. Faliero, who urges his nephew to "think upon the cause" (I, ii, 272), subsequently offers a diagnosis that turns on Mandeville: "Our private wrongs have sprung from public vices" (III, ii, 154). He specifies the crisis twice, each time identifying it with his election as Doge: "Their own desire, not my ambition made / Them choose me for their prince, and then farewell all social memory. . . . [N]o friends, no kindness, / No privacy of life—all were cut off" (III, ii, 325-27, 348-49). To be made the Doge is to feel the full imposition of the public in the joke of sovereignty; to assume the ducal authority is to submit to the constraint of an absent power which the sovereign can never possess but must always represent. As representation the sovereign is incapacitated—not deprived of power exactly, for to become doge is to learn that one cannot lose what no one has, but stripped of the watery, bourgeois surrogate for power, privacy. Consequently, the provocation of Steno's gibe, according to Faliero, lay in its final spoliation of the one fragile refuge of privacy that remained to him, his domestic life with Angiolina.

Given the synonymity of the public and the theatrical, Faliero's account squares with my own, except in its insistence on an opposition between the private and the public and on some dramatic moment in which the former is violated by the latter. But such a theory cannot be credited. Certainly Steno's lampoon does not violate any privacy; for in the dialogue between Faliero and Angiolina in which they recall their betrothal, arranged by Angiolina's dying father, it is evident that nothing that could be called privacy ever subsisted between them, no subjective space in which a theoretical liberty could be exercised. Faliero reminds her, '[Y]ou had / Freedom from me to choose, and urged in answer / Your father's choice." Angiolina agrees: "My lord, I look'd but to my father's wishes. . . ." (II, i, 322-24, 342). A choice so given is no choice at all; and the freedom of a virtuous woman is not liberty, since virtue is a fixed source of light:

> Vice cannot fix, and virtue cannot change.
> The once fall'n woman must for ever fall;
> For vice must have variety, while virtue
> Stands like the sun, and all which rolls around
> Drinks life, and light, and glory from her aspect. (II, i, 394-98)

The helos of that sun, who fixes the woman within a solar system of virtue, is the father, whose wishes have the authority of a cosmological given. Thus in its form Faliero's marriage "proposal" to Angiolina, made at the behest of her father, recapitulates the bind in which *he* was placed by his election as Doge: in proposing

marriage he cuts himself and his wife off from all "social memory." Any proposal
made by authority addresses a subject whose choice can only be nominal, since
to reject the proposal would be to remove oneself from the line of the father
which confers the very possibility of choice. There is no power to choose what is
not authorized; but it follows that authority is delegated every power except that
of conferring the power freely to choose. Every well-formed statement in Venice
is a variant of Angiolina's "My Lord, I look'd but to my father's wishes," even, or
rather especially, Faliero's pathetically curtailed self-assertion, "I will be what I
should be, or be nothing. . . ." (II, i, 453). The ironical equivocation of that
"should" displays the blind vanity of the will which indulges the fancy of a destiny that is different from that which is designed by the father, who has said and
is continually saying the same thing. Embedded in the inexorable conjunction
of "will" and "should" is the endless reiteration of the compliance of all subjects
with the wish of a father who wishes to identify himself with a father ideal making the same wish — a circuitous submission to an ideal authority which is faulted
by its structural incapacity to will anything but what it should, a circuit which, in
its dynamic iterability, is the expression of an absent cause.

The play gives us no grounds to think that the virtuous Angiolina is un-
faithful; indeed, Byron takes pains to dispel the possibility that anyone in
Venice could suspect her. Steno's slander, then, is by all accounts impotent: it
exposes nothing nor does it propagate rumor. Indeed, Faliero's irate response, a
"fury [that] doth exceed the provocation, / Or any provocation" (I, ii, 136–37),
does not take the form of a repudiation of the incredible charge of wifely infidelity but of a denial of his own passion for his wife:

> 'T was not a foolish dotard's vile caprice,
> Nor the false edge of aged appetite,
> Which made me covetous of girlish beauty,
> And a young bride: for in my fieriest youth
> I sway'd such passions; nor was this my age
> Infected with that leprosy of lust
> Which taints the hoariest years of vicious men,
> Making them ransack to the very last
> The dregs of pleasure for their vanish'd joys;
> Or buy in sefish marriage some young victim,
> Too helpless to refuse a state that's honest,
> Too feeling not to know herself a wretch. (II, i, 310–21)

The lust that Faliero denies is the obverse of the innocent "patriarchal love" he
affirms (III, i, 363). Steno's scrawl does not discover, let alone cause, any infidelity; it marks the exclusion of any physical passion from the Venetian patriarchy

that could be anything other than vicious by bringing to visibility the incestuous format imposed on all private relations between husband and wife, "father" and "daughter." The determination in the last instance is not the father, but a discourse that puts any man, any husband, any sovereign in the position of a father who can have no desire except that which is already scripted as incestuous. Steno's mark is a provocation not because it speaks of facts but because it signifies at all levels a proscription of desire.

All relations in Venice, even the most intimate, are statements in a discourse which allows for no digression or, what is the same thing, no unintentional, nonhierarchical, wordless sensuality. The linkage is Milton's, from *Paradise Lost*, Book 8: "hee, [Eve] knew would intermix / Grateful digressions, and solve high dispute / With conjugal Caresses, from his lip / Nor Words alone pleas'd her" (lines 54–57 [sic]). Milton suggests a connection between digression and prelapsarian sexuality, intimately cohabitating within an unrepresentable zone of human freedom, here specifically dissociated from a discourse only not yet totalitarian. Of course, that "not yet" is disputable; and Byron's Cain does dispute it. Cain and his wife Adah are congruent with Faliero and Angiolina in the lack of that ability to digress either verbally or sexually that Milton attributes to the first couple. But Cain exceeds Faliero in his bitter demystification of any association of that digressive capacity with choice, which Cain recognizes must have been as much an illusion for his parents as it is for him: choice can only be intelligible within an ordered discourse that specifies the options and which choice merely elaborates, according to the secret discipline of an algorithmic logic. Edenic digression, like unfallen sexuality, is, as C. S. Lewis uneasily observed, no legitimate option because it occurs on the outside or rather on the margin, the outsiding of the inside, of theological discourse. Byron's *Cain* interprets that most peculiar of all biblical narratives as the reinscription by main force of that margin within the providential economy. As for Cain so for Faliero: digression, like a nondiscursive sexuality, is impossible. It is only an apparent paradox to assert, however, that from the "point of view" of power everything that occurs in Venice, all actions and words of all parties, the whole discourse of society, is nothing but digression. Digression, like theatrical representation, is empty, purposeless speech. It is ordinarily staged as a respite or recreation (what Coleridge in *The Friend* calls a "Landing Place" or what Kant in *The Critique of Judgment* calls the "aesthetic") within a teleological order of executive decisions and effective actions. The text of *Marino Faliero*, however, extends the digressively theatrical to include *all* social and political speech and behavior, which is not framed by any supervisory purpose, and which is distinguished from theatrical representation proper only in that it is both mystified in its production and afflicted with nostalgia, uttered by actors who believe in their parts.

This conception of power, with its implication of a bifocal view of digression, is strongly thematized in Shelley and is most salient in *Prometheus Unbound*, where the "dramatic" crux is the distinction between two kinds of digression each of which is the expression of a power that is always elsewhere. The problem, to put it crudely, is to transform a pernicious digression—the discourse of causes and effects, of hierarchy, of fathers—into a benign digression: the masque, the love duet, innocent tales let slip in an unseen cave, unthought melodies gently noting the passage of eternity. For Shelley, unlike Byron, art is not in question—it subsists on both sides of the fault line—but the status of theater as a human art surely is: the vector of the "action" of *Prometheus Unbound* aims at transforming classical drama into Promethean masque, tragedy into Ovidian metamorphosis. The most intense narrative in all of romantic poetry is surely the first four scenes of Act II, Shelley's strenuous overrepresentation of the fault, where, in spendthrift futility, he endeavors to forge a crossing from Prometheus to Asia, from father to power, from curse to love.

In the decidedly postlapsarian state of Venice there are neither mountains nor chasms (those dazzling fragments of the fall, which could stimulate the excited revery of theodicy or apocalypse); discourse abides no interruptions but overlays and canalizes all relations; a king can talk to but not touch his wife, whose very virtue consists in her abstraction into a cipher that saves all place in a political order empty of social memory. One has the language of causation, the appearance of causation, but the feeling (insofar as one can be said to feel) that one is the mechanical instrument rather than the producer of effects. In *Marino Faliero* Byron is not stating a problem in political science, in any science at all. Venice is not a mixed government in which a grasping and decadent oligarchy dangerously constrains the legitimate power of the sovereign and immorally oppresses its lower class; on the contrary, it is a government totally unified and elaborately articulated under the sign of the father. What constraints apply are not the fault of the patrician, the patriot, or the patriarch; they inhere in the paternal root. The father attains, exercises, and preserves his authority only at the expense of all social memory, the recollection of a feeling that was not merely instituted— a fee which is extorted from his as the price for social order. There is no choice without the father and no real choice with the father; the father gives all freedom; the father has no freedom to give. That he is the emblem of all authority but only the representation of power is the fault in the father.

The wish for privacy is a wish to have a will, to feel, to have some source of power of which one is in control rather than to be the representative through which a power, which is always elsewhere, flows. This wish for an uncharactered, authentically affective and effective subjectivity can only be inordinate, since the private has no place in a society where every place has already been overwritten by a reticulative discourse. Or, if the private does have a place, as in some sense it must, since it is named over and over again, that place is posited and deployed as the name of the (in)violable in a metaphorics of shame which motivates the drama of social life. Here is the honorable house of Faliero: his name, his shame. The wish for privacy (to be together with a woman just feeling) and the eclipse of privacy (feeling encoded as incestuous desire) occur in the same moment; they are the same gesture, a metaphor in which the vehicle traduces its tenor. As soon as something inner and secret is defined it is already imprinted with a scene that coordinates it with a discourse which proscribes the *socius* and prevents all social feeling.

We can agree with Faliero then that Steno's ribaldry is not the cause of the civil disturbance in Venice. Yet Faliero wants to go further, to claim that the scrawl is nothing at all. He calls it the "mere ebullition of vice" (III, ii, 403)—a figure that oddly anticipates the trope that T. S. Eliot would later use to characterize Byron's poetry: "We have come to expect poetry to be something very concentrated, something distilled; but if Byron had distilled his verse, there would have been nothing whatever left." Cavalier chemist, Eliot employs a scientific metaphor that both stigmatizes Byron and repudiates the laws of physics: could even a Paracelsus have imagined a distillation that would leave nothing? The suave Eliot seems offhandedly to admit the notorious Byronic nihilist at the back door. In this he is an ally of Faliero, whose contemptuous characterization of Steno keynotes a critique of Venetian corruption and a program for its elimination:

> The whole must be extinguished; — better that
> They ne'er had been, than drag me on to be
> The thing these arch-oppressors fain would make me. (I, ii, 321–23)

Although vice itself, the vile substrate from which poisonous ebullitions like Steno's effervesce, Venice is queerly figured as compounded of the same fantastic element as Steno's scrawl; it is a something that can be reduced into nothing. This view of Venice has been called "organic," but it is surely a root and branch organicism, indistinguishable from the sort of nihilism that shadows a swollen, frustrated, so-called "Byronic" narcissism. Faliero's "political" program is indistinguishable from the project of the ego to which I have already referred: "I will be what I should be, or be nothing," a zero-sum egoism which allows for no action that is not the doomed extension of a wish, or the wishful extension of a doom. Faliero is thus like Eliot, who flaunts a magical power to extinguish, which he, however, graciously restrains. And like, curiously enough, a more efficient practitioner of the art of extinction, Robert Elliston, manager of Drury Lane, who in his application for a license for *Faliero*, which he had assiduously cut to eliminate all traces of contemporary political comment, stressed that "we have so curtailed [the play] that I believe not a single objectionable line can be said to exist." Elliston regarded the political gestures of *Faliero* as a "mere ebullition of vice," a digression from an innocuous Byronic entertainment that might be distilled, that, he claimed, he *had* distilled into nothing.

Hence when, at the end of the play, members of the populace, frustrated in their desire to get within hearing distance of the exchanges at Faliero's execution, "curse . . . the distance" and vent the forlorn wish, "would we / Could but gather one sole sentence" (IV, iv, 11–14)—as if that sentence would distill and resolve the confusing events that have been acted out in the streets of Venice—they are in the same situation as the Drury Lane spectators who watched the mutilated result of Elliston's censorship (which did not include this final scene). All objectionable sentences have been lopped off and hauled away; nothing salient remains. *This is no loss.* There could be nothing truly objectionable in a sentence spoken by Faliero or any actor who might impersonate him. Indeed, the play demonstrates the homology between gathering, distillation, and extinction: there is no substantive difference between the fetishism of distillation, whether it be the Eliotic notion of a crystalline touchstone or the popular wish to gather a single explanatory sentence, and the murderous ambition to extinguish all, to censor the objectionable out of existence. Essence and nothingness turn on the same idealist pivot. The twin beliefs in a distillation that will return either to an essence or to nothing partake of the same alchemical faith, the same mystery-mongering politics. The very attempt to look for a sentence is to look to one's father's wishes.

What remains is the black veil, neither essence nor nothing. It is the mark beyond the sentence of Faliero and its execution—something added to the sacrificial machinery of the state in order economically to seal once and for all the flawlessly sufficient hegemony of the state machine. Intended as an *index expurgatorius* which would put a stop to all further talk, the black veil was itself censored by Elliston; indeed, it is the sign in the play of that censorship, which the veil anticipates and entails as the type ordains and is (all but) cancelled by its antitype. Venetian censorship is expunged by a new censorship, which may disable the play as theater but realizes it as a text that has a forcefulness which is not under the control of the monopolistic discourse of patriarch, patrician, and patriot. The veil marks and its censorship remarks the necessity of a certain craftsmanship of repression. The mark of the veil and the censorship of Elliston attest, however unwittingly, to a strength that belongs to texts apart from their meaning, that, indeed, satirizes theatrical professions of meaning by virtue of an indelibly contingent position. That position is written into the play as something that is not and could not be represented in the play and therefore, of course, could never be censored from the performance of the play: Steno's squib, the text that produces all the action, while causing nothing. Steno's offstage scrawl is the parody of that invisible power which expresses itself in the well-formed statements that in their monotonous reiteration constitute Venetian political life, a parody which can be named satiric not only because its position, wholly without authority, is contingent, thus describing a border or margin of the hegemonic, but also because it is forceful, a force attested to rather than sealed by the institutional reproduction of the mark in both the black veil and the censor's erasure — each of which is a self-inflicted pasquinade that belies the power of the master discourse to discipline all signs to its standard of propriety.

Not a proper cause, the strength of the mark is wholly contingent. The path that connects the black veil and the inky scrawl is no vector of necessity but a digressive association that follows the fault of authority from displace to displace, motivating the turgid metaphorics of blood and contamination desperately imposed by rebel and ruler and exposing the futility of Faliero's hope to purify Venice by sounding the clarion in the tower of St. Mark — as if a single sound could sublate what is not a contradiction but a fault in diction itself; as if one mark, no matter how ringing, could abolish another. Neither a distillate nor nothing, the offstage pasquinade is a literal *steno-graph*, an abbreviation, which is itself faulted, which takes discourse to its bottom line, a stroke of the pen, in a strategic place, and which inscribes that line as a site of possible interpretations, coincidences, disruptions, and evasions. A scrawl on the throne that is talked about and dismissed but never fully represented or erased; a play that is appropriated from manuscript, censored, performed, and retired but that insists *on* and persists *in* its forceful materiality — each is a stenograph that appears as the irreducible material occasion for a theater in which sentences tagged to various authorities try to claim or assign power. The strength of this stenograph is to mark all such utterances as inconsequential digressions from an unspeakable fault.

I would claim that *Marino Faliero* is a poetics of satire in abbreviated form. Byron's satire, like all satire, finds fault; what distinguishes Byron's satire is that what it finds is what it *is*. The only possible power that can accrue to satire in a disciplinary society managed by a discourse that remains invisible, a power that no one can speak, is to mark the digressiveness of all authoritative utterance by an abbreviation without authority that contingently produces its own reproduction as the track of its own aboriginal digression. If the fault of Byron's poetry is its digression, a digression that invokes no authority, nor prospects any teleology, that fault is its indubitable strength. Byron's digression is the stenographic signifier that cannot be gathered into one sole sentence, that cannot be disciplined; this, I say, is a political act, if not, in the absence of any shibboleth, a political program. If, then, Byron participates in what Richard Sennett calls "the fall of public man," he does not reify a zone of "privatized freedom" as a transcendent refuge of the self from the arena of public expression and display; rather he dramatizes the yearning for such a refuge and the futility of that yearning, shows that the notion of a secret place of self-expression and unencumbered personal relations, of any sort of transcendence, is an illusion that is constituted by and functional within a pervasive disciplinary discourse. Byron opposes every explanation of the private that is in any way systematic but observes the impossibility of proposing any alternative that would not be subject to "this cursed attempt at representation." His undisciplined practice is to inscribe in public a stenograph that, whether it be the text of a play, a mock confessional "I," a potentially endless series of cantos, or merely his adopted initials "N.B.," is a material force.

In my view it is less important that Byron was "born for opposition," than that he was made for apposition: to *add, juxtapose, apply*. His is the only poetry that we can place in apposition to the writings of a Pope: he is the true, if necessarily contingent and unpropertied heir of that poet who could spawn only bastards. Taking on Pope's power without his authority, the scapegrace stenographer puts his master, all masters, to shame. A stenograph that is a digression, a digression that is a stenograph — that is how *Marino Faliero* characterizes *Don Juan*; that is the mark of Byron, the fault of his satire.

Chronology

1788	George Gordon Byron born, January 22, in London, to Captain John ("Mad Jack") Byron and Mrs. Byron (formerly Catherine Gordon of Gight).
1790	Mrs. Byron, her fortune spent by her husband upon lavish living, takes her son to Aberdeen.
1791	Captain Byron dies at thirty-six in France.
1792	George Gordon attends day school in Aberdeen.
1798	Inherits the title of his granduncle, the fifth Lord Byron ("Wicked Lord") and moves to Newstead Abbey, Nottinghamshire, Byron family seat.
1798–99	Tutored in Nottingham; clubfoot treated by a quack doctor. Byron initiated into sex by a Scots maid, who also mistreats him.
1799–1801	Attends boarding school at Dulwich, near London.
1801–05	Byron attends Harrow School and spends his vacations with Mrs. Byron at Southwell.
1803	First romance with Mary Chaworth of Annesley Hall, grandniece of Lord Chaworth, who had been killed by the "Wicked" Lord Byron in a duel.
1804	Begins correspondence with his half-sister, Augusta.
1805	Enters Trinity College, Cambridge.
1806	*Fugitive Pieces*, first poems, privately printed.
1807	*Hours of Idleness* published. Byron is drawn into a Cambridge circle of young intellectuals and political liberals.

1808   *Hours of Idleness* attacked in the *Edinburgh Review*. Byron re-
        ceives master's degree at Cambridge in July and moves to Lon-
        don, fully engaged in a life of sensuality.

1809   Takes seat, March 13, in the House of Lords. Publishes *English
        Bards and Scotch Reviewers* in retaliation against the *Edinburgh
        Review*; Byron points to Pope and Dryden as the standards for
        English poetry. With John Cam Hobhouse he departs in July for
        a journey through Portugal, Spain, Albania, and Greece. Com-
        pletes first canto of *Childe Harold's Pilgrimage* in Athens.

1810   Finishes second canto of *Childe Harold*, March 28. Travels in
        Turkey and Greece. Swims Hellespont, May 3. Lives in Athens.

1811   Returns to England in July. Mother dies in August.

1812   Gives three liberal speeches in the House of Lords. *Childe
        Harold*, published in March, brings immediate fame, and Byron
        becomes the darling of London's fashionable women. Affair with
        Lady Caroline Lamb.

1813   Begins affair in June with his half-sister, Augusta Leigh. Pub-
        lishes first Oriental tales, *The Giaour* and *The Bride of Abydos*.

1814   Publishes *The Corsair* and *Lara*. Becomes engaged in September
        to Anabella Milbanke.

1815   Byron marries Annabella Milbanke, January 12. Hounded by
        creditors, he flies into frequent rages. Daughter, Augusta Ada,
        born December 10.

1816   Lady Byron leaves Byron January 15; formal separation signed
        April 21. Byron, on April 25, leaves England forever. Spends
        summer in Switzerland with Shelley, Mary Godwin, and Claire
        Clairmont, with whom he has an affair. Publishes Canto III of
        Childe Harold and *The Prisoner of Chillon*. Begins *Manfred*.
        Travels to Italy.

1817   Allegra, daughter by Claire Clairmont, born January 12. Byron
        resides in Venice and engages in a liaison with Mariana Segati.
        Visits Florence and Rome; completes *Manfred* and works on
        fourth canto of *Childe Harold*; experiments in *Beppo* with collo-
        quial *ottava rima* on the theme of Venetian life.

1818   Begins liaison with Margarita Cogni; abandons himself to dissi-
        pation in Venice without losing literary energy. *Beppo* published

in February. *Childe Harold* IV published in April. Begins *Don Juan*; finishes Canto I in September.

1819   Weary of debauchery, Byron meets Teresa, Countess Guiccioli in April, his last liaison. Spends fall with Teresa at La Mira and continues *Don Juan*; the affair is countenanced by her husband. Thomas Moore visits Byron and is given the gift of Byron's memoirs. *Don Juan* Cantos I and II published in July.

1820   Byron lives in Guiccioli palace in Ravenna. Continues *Don Juan*; writes first of poetic dramas, *Marino Faliero*. Teresa's application for separation from Count Guiccioli granted by the Pope in July. Byron visits Teresa at Gamba family villa at Filetto; becomes involved in revolutionary Carbonari struggle against Austrian rule in Italy.

1821   Carbonari movement defeated. The Gambas, Teresa's family, banished to Pisa. Outbreak of Greek war for independence interests Byron. *Don Juan* Cantos III, IV, V published in August, and Byron promises Teresa not to continue *Don Juan*. In September writes *Vision of Judgment*. Joins Gambas and Shelley in Pisa in November. *Cain* published in December.

1822   British outcry against *Cain* and *Don Juan* increases. Teresa consenting, Byron resumes *Don Juan*. Leigh Hunt and family lodged in Byron's Pisa house. Shelley drowns in the Bay of Lerici. Byron joins exiled Gambas in Genoa. *Vision of Judgment* published in October; British outcry excessive. Byron changes to John Hunt as publisher.

1823   London Greek Committee enlists Byron's aid on behalf of Greece. Byron sails in July for Greece; becomes severely ill after strenuous excursion to Ithaca. Sets sail for Missolonghi on December 30. *Don Juan*, Cantos VI to XIV, published.

1824   Byron hailed in Missolonghi on January 4 as a deliverer. On January 22 writes "On This Day I Complete My Thirty-Sixth Year." Tries to form artillery corps to send against Turkish-held stronghold of Lepanto. Cantos XV and XVI of *Don Juan* published in March. Byron gravely ill on April 9; incompetent doctors insist on repeated bleedings; dies on April 19. Mourned by Greeks as a national hero. Regarded throughout Europe as "the Trumpet Voice of Liberty," Byron is buried July 16 in Hucknall Torkard Church near Newstead.

Contributors

HAROLD BLOOM, Sterling Professor of the Humanities at Yale University, is the author of *The Anxiety of Influence, Poetry and Repression*, and many other volumes of literary criticism. His forthcoming study, *Freud: Transference and Authority*, attempts a full-scale reading of all of Freud's major writings. A MacArthur Prize Fellow, he is the general editor of *The Chelsea House Library of Literary Criticism*.

G. WILSON KNIGHT was formerly Professor of English at the University of Leeds. He has written extensively on both Shakespeare and Byron and is one of the leading British literary critics of this century. His works include *The Wheel of Fire, The Starlit Dome*, and *The Burning Oracle*.

NORTHROP FRYE is University Professor at the University of Toronto and one of the best-known literary critics in North America. Among his many works are *Fearful Symmetry: A Study of William Blake* and *Anatomy of Criticism*.

GEORGE M. RIDENOUR is Professor of English at the City University of New York. He is the author of *The Style of "Don Juan."*

LESLIE BRISMAN is Professor of English at Yale University. His works include *Romantic Origins* and *Milton's Poetry of Choice and Its Romantic Heirs*.

MICHAEL G. COOKE is Professor of English at Yale University. Among his works are *Acts of Inclusion: Studies Bearing on an Elementary Theory of Romanticism* and *Afro-American Literature in the Twentieth Century*.

SHEILA EMERSON is Assistant Professor of English at Tufts University. She has published essays on Wordsworth and Ruskin, and is the author of the forthcoming *Ruskin: The Genesis of Invention*.

PETER J. MANNING is Associate Professor of English at the University of Southern California, Los Angeles. He is the author of a number of works on Byron, including *Byron and His Fictions*.

JEROME CHRISTENSEN is Professor of English at The Johns Hopkins University. He is the author of *Coleridge's Blessed Machine of Language* and a forthcoming study entitled *Hume's Practice*.

Bibliography

Blackstone, Bernard. *Byron: A Survey*. London: Longmans Group Ltd., 1975.

Bloom, Harold. *The Visionary Company*. Rev. ed. Ithaca, N.Y.: Cornell University Press, 1971.

Bottral, Ronald. "Byron and the Colloquial Tradition in English Poetry." In *English Romantic Poets*, edited by M. H. Abrams. New York: Oxford University Press, 1960.

Bowra, C. M. *The Romantic Imagination*. Cambridge: Harvard University Press, 1949.

Boyd, Elizabeth F. *Byron's "Don Juan": A Critical Study*. New Brunswick, N.J.: Rutgers University Press, 1945.

Brisman, Leslie. *Romantic Origins*. Ithaca, N.Y.: Cornell University Press, 1978.

Calvert, William. *Byron: Romantic Paradox*. Chapel Hill, N.C.: University of North Carolina Press, 1935.

Chew, Samuel C. *The Dramas of Lord Byron*. Baltimore: The Johns Hopkins University Press, 1915.

Cooke, Michael G. *Acts of Inclusion: Studies Bearing on an Elementary Theory of Romanticism*. New Haven: Yale University Press, 1979.

————. *The Blind Man Traces the Circle: On the Patterns and Philosophy of Byron's Poetry*. Princeton: Princeton University Press, 1969.

De Almeida, Hermione. *Byron and Joyce through Homer: "Don Juan" and "Ulysses."* New York: Columbia University Press, 1981.

Eliot, T. S. *On Poetry and Poets*. New York: Farrar, Straus & Cudahy, Inc., 1957.

Elledge, W. Paul. *Byron and the Dynamics of Metaphor*. Nashville: Vanderbilt University Press, 1968.

Frye, Northrop. *Fables of Identity: Studies in Poetic Mythology*. New York: Harcourt, Brace & World, Inc., 1963.

Gleckner, Robert F. "From Selfish Spleen to Equanimity: Byron's Satires." *Studies in Romanticism* 18 (1979): 173–205.

————. *Byron and the Ruins of Paradise*. Baltimore: The Johns Hopkins University Press, 1967.

Hilles, Frederick W., and Harold Bloom, eds. *From Sensibility to Romanticism: Essays Presented to Frederick A. Pottle.* New York: Oxford University Press, 1965.

Joseph, M. K. *Byron the Poet.* London: Victor Gollancz, Ltd., 1964.

Jump, John D. *Byron.* London and Boston: Routledge & Kegan Paul, Ltd., 1972.

———. *Byron: A Symposium.* London: Macmillan & Co., 1975.

Kernan, Alvin. *The Plot of Satire.* New Haven: Yale University Press, 1965.

Knight, G. Wilson. *The Burning Oracle.* New York: Oxford University Press, 1939.

———. *Byron and Shakespeare.* New York: Barnes & Noble, Inc., 1966.

———. *Lord Byron: Christian Virtues.* London: Routledge & Kegan Paul, Ltd., 1952.

———. *Poets of Action.* London: Methuen & Co., Ltd., 1967.

Kroeber, Karl. *Romantic Narrative Art.* Madison: University of Wisconsin Press, 1960.

Leavis, F. R. *Revaluation: Tradition and Development in English Poetry.* London: Chatto & Windus, Ltd., 1936.

Lovell, Ernest J. *Byron: The Record of a Quest.* Austin: University of Texas Press, 1949.

———. "Irony and Image in *Don Juan.*" In *English Romantic Poets,* edited by M. H. Abrams. New York: Oxford University Press, 1960.

Manning, Peter. *Byron and His Fictions.* Detroit: Wayne State University Press, 1978.

———. "*Don Juan* and Byron's Imperceptiveness to the English Word." *Studies in Romanticism* 18 (1979): 207–33.

Marchand, Leslie A. *Byron: A Biography.* 3 vols. New York: Alfred A. Knopf, Inc., 1957.

———. *Byron's Poetry: A Critical Introduction.* Cambridge: Harvard University Press, 1968.

Marshall, William H. *The Structure of Byron's Major Poems.* Philadelphia: University of Pennsylvania Press, 1962.

Martin, Philip W. *Byron: A Poet Before His Public.* Cambridge: Cambridge University Press, 1982.

McGann, Jerome J. *The Beauty of Inflections: Literary Investigations in Historical Method and Theory.* Oxford: Oxford University Press, 1985.

———. *"Don Juan" in Context.* Chicago: University of Chicago Press, 1976.

———. *Fiery Dust: Byron's Poetical Development.* Chicago: University of Chicago Press, 1968.

Mellor, Anne K. *English Romantic Irony.* Cambridge: Harvard University Press, 1980.

Praz, Mario. *The Romantic Agony*. London: Oxford University Press, 1933.

Ridenour, George M. *The Style of "Don Juan."* New Haven: Yale University Press, 1960.

Robinson, Charles E., ed. *Lord Byron and His Contemporaries: Essays from the Sixth International Byron Seminar*. East Brunswick, N.J.: Associated University Press, 1982.

————. *Shelley and Byron: The Snake and the Eagle Wreathed in Fight*. Baltimore: The Johns Hopkins University Press, 1977.

Rutherford, Andrew. *Byron: A Critical Study*. Stanford: Stanford University Press, 1961.

Stürzl, Erwin A., and James Hogg, eds. *Byron: Poetry and Politics*. Salzburg, Austria: Institut für Anglistik und Amerikanistik, 1980.

Thorslev, Peter L., Jr. *The Byronic Hero: Types and Prototypes*. Minneapolis: University of Minnesota Press, 1962.

Trueblood, Paul G. *The Flowering of Byron's Genius*. Stanford: Stanford University Press, 1945.

————. *Lord Byron*. New York: Twayne Publishers, Inc., 1969.

Vassallo, Peter. *Byron: The Italian Literary Influence*. New York: St. Martin's Press, Inc., 1984.

West, Paul, ed. *Byron and the Spoiler's Art*. London: Chatto & Windus, Ltd., 1960.

Wilkie, Brian. *Romantic Poets and Epic Tradition*. Madison: University of Wisconsin Press, 1965.

Woodring, Carl. "Nature, Art, Reason, and Imagination in *Childe Harold*." In *Romantic and Victorian*, edited by W. P. Elledge and R. L. Hoffman. Rutherford, N.J.: Fairleigh Dickinson University Press, 1971.

Acknowledgments

"Introduction" (originally entitled "George Gordon, Lord Byron") by Harold Bloom from *The Visionary Company* by Harold Bloom, © 1961 by Harold Bloom, 1971 by Cornell University Press. Reprinted by permission of Cornell University Press.

"The Two Eternities" (originally entitled "The Two Eternities: An Essay on Byron") by G. Wilson Knight from *The Burning Oracle: Studies in the Poetry of Action* by G. Wilson Knight, © 1939 by Oxford University Press. Reprinted by permission of Methuen & Co. Ltd.

"Lord Byron" by Northrop Frye from *Major British Writers*, Enlarged edition, Vol. 2, edited by G. B. Harrison, © 1959 by Harcourt Brace Jovanovich, Inc. Reprinted by permission of the publisher.

"Byron in 1816: Four Poems from Diodati" by George M. Ridenour from *From Sensibility to Romanticism: Essays Presented to Frederick A. Pottle*, edited by Frederick W. Hilles and Harold Bloom, © 1965 by Oxford University Press, Inc. Reprinted by permission.

"Troubled Stream from a Pure Source" (originally entitled "Byron: Troubled Stream from a Pure Source") by Leslie Brisman from *Romantic Origins* by Leslie Brisman, © 1978 by Cornell University. An earlier version of this essay appeared in *ELH* 42, no. 4 (Winter 1975). Reprinted by permission of Cornell University Press and The Johns Hopkins University Press.

"*Don Juan*: The Obsession and Self-Discipline of Spontaneity" (originally entitled "Byron's *Don Juan*: The Obsession and Self-Discipline of Spontaneity") by Michael G. Cooke from *Studies in Romanticism* 14, no. 3 (Summer 1975), © 1975 by the Trustees of Boston University. Reprinted by permission.

"Byron's 'one word': The Language of Self-Expression in *Childe Harold* III" by Sheila Emerson from *Studies in Romanticism* 20, no. 3 (Fall 1981), © 1980 by the Trustees of Boston University. Reprinted by permission.

"The Hone-ing of Byron's *Corsair*" by Peter J. Manning from *Textual Criticism and Literary Interpretation*, edited by Jerome J. McGann, © 1985 by the University of Chicago. Reprinted by permission.

"*Marino Faliero* and the Fault of Byron's Satire" by Jerome Christensen from *Studies in Romanticism* 24, no. 3 (1986), © 1985 by the Trustees of Boston University. Reprinted by permission.

Index